ENRICO DONATI

Surrealism and Beyond

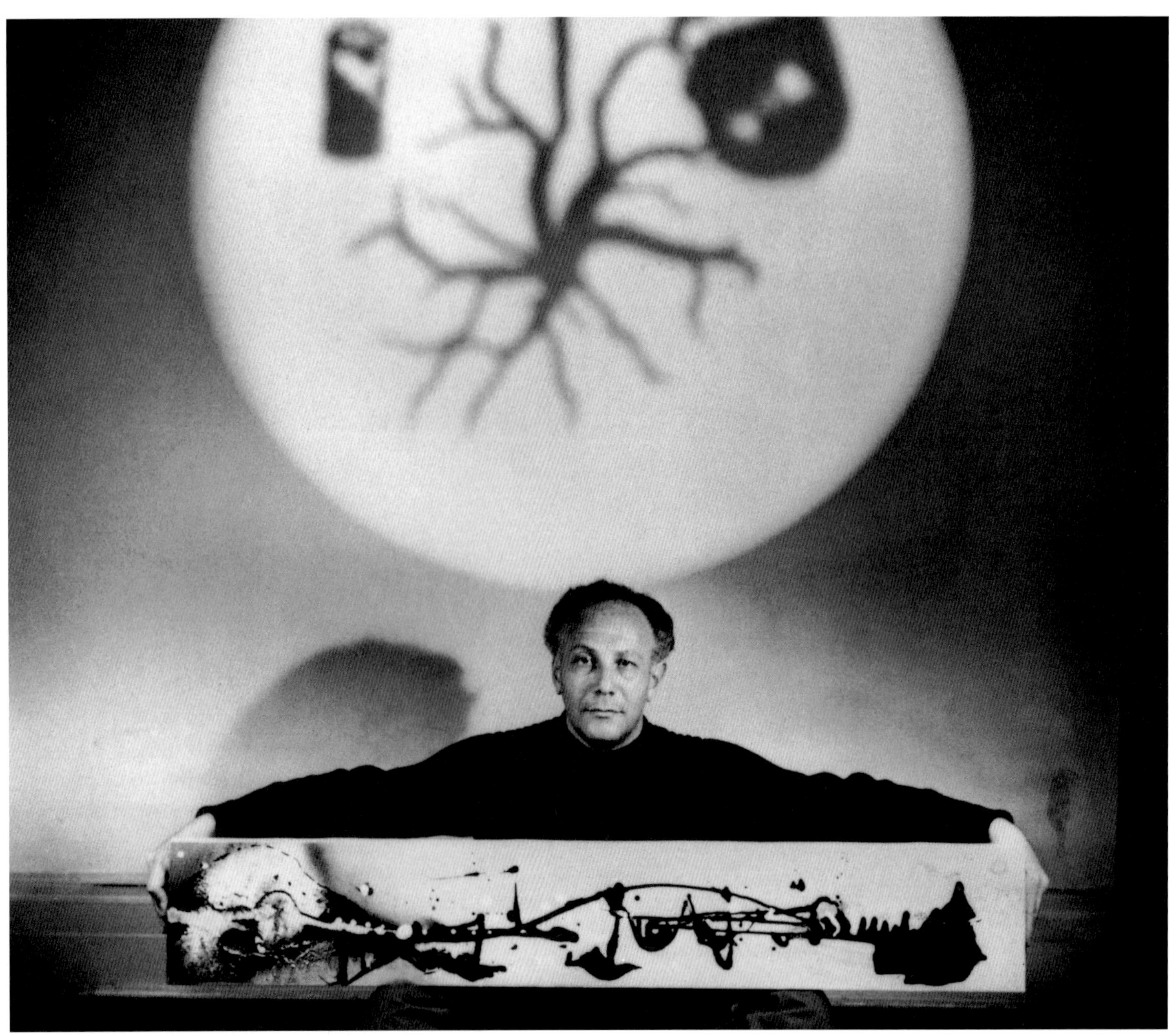

Donati at Alexandre Iolas Gallery, New York, 1952.

ENRICO DONATI

Surrealism and Beyond

THEODORE F. WOLFF

Hudson Hills Press / NEW YORK

FIRST EDITION

Text © 1996 by Theodore F. Wolff

Illustrations © 1996 by Enrico Donati

All rights reserved under International and Pan-American Copyright Conventions.

Published in the United States by Hudson Hills Press, Inc.,
Suite 1308, 230 Fifth Avenue, New York, NY 10001–7704.

Distributed in the United States, its territories and possessions, Canada,
Mexico, and Central and South America by National Book Network.

Distributed in the United Kingdom, Eire, and Europe by Art Books International Ltd.

Exclusive representation in Asia, Australia, and New Zealand by EM International.

Editor and Publisher: Paul Anbinder

Copy Editor: Phil Freshman

Editorial Assistant: Faye Chiu

Proofreader: Lydia Edwards

Indexer: Karla J. Knight

Designer: Betty Binns

Composition: Angela Taormina

Manufactured in Japan by Toppan Printing Company.

Special thanks must go to Kathleen Hill for the thorough manner in which she
assembled and organized all relevant pictorial and archival material.

Library of Congress Cataloguing-in-Publication Data

Wolff, Theodore F.
    Enrico Donati : surrealism and beyond / Theodore F. Wolff.
      p.   cm.
    Includes bibliographical references and index.
    ISBN 1–55595–138–4 (alk. paper)
     1. Donati, Enrico, 1909—Criticism and interpretation.
2. Surrealism. I. Title.
ND237.D62W64 1996
759. 13—dc20   96–17759
                                                CIP

Contents

Plates

Works indicated with an asterisk (*) are reproduced in color.

ENRICO DONATI

Surrealism and Beyond

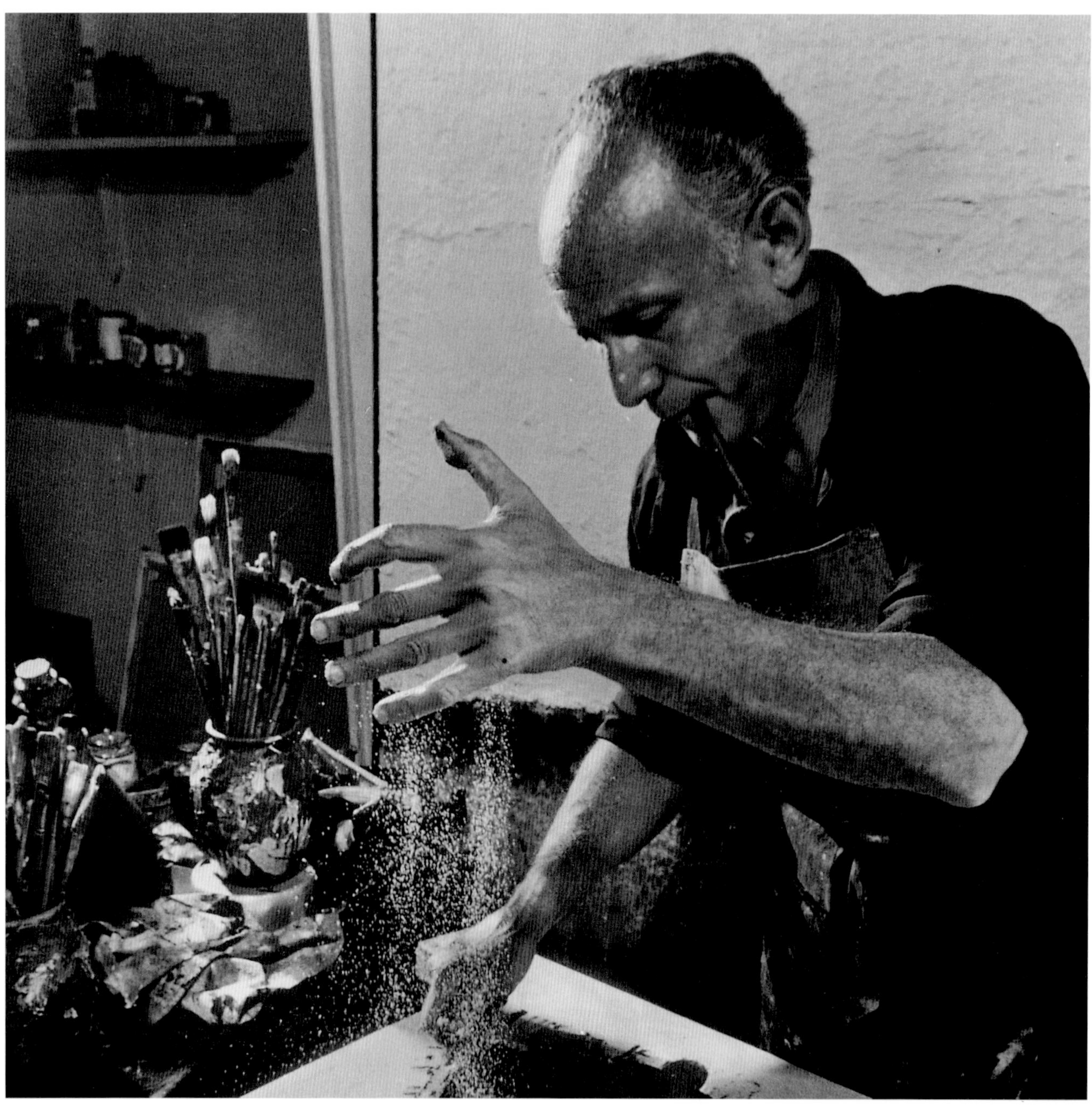

Donati, 1951.

The Fossil and the Stone

Some artists have the good fortune to appear at exactly the right time and place. One thinks of Jackson Pollock hitting his stride at precisely the moment his revolutionary approach to painting was most likely to be taken seriously by the American art community. And of Andy Warhol bursting upon the scene with his iconoclastic Pop Art images just as large numbers of art critics and curators were becoming bored with the high-minded seriousness of Abstract Expressionism.

Another midcentury beneficiary of this fortuitous conjunction of talent and timing was a young and exceptionally gifted Italian artist who had moved from Paris to New York in 1940. Thoroughly trained in traditional painting methods and fully aware of the latest developments in avant-garde European art, Enrico Donati, nevertheless, was completely unknown to the art world at large.

That would soon change, however. Recognition of his abilities by the renowned art historian Lionello Venturi led to a meeting with André Breton in 1942. Impressed by Donati's paintings, Surrealism's founder and pontifical grand master pronounced him a Surrealist on the spot and mustered him, as a younger peer, into the august company of such luminaries as Marcel Duchamp, Max Ernst, and Yves Tanguy.

Breton's final stamp of approval came in 1944 when he wrote an enthusiastic preface for the catalogue accompanying Donati's third New York exhibition. After reporting glowingly on the young painter's creative vision, Breton proclaimed, "I love the paintings of Enrico Donati as I love a night in May."[1]

Only a similar declaration from Picasso could have meant as much to a young Surrealist, or have had as great an impact on his career. Not only was this high praise from the only person able to confer "official" recognition as a Surrealist, but it also came at a time when that movement was deeply divided and desperately in need of someone capable of reconciling its differences.

With these words and his continued personal and "official" support, Breton helped launch Donati's long and successful career—a career that not only survived Surrealism's unfortunate demise a few years later but that also has continued on unabated and in increasingly significant and fascinating ways right down to the present.

Few artists living today, in fact, have had as long and distinguished a career. It already has spanned more than five decades, produced a considerable number of works of genuine art-historical importance, and enriched numerous museum, corporate, and private collections with paintings of outstanding character and quality.

Never one to rest on his laurels, Donati continues to work as hard today in his late eighties as he did when he was an ambitious youngster. Hard work, in fact, coupled with a rare talent and a fertile imagination, have played a much greater role in his success than timing—crucial as the latter may have been in the initial stage of his career. His Surrealist period, after all, lasted barely eight years. After that, he was on his own. And yet his career has never faltered, never surrendered to fashion or sensationalism, and never dwindled into mere commercialism.

Throughout, Donati has remained uncompromisingly independent. Even as a Surrealist he was his own man. Breton proclaimed him a member of the group after recognizing him as a kindred spirit, not because Donati had asked to join. And once he was a member, he followed his own path—even to the extent of deviating dramatically at times from what was expected of a Surrealist.

This spirit of independence was not so much an act of defiance as a natural extension of his personality. Even as a young boy, he recalls, he felt free to express himself as he wished as long as he respected his family's values and position. He recalls his childhood as a "happy and carefree" one and his parents, Federico and Janna Donati, with affection.[2] His birth, in 1909 in Milan, Italy, completed the family circle. There were no other children, a fact to which he attaches no special significance so far as his evolution as an artist is concerned. What he does remember as important was the regard in which his father was held in Milan as a distinguished scholar, and that his mother had a modest talent for copying Old Master paintings. Occasionally, he adds, visitors to their home were fooled by the accuracy of what she produced.

As for young Enrico himself, while he drew a little and says he was "quite good" at it, his main interest as a boy was in playing the piano and in composing music.

Music, in fact, continued to hold a much greater fascination for him than the visual arts, even after he had become a young adult. Family considerations, however, prevented him from pursuing it as a career—at least until after he had acquired a respectable academic degree. And so, with typical Donati practicality, he enrolled at the University of Pavia in 1928 and left there the following year with a doctorate in what today would be called sociology.

Free now to do as he pleased, Donati turned his attention once again to his first love. He signed up for a course in musical composition at the Milan Conservatory, completed it without difficulty, and decided that the time had come to begin his career as a serious composer.

Since he believed Paris was the only place for an aspiring musician, the early 1930s found him hard at work in a ninth-floor walk-up studio in Montmartre writing avant-garde music. Much as he tried, however, success would not come his way. It was not that what he wrote lacked quality, he insists, only that it failed to impress the right people.

Even when he was at his busiest composing, he still found time for his other interests. He painted a little, drew whenever he could, and, when he was not otherwise engaged, visited the galleries and museums of Paris. It was at the former that he first saw the work of the Surrealists whose ranks he would join a few years later. (He was not able, however, to meet any of them in person.) And it was at the latter that he studied the great art of the past and present.

One museum held a special fascination for him. The Musée de l'Homme on the Place du Trocadéro exhibited a rich assortment of anthropological odds and ends, including a number of Native American artifacts. These struck such a profoundly sympathetic chord in Donati that he decided to travel to the American Southwest in order to become more familiar with the culture that had produced them.

He left Paris in 1934 with Claire Javal, whom he had just married, and with the intention of returning with as many Native American artifacts as he could obtain. Since his plan was to barter rather than to buy, he took with him a selection of items he felt were particularly suitable for trading with native craftsmen. These included Venetian beads, feathers from European pheasants (he had noticed that the European bird's feathers differed significantly from those of its

American cousin), and Swiss army knives, especially those with the largest number of features.

His strategy worked remarkably well with the Apache, Hopi, and Zuni whom he visited for roughly three months on their reservations, as well as with the Eskimos in Canada's Hudson Bay region. Their method of bartering surprised him, however. They were friendly enough but not inclined to talk. Items for trade were left out overnight, and in the morning something special would be found in their place.

Donati returned to New York after a few weeks in Canada with a sizable collection of unusual objects, many of which still grace the walls of his large Central Park South studio. There, kachina dolls and Eskimo masks compete for attention with works from other "primitive" societies, several of Donati's startling Surrealist sculptures, and a constantly changing selection of the artist's older and more recent paintings. Seeing them together in this fashion, one senses the subtle interconnections that exist among these works, "primitive" and "modern" alike, and begins to suspect that the objects Donati collected long ago in the United States and Canada challenged his imagination to the point where he was led to seek out and to express similar but hitherto unsuspected dimensions of creativity within himself.

This should not be viewed as evidence that Donati was directly influenced by these artifacts, however. One looks in vain for the thematic and stylistic parallels that exist, for instance, between some of Picasso's and Matisse's images and African art. In addition, Donati's use of color is much too personal, even idiosyncratic, to have been derived from outside sources. And yet, one cannot help noticing a pronounced similarity of spirit and intent. It makes itself felt in many ways and at every stage of his career: in the provocative, primal imagery of his Surrealist days, in the color-drenched, enigmatic icons of his middle period, and in the magical, richly patterned pictorial riddles of his later years. To all of these works certain words—*magical, enigmatic, primal,* and *provocative*—invariably apply, words that can be applied with equal justification to much of what is best and most significant in Native American art.

Back in New York after his Canadian trip, however, Donati was less concerned about the future course of his art than about returning to Paris to pick up a few possessions for a more extended stay in America. "I met the Indians," he says by way of explaining his decision to return, "and now I wanted to meet the people of New York."

For the following two years in Manhattan, Donati was involved in a variety of activities, most of which concerned art in one way or another. Having given up his dream of a musical career, he now turned his attention to how he could best utilize his talent for drawing. He tried his hand at commercial and fine-art printing and mastered the various engraving processes, but he ultimately found the field unrewarding. Other attempts at channeling his skills led to similar disappointments, and so, in 1936, he and his wife decided to return to Europe.

Back in Paris, Donati finally committed himself wholeheartedly to painting. He enrolled at the "very academic" École de la rue de Berri, not because he expected to like it there but because he wanted a solid professional background upon which to build his future career as a painter. He was right on both counts. His years at the school were not happy ones, yet he acquired as thorough a technical background as anyone could wish.

When war broke out in September 1939, plans once again had to be changed. The United States seemed the safest place for a young family of four—daughters Marina and Sylviane had been born in 1936 and 1938, respectively—and so the Donatis packed their belongings and headed for New York, this time for good.

Donati was glad to be back in the city that was fast becoming the temporary home for many of Europe's finest and most advanced painters and sculptors—all of whom had fled their respective countries because of Hitler. The presence in New York of Marc Chagall, Salvador Dalí, Marcel Duchamp, Max Ernst, Fernand Léger, Jacques Lipchitz, Piet Mondrian, and Yves Tanguy—to name only a few—transformed it almost overnight from a provincial art city into one of the most cosmopolitan art centers of the Western world.

The presence of these artists also affected the work of their American counterparts. Not immediately, perhaps, nor to any significant extent so far as most members of the art community were concerned. (American art, after all, would remain militantly conservative for several more years.) But certainly in the long run, and most specifically in the case of a few forward-looking individuals who had learned the lessons of European modernism—often directly from these masters—and would soon come to prominence as the original members of the influential New York School.

Donati felt both at home and stimulated in this environment, especially when he realized that several of the Surrealists whose work he had admired in Paris were also living in the city. The presence of Breton, Ernst, and Tanguy was of special significance to him at this time since his own work was becoming increasingly interior and subjective.

This new direction in his work was partly the result of his decision to devote himself exclusively to painting, but mostly it was the outcome of his recent intensive probings into the mysteries of the creative act. He was particularly fascinated by the cyclical process of regeneration, by the passage from life, through death, into life again that occurs regularly in nature but also in art and myth. The relationship between myth and nature had always intrigued him, and in that context, he remembered something that had struck him forcibly when he had first come upon it. He recalled learning, while still in Europe and long before he had considered himself a painter, about the mythological mandragora root—or mandrake root, as it is more commonly known—and its alleged supernatural powers. Part of its original fascination for him derived from the fact that an actual poisonous plant of the nightshade family had achieved mythological status. But its greatest attraction at this later date, and the reason it was relevant to his investigations into the phenomenon of creativity, lay in its extraordinary regenerative and transformative capabilities.

In mythology, the mandrake plant, which was said to take root under the gallows and to be nurtured by the executed criminal's sperm, grew in the image of the man who gave it life. Upon maturity, it had the ability to bestow passion, fecundity, and riches on those who treated it respectfully. If pulled from the earth, however, it screamed and those within earshot went mad.

All this fitted in beautifully with Donati's exploration at the time of the mysteries and mechanics of life, death, and the creative process—as well as his search for an effective personal imagery for his art. In the mandrake root he struck pay dirt. As a metaphor for his thoughts and intentions as an artist it was both appropriately precise and probing and sufficiently ambiguous and loaded with metaphysical implications to induce the viewer of his paintings to respond in exactly the intrigued but mildly perplexed manner Donati desired. In this he was already proving himself closely aligned with the Surrealists, for they also were more concerned with the primal, deeply interior, and apparently irrational dimensions of the human psyche—and with alerting viewers to their existence—than they were with the depiction of surface reality, regardless of how engaging it might be.

While mankind, in general, preferred not to confront these areas or pretended they did not exist, Donati perceived them as significant wellsprings of creativity. At the same time, he understood that if what he was to produce from these sources was to be art and not merely another form of science-fiction illustration, it would have to derive from them honestly and with full regard for the difficult and often disturbing questions they raised.

Thus the mythologically charged mandrake root, with its multiple associations with death, procreation, rebirth, and metamorphosis, and its capacity to assume a variety of colorful and exotic forms, became the metaphor around which Donati invented, as he put it, "a mandragora world of my own."

That world would not come fully into its own for just under two more years. Donati needed time to transform impulse and idea into imagery and to bring his working methods into sharper focus. But when, in 1942, everything he hoped for did fall into place, it triggered a series of events that dramatically altered the course of his life.

The process of transformation began with Donati's friendship with Camilo Egas, an Ecuadoran Surrealist, who was codirector of the gallery at Manhattan's New School for Social Research. Egas liked his Italian friend's latest paintings and exhibited them in his gallery. The art historian Lionello Venturi saw the show, liked it immensely, and gave Donati his card as an introduction to André Breton.

Donati remembers it this way: "I was just a kid, . . . but Breton accepted me into the Surrealist movement. Suddenly I was surrounded by giants—Max Ernst, Tanguy, all of the big guys. Matta and I were the youngest of this group of the most *impossible* characters. But we got along very well. From then on I started having shows."[3]

Donati's induction into the movement had social as well as artistic ramifications. "We were together every day. We had lunch at Larré, a restaurant on West Fifty-sixth Street across from the two rooms where Breton lived. It was an open table for all of us to come and go. Tanguy came down from Woodbury,

Seligmann came down, Sandy Calder, Max Ernst. . . . Our table was right at the window."4

One can well imagine the effect all this had on the young artist. Merely being in the presence of such glamorous art-world figures was wonderful enough. Being accepted by them as an equal must have seemed like the wildest, most impossible dream come true. Even now, more than fifty years after these events, Donati remembers it all with great clarity: "It was a beautiful time. Our futures seemed so bright. We worked hard, but we also had fun. And they were all such great guys."

The reason for Donati's inclusion in this brilliant but idiosyncratic group, of course, was the nature and quality of his work. That he was a Surrealist was beyond question. Two examples from this period, in particular, *Le philtre* (1943) and *Trouble-fête* (1944), immediately establish him as such—unless, not unreasonably, the latter painting causes one to wonder if Hieronymus Bosch had not returned in modern guise. But even that early Flemish master of the fantastic would have been hard pressed to devise so wildly imaginative a scene, one in which water and air are interchangeable, grotesque swimming and flying creatures bearing only the slightest resemblance to their biological prototypes preen and prance about for no discernible reason, and the world itself seems to have gone mad.

As for quality, there also was no doubt. Donati must have surprised his colleagues with the passion and authority of his vision. No matter how complex, even convoluted, his early Surrealist compositions may appear—and *Trouble-fête* is a good example—careful examination will reveal a singleness of purpose behind that complexity that pushes unremittingly for particular pictorial objectives while also taking full advantage of any accidental painterly effects that occur along the way.

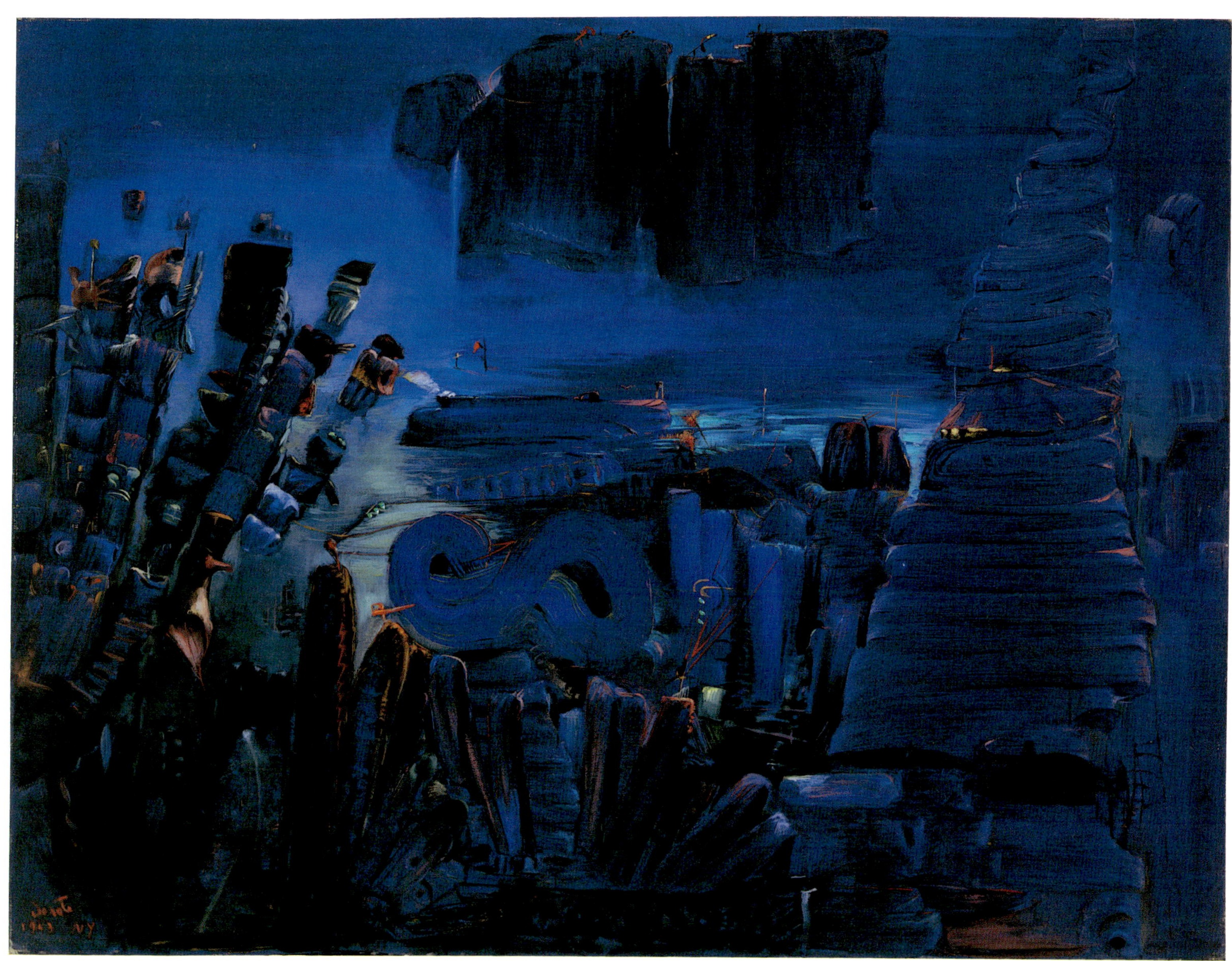

Snake Blue: Homage to Egas,
1943
Oil on canvas
30 × 40
Private collection

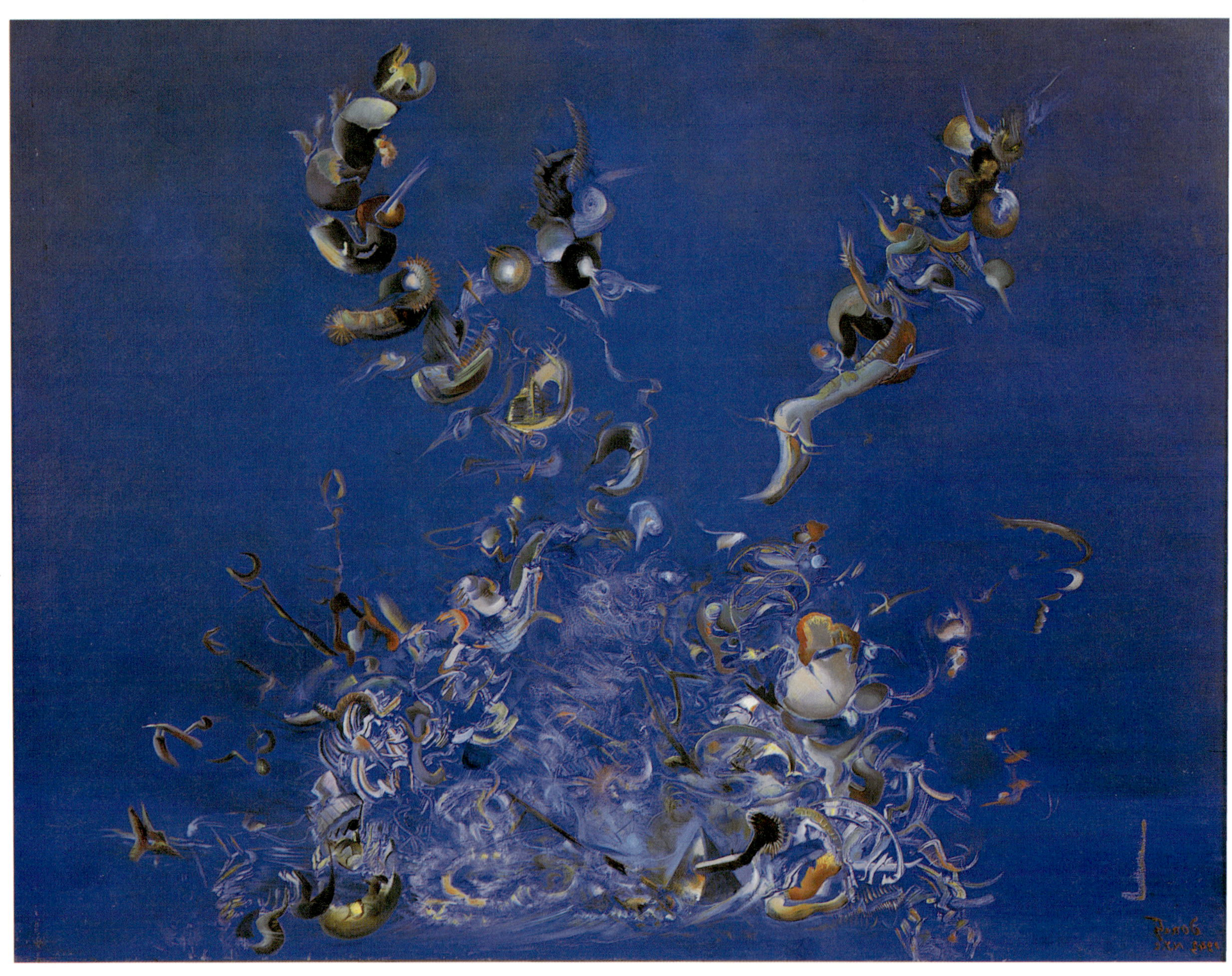

Le philtre (The Filter), 1943
Oil on canvas
30 × 40
Collection Marina Donati, Paris

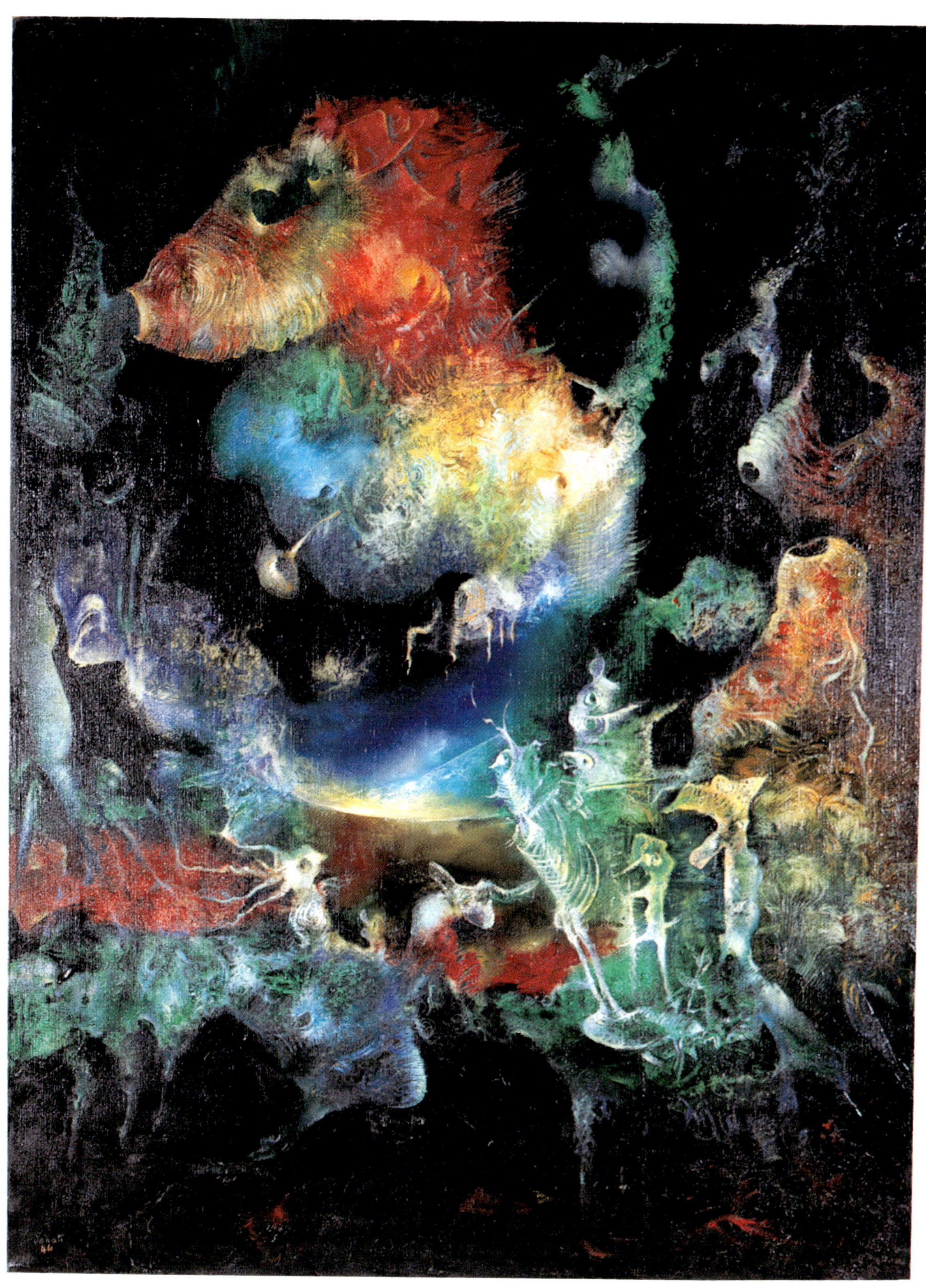

Trouble-fête (Killjoy), 1944
Oil on canvas
40 × 30
Private collection

Few painters of his generation had as direct a line into their subconscious as Donati—or as uncanny an ability to make the nature and substance of that communication known to others. There can be little doubt, when confronted by such paintings as *Gore and Mandra Jr.* (1944) and *Minotaure* (1945) or such provocative black-and-white pen drawings as *La chauve-souris* (1945) and *La création du monde le huitième jour* (1945), that, in them, Donati produced remarkably authentic and only slightly edited accounts of what he had sensed and "seen" at his deepest, most intuitive level.

Now while such subjective imagery may have been disturbing to some, it was received with enthusiasm by others. Breton, as already noted, proclaimed to the world that he loved Donati's paintings as he loved a night in May. The French critic and writer Maurice Nadeau, after declaring rather colorfully that he saw the art of Donati as "an airy and insolent flower rising from amidst the sunken ribs of a skeleton crumbling in the dust," went on to claim that "Donati's painting . . . shuns all mannerisms, whether of abstraction, figuration or even of Surrealism. He restores to the last its primal vigor which was perpetual conquest and liberation and to its revolution he adds a spiral unwinding to the infinite."[5] And the American art critic Nicolas Calas wrote simply, "Donati's paintings are love songs."[6]

At least some of this enthusiasm reflected the hope that Donati could heal the rift that had long divided Surrealist painters. The separation was between those who remained dependent on the world of appearance and those who discovered their imagery by means of automatic drawing or the utilization of "accidental" effects. Breton, in particular, thought Donati was just the person for the task, and he devoted much of his famous preface to the catalogue for the 1944 exhibition at the Passedoit Gallery in New York to explaining why.

Facing page
Gore and Mandra Jr., 1944
Oil on canvas
30 × 25
Collection James Pinz

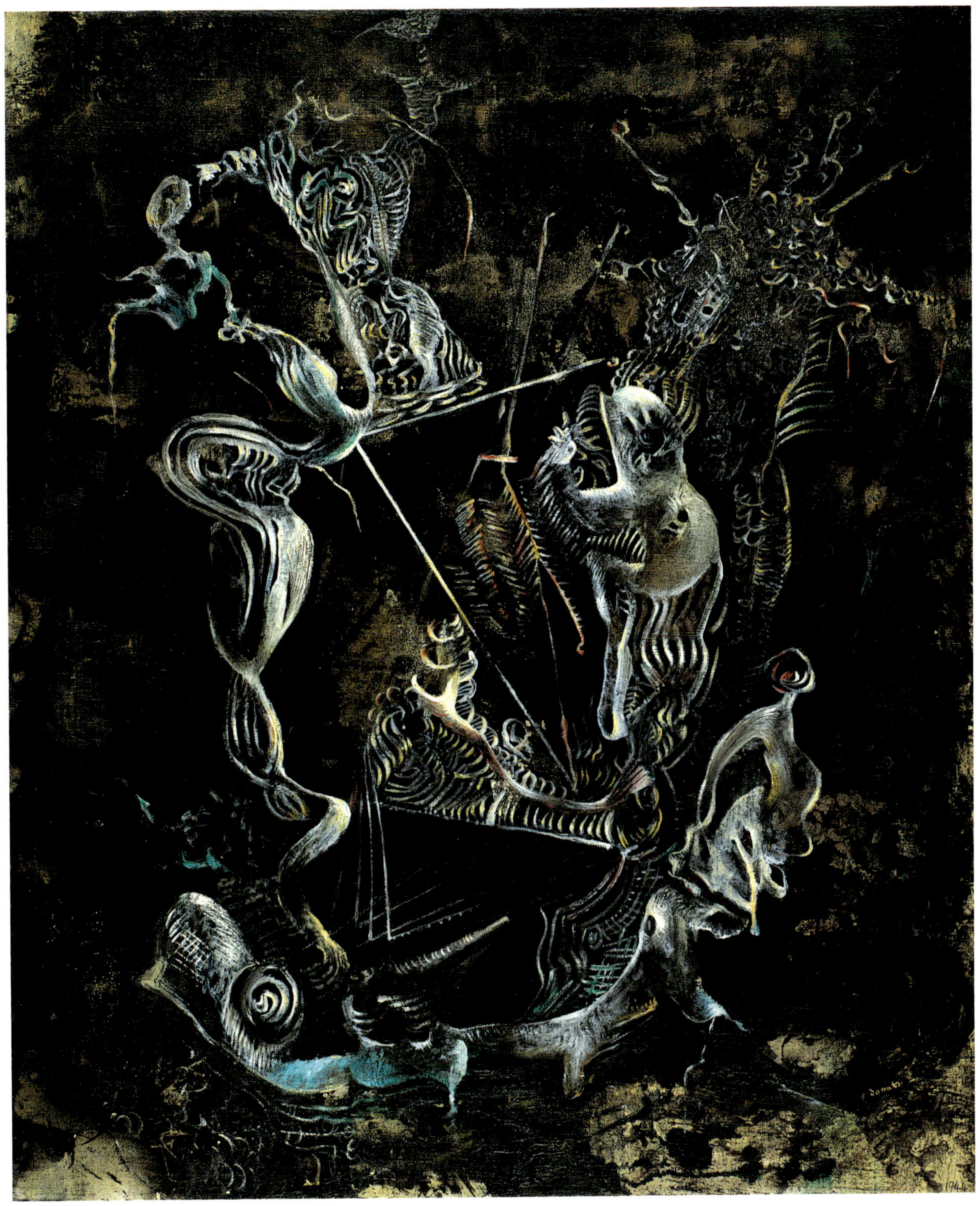

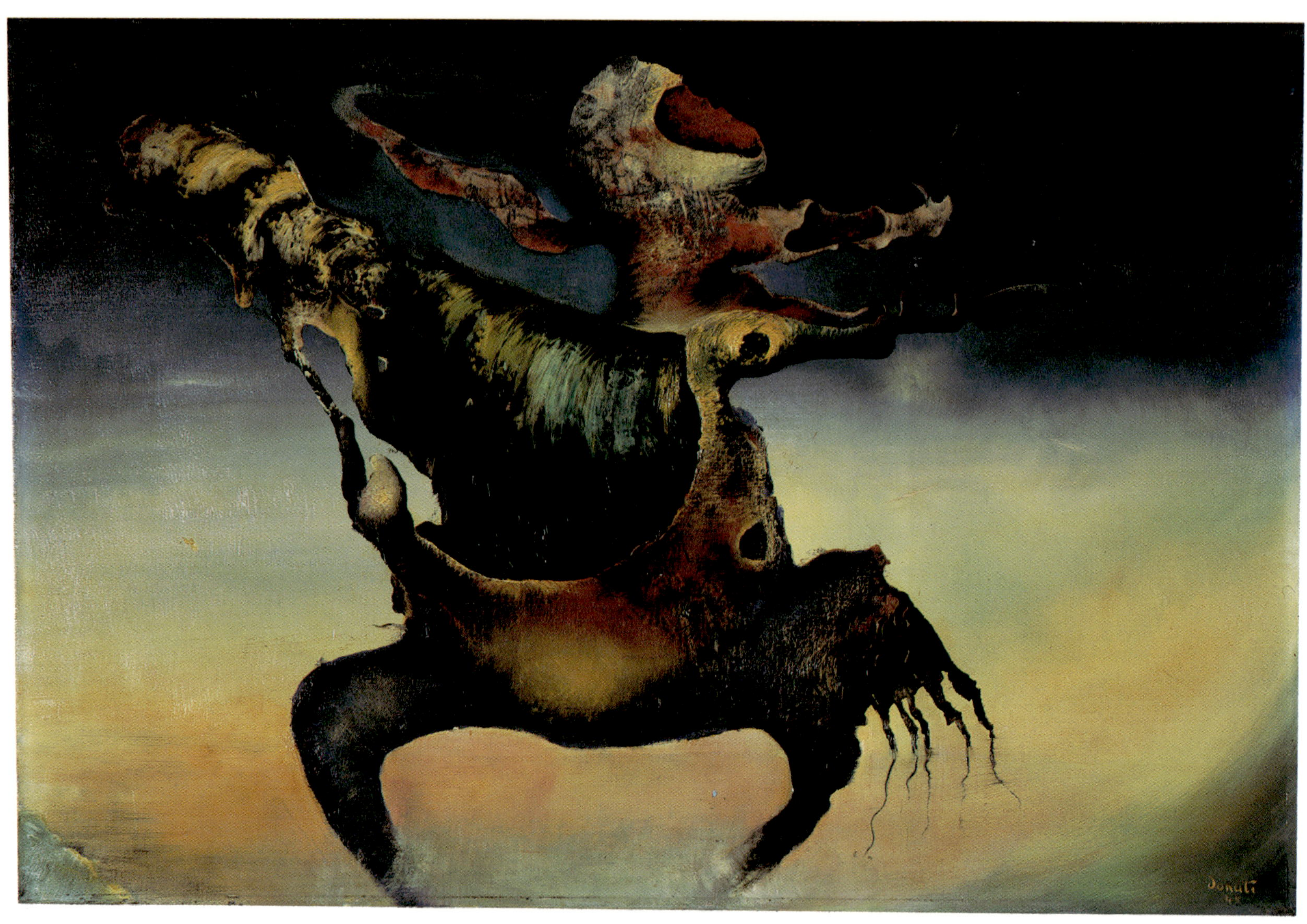

Minotaure, 1945
Oil on canvas
20 × 30
Private collection

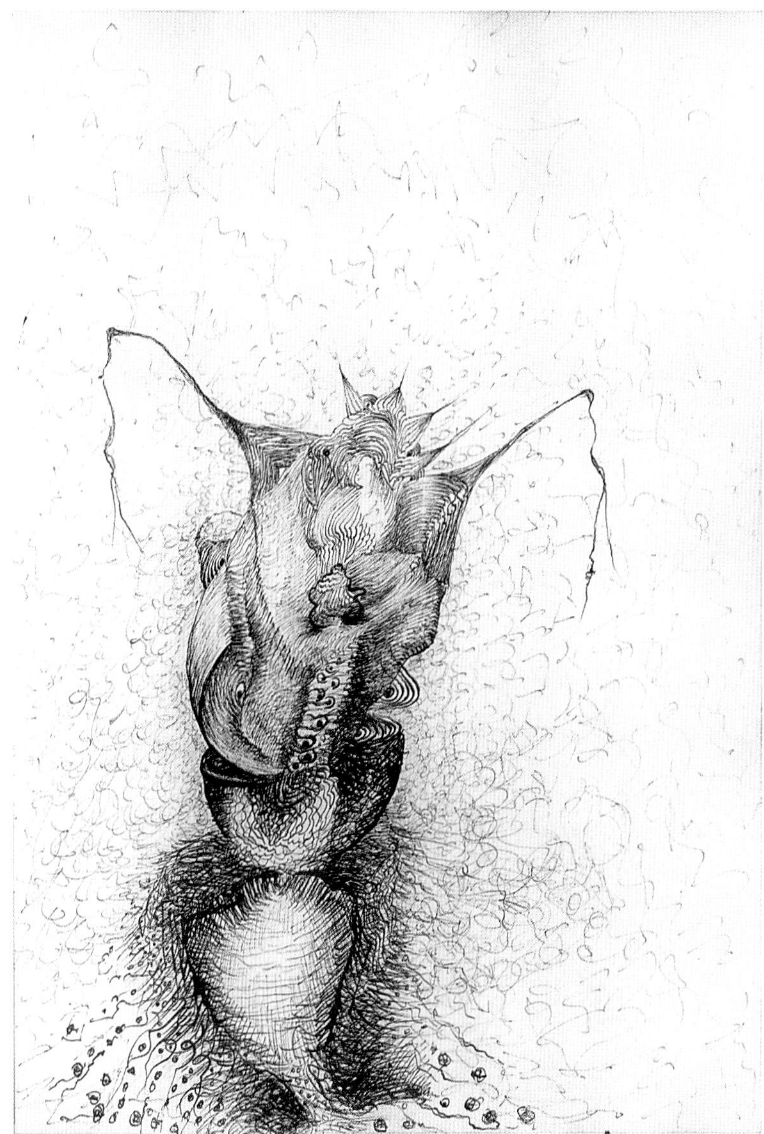

La chauve-souris (The Bat),
1945
Pen and ink on paper
9³/₄ × 6⁵/₈
Private collection

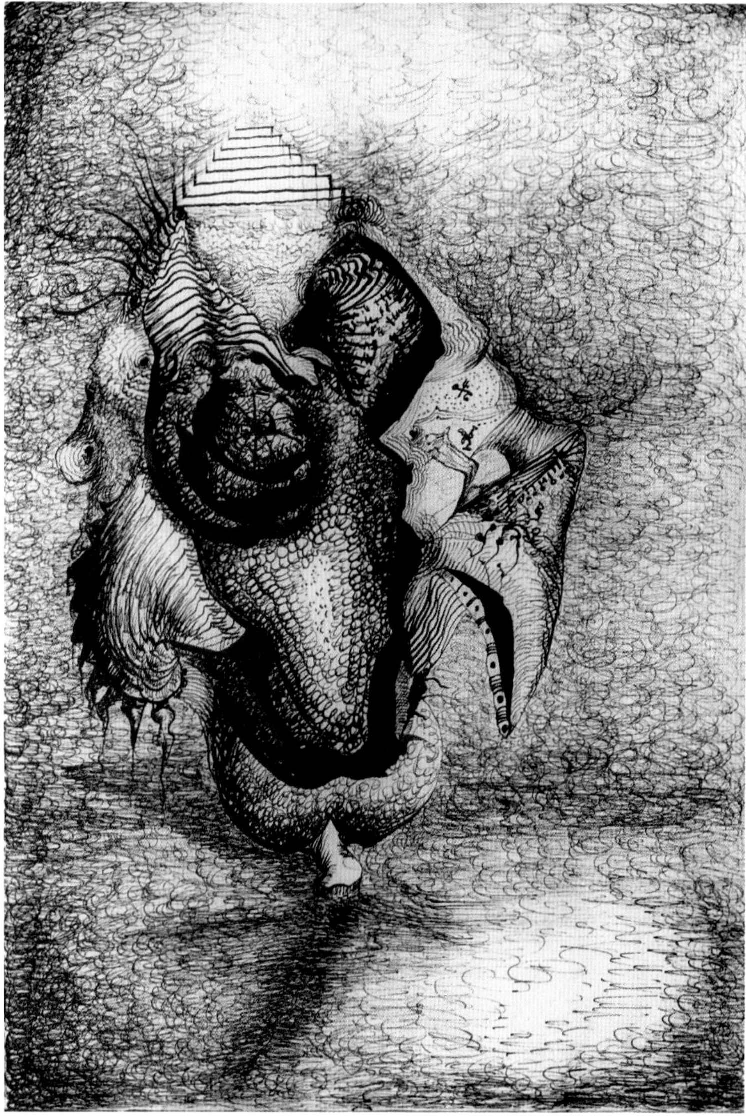

He began by defining the rift. "The quarrel . . . is the one which divides the two equally irreconcilable defenders of the two systems of figuration: the artist who insists on keeping a direct contact with the outer world and, however violently he disrupts that world, always takes his bearings from it," and his opponent, "who breaks with appearances, or at least the most familiar ones, and, claiming to have freed himself from the restraints of conventional space, demands that the painting take an objective value from itself alone."

Breton then went on: "Meanwhile, Enrico Donati has intervened in the thick of the fray. His background kept him aloof from the struggle that is still going on and it is immediately clear that his message is above all a message of harmony. It is indeed a message of harmony—were we only to judge by the favor with which he has been received in the two camps. Furthermore, by maintaining an equilibrium between the two rival worlds, instinctively rejecting any dissociation of vision, he avoids being ostracized by either side." And finally, using more typically Surrealist language, Breton affirmed: "It is a message of harmony because it conquers its most defiant adversaries by the quality of its light, . . . because the dynamism which carries it off . . . is always exerted in an upward sense, and gives above all the feeling of hatching, of breaking forth."[7]

Despite Breton's high hopes, the Surrealists, on the whole, ignored Donati's "message of harmony." Few who knew the situation were surprised. The Surrealists, after all, were famous for their carefully nurtured individualism. And besides, many of them argued, Breton's conclusions about the reconciling nature of Donati's work sounded a little too much like wishful thinking. Donati was a wonderful painter, no doubt about that, and his paintings had won the respect of both camps. But to envision him as a kind of savior, as someone capable of healing the rift between Surrealism's two rival factions, was unrealistic and asking too much of this talented but still youthful artist.

Meanwhile, Donati quietly kept on working—and in the process produced some of the finest and most original paintings of his career. *St. Elmo's Fire* and *Tentation d'Icare,* both from 1944, evoke the mystery and horror of the tales told long ago about the mandrake root's fearsome supernatural powers, but in ways that engage the viewer's serious and fascinated attention much more than they repel. Donati's artistry was such that even death and decay were transformed into something peculiarly alive and beautiful—perverse and somewhat intimidating though that beauty might be. In *St. Elmo's Fire,* a vaporous nocturnal light burns and glows with precisely the rich phantasmagoric colors one imagines present under the gallows when the mandrake plant assumes the form of the hanged man above it. And in *Tentation d'Icare,* twisted organic structures of indeterminate biological origin conjure up an exquisitely delineated and wondrously detailed world in which nothing is quite what it seems.

The ambiguity and often unconscious multiplicity of meaning that characterized Donati's work during this period are especially apparent in his more compact but equally "mandragoric" *L'oiseau-éponge* (1946) and in the already-mentioned *Gore and Mandra Jr.* (The latter title, of course, is a play on *mandragora.)* While the artist's thematic intentions in these paintings may not be clear, the mood and emotional response he wanted to induce are unmistakable.

Painting pictures that provoked such ambivalent and subjective reactions was one thing. Finding appropriate titles for them was quite another, especially since so many of Donati's images sprang directly, and in some cases almost full-blown, from his subconscious. Fortunately, Breton relieved him of this duty by volunteering for the task. He began in 1942, and continued until well into the 1950s, to come up with a series of provocative and often outrageous titles in French that added a great deal to the aura of mystery and enchantment that surrounded Donati's work.

Following pages

St. Elmo's Fire, 1944
Oil on canvas
36½ × 28½
The Museum of Modern Art, New York. Given anonymously

Tentation d'Icare
(Temptation of Icarus), 1944
Oil on canvas
30 × 25
Courtesy Horwitch Newman Gallery, Scottsdale, Arizona

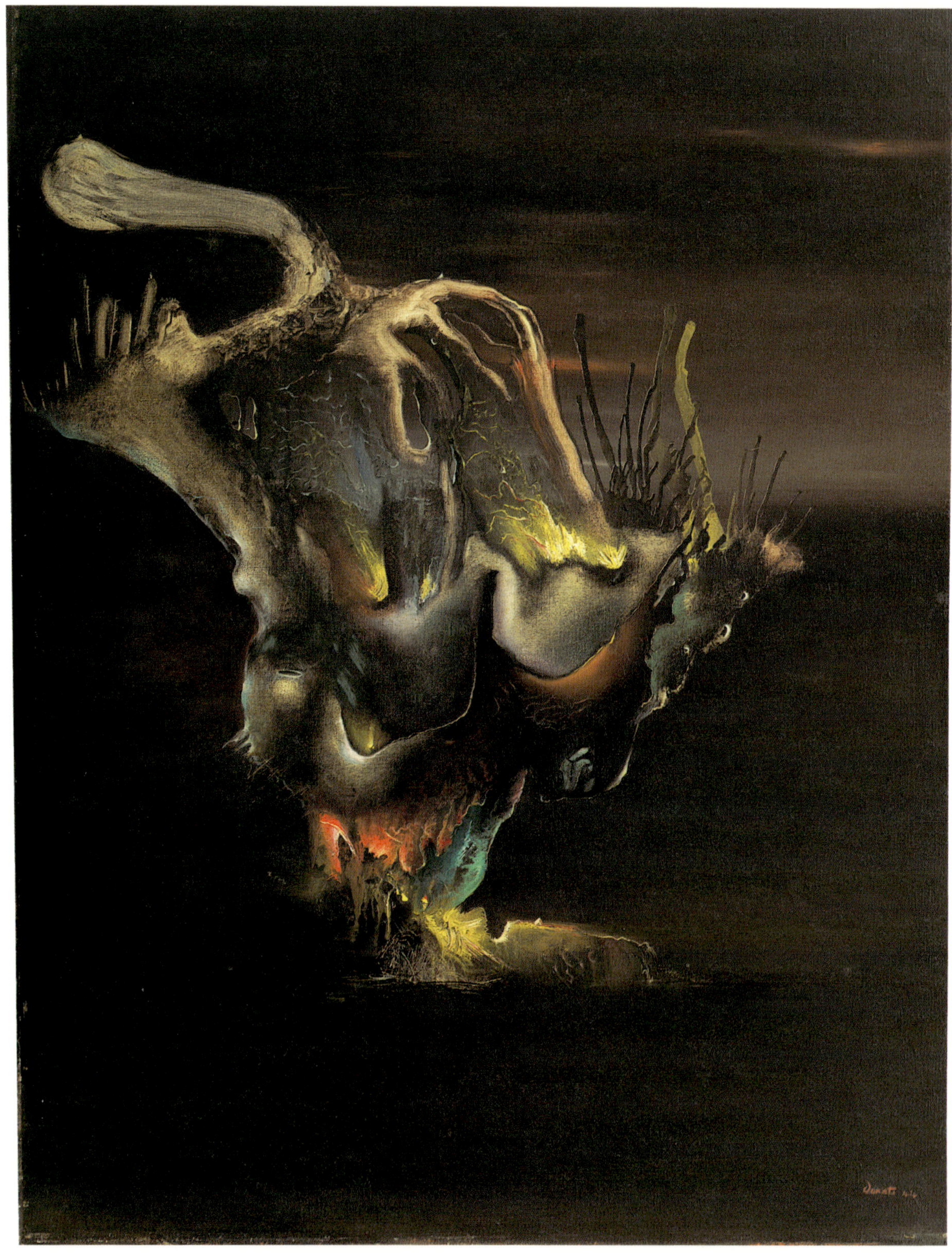

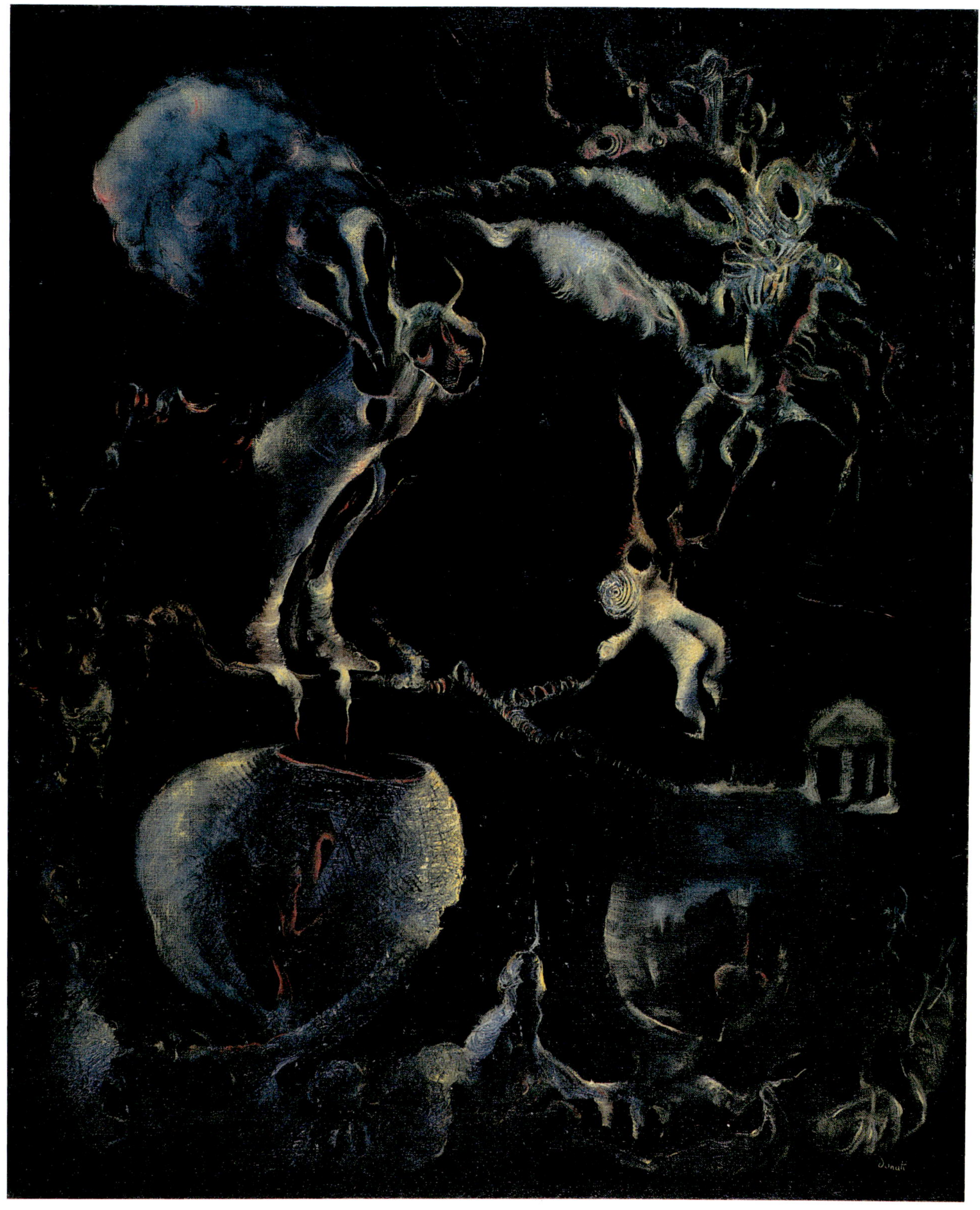

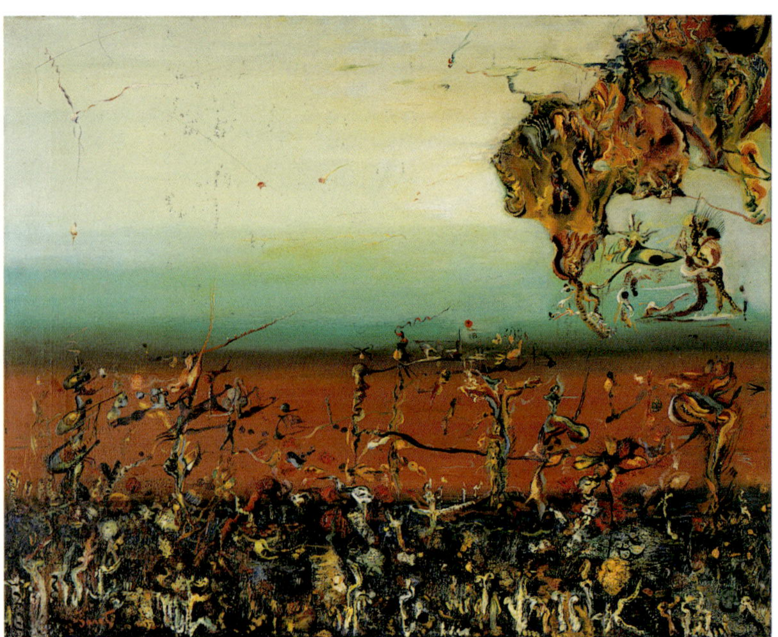

Émotion con moto

(Emotion with Motion), 1944

Oil on canvas

32 × 28

Private collection

L'oiseau-éponge

(The Sponge-Bird), 1946

Oil on canvas

20 × 24

Collection Dr. James A. Jordan,
Fort Lauderdale, Florida

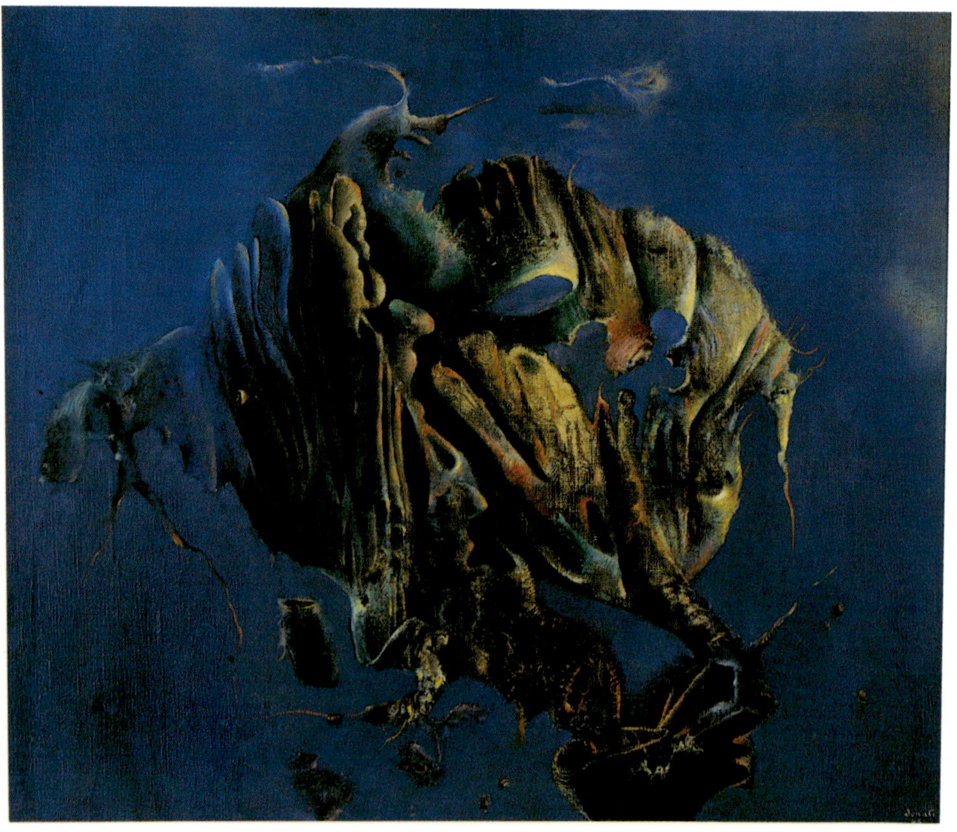

According to the writer Alan Jones, "(E)ach of these titles can be said to qualify as the shortest (and uncollected) Surrealist poems by André Breton. . . . Like a *cadavre exquis,* this interaction between painter and poet embodies all of the Surrealist spirit of spontaneous combustion of the psyche occurring in the highly charged electrical field between multiple creative forces."[8]

This spirit of cooperation took other forms as well. In 1945 Duchamp and Donati collaborated on the installation of a window display at Brentano's New York bookstore for the second edition of Breton's book *Le Surréalisme et la peinture,* which included a chapter dedicated to Donati's paintings. Donati's major contribution consisted of a startling half-feet/half-shoes sculpture entitled *Shoes,* which was based on the Magritte painting that graced the book's cover. Even more disturbing—at least to the bookstore's owner—was a headless female manikin reading a book. Outraged, Mr. Brentano demanded the entire display be removed. Delighted by the trouble they had caused, Duchamp and Donati immediately transferred the display to the Gotham Book Mart.

A much more significant event was the *Exposition Internationale du Surréalisme,* which Donati helped Duchamp organize in 1947 at the Galerie Maeght in Paris. This would prove to be Surrealism's last big public event before it entered the history books. And while most of those who participated in it probably did not know how close the movement was to extinction, they nevertheless did all they could to make it a memorable occasion. Among Donati's contributions to the exposition were *Carnaval de Venise* (1946), one of the most spectacular of his Mandragora canvases, and three pieces of sculpture, *Fist* (1946), *Evil Eye* (1947), and *Pour un autel* (1947). Of these, *Fist,* with its two fishy glass eyes protruding from the center of a clenched fist, struck the most provocative note. It was *Evil Eye,* however, which occupied a special place in the exposition's *Salle des Superstitions,* a room designed by Frederick Kiesler and filled with strange and exotic objects selected by Duchamp, Donati, Ernst, Matta, Miró, and Tanguy.

Donati was involved in other projects with Duchamp in 1947. The two collaborated on the cover of the catalogue accompanying the Paris exhibition *Le Surréalisme en 1947,* each copy of which included a glued-on foam-rubber breast. And shortly thereafter, Donati worked with this mentor on the *Nude Descending the Staircase* sequence in Hans Richter's film, *Dreams That Money Can Buy.*

On the creative front, however, things were not quite so productive. World War II was over, many of Donati's Surrealist friends had returned to Europe, and Surrealism itself was dying. Furthermore, he had begun to have misgivings about his own work. He felt that his paintings had become too romantic, too

Shoes, 1945
Oil on leather shoes
5¾ x 11¼ x 7¾
Private collection

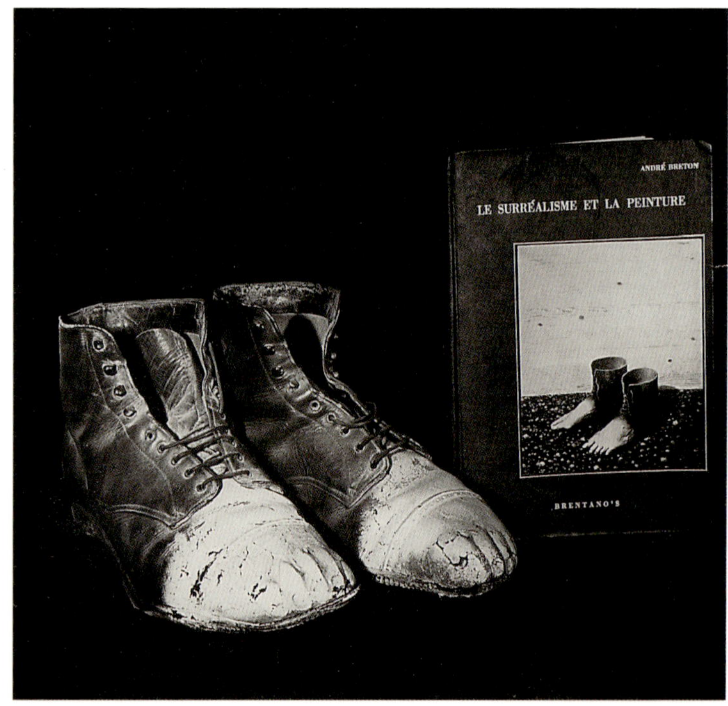

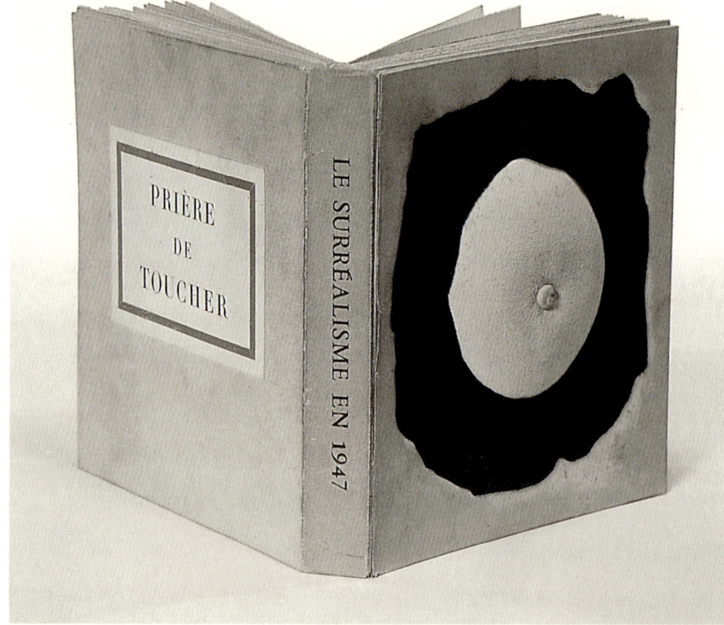

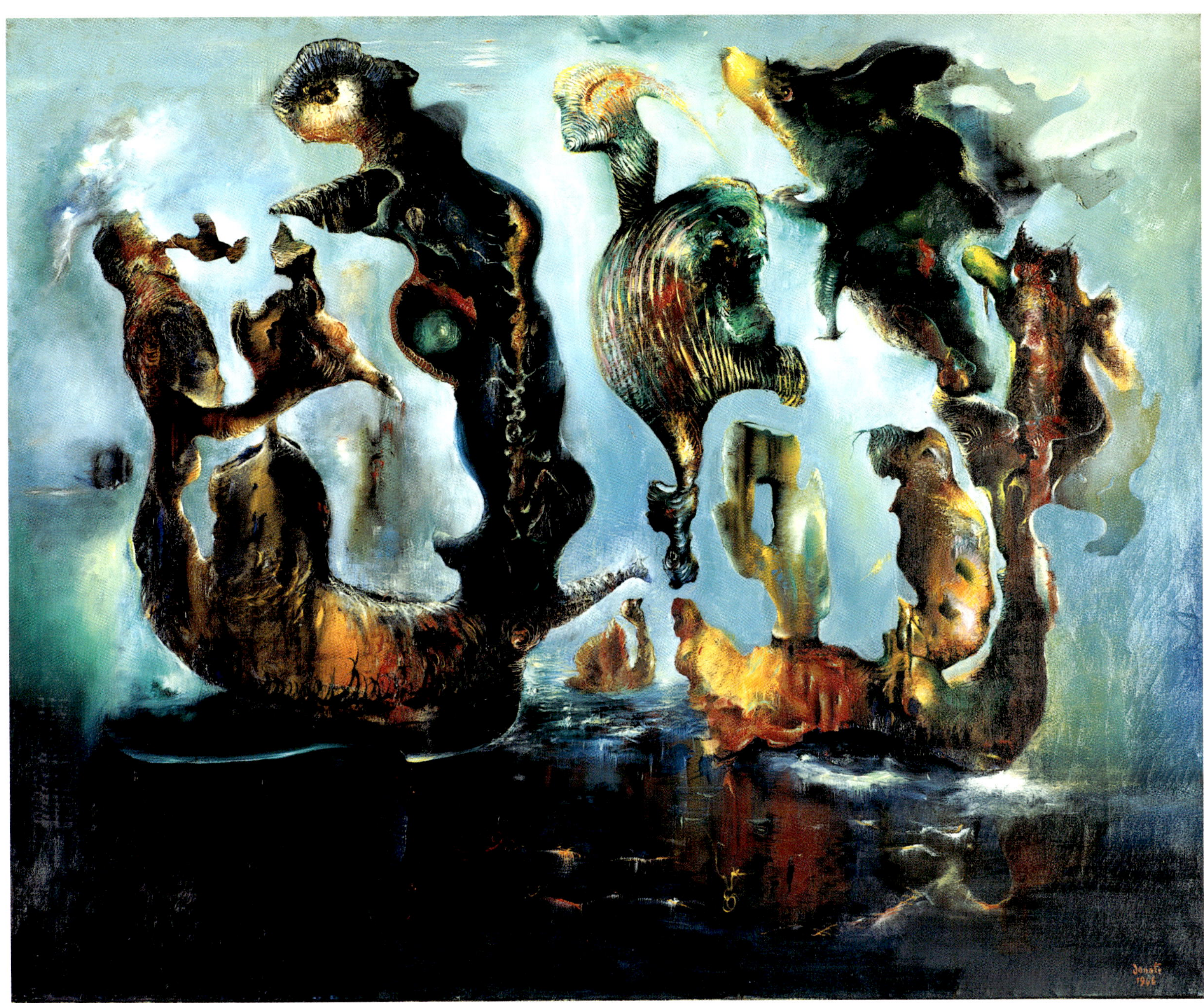

Carnaval de Venise
(Carnival of Venice), 1946
Oil on canvas
40 × 50
Private collection

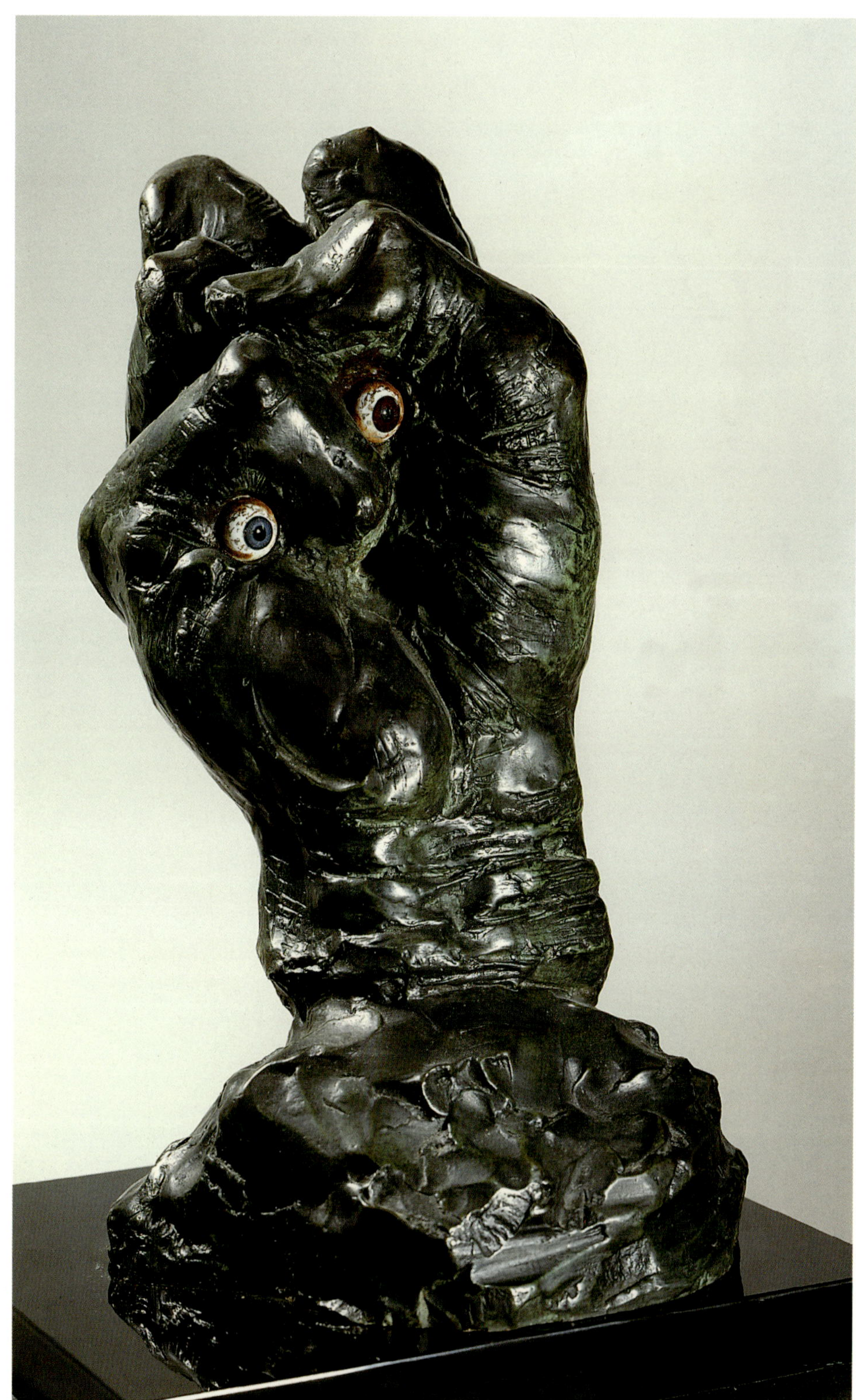

Facing page

Evil Eye, 1947
mixed media
9¾ x 11½ × 7
Private collection

Fist, 1946
Bronze and glass eyes
17 x 10½ x 10
Collection V. Michael Hogan

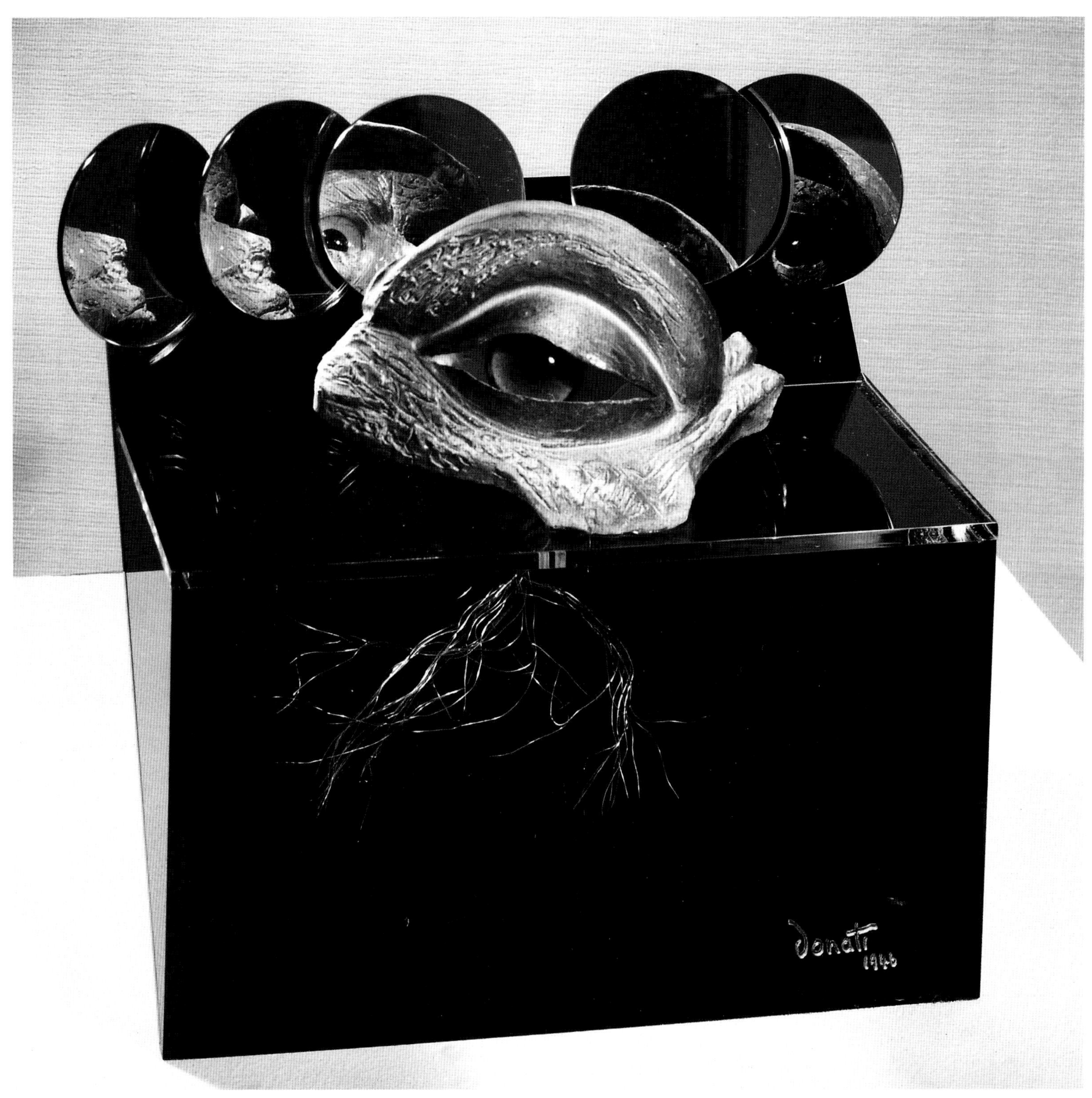

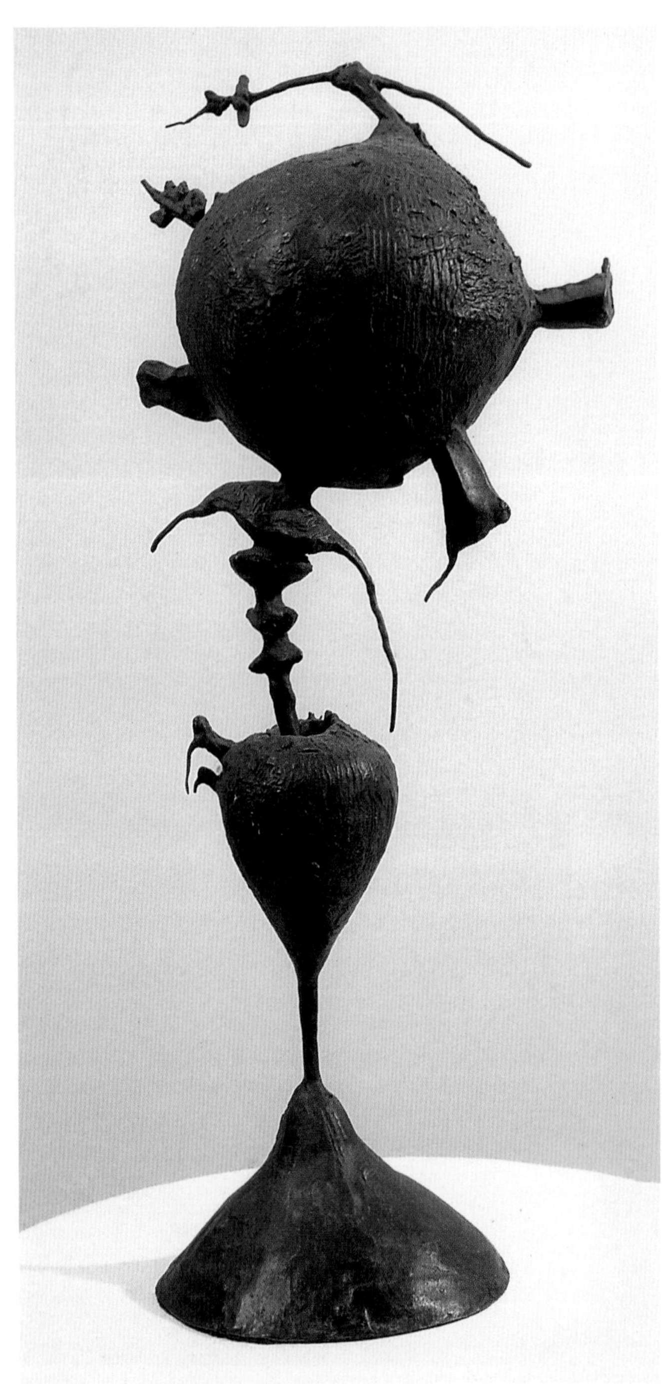

Pour un autel, 1945
Bronze
19 × 8 × 5¹⁄₂
Private collection

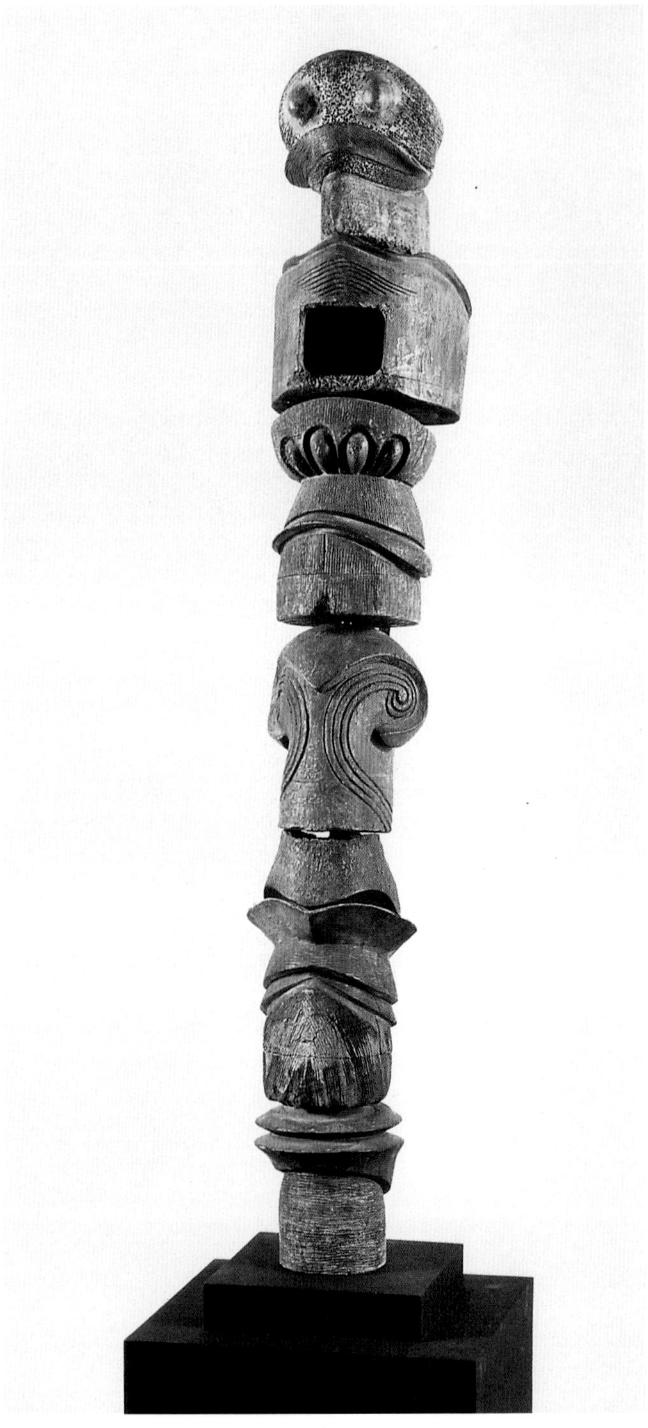

Totem (Hommage à Julius),
1945
Wood
53³⁄₄ × 9¹⁄₂ × 9¹⁄₂ (irregular)
Private collection

pleasing in color, even a bit too sentimental, and that it was time to discipline himself, to impose certain restrictions on how and what he painted.

In short, Donati felt the need both for a corrective for his work and for greater control over the creative act. And small wonder. Automatism was a perfectly good way to produce art, but it *did,* after a while, leave the feeling that one was not fully in control, that one's paintings "happened" more often than not with very little, if any, conscious effort on one's part.

And of no one must this have been more true than Donati. With his extraordinarily direct line into his subconscious, and his uncanny ability to "report back" directly to others what existed there, he must have been particularly vulnerable to this feeling of not being sufficiently in charge of what he produced.

But while he realized the need to break away from a creative mode that was threatening to engulf him, and to experiment with other methods and approaches, he found such a move easier to contemplate than to put into effect. For one thing, there was the matter of his reputation. Would he still be held in such high regard by those he admired most? Or would they and the art world turn their backs on him if what he painted failed to meet their expectations?

It was a difficult decision but one he could not avoid making. What he *could* avoid, however, was public awareness of what he was attempting. And so, from 1947 to 1949 Donati withdrew within himself to experiment.

The imagery and style of the works from 1947 and 1948 that Donati began showing to his friends when he resurfaced in 1949 were dramatically different from anything he had produced before. The appearance of his art changed. Amorphous, organic forms became crystalline and aggressively geometric. Objects, which previously had floated or swum randomly within dense, vaguely defined space, were now crisply delineated and precisely located against backgrounds of evenly applied flat paint. And the provocatively blended colors for which he had become so well known were now carefully isolated and compartmentalized within clusters of circles, triangles, and squares.

No wonder he was concerned about the reaction of his peers and the public, or even, at times, as he now admits, about the validity of this new approach. There had been hints, of course, a year or so earlier, of what was to come. But apparently his 1946 canvas *La méduse, l'araignée s'aimant,* while already largely geometric in form, was still sufficiently biomorphic not to reveal the direction his art was taking. And *La prière de l'araignée,* which he had begun in 1946 but did not complete until the following year, was so obviously a radical departure that Donati kept it hidden from view.

In fact, none of these new works—there would be some thirty-five in all— would be seen at the time by anyone except a few close friends (Breton, Calas, Duchamp, and Matta), and none would be exhibited until 1987 when the Zabriskie Gallery in New York assembled twelve of them for a show.

Startlingly different as his new paintings may have appeared, it was not until late 1947 and early 1948 that the truly significant changes he had envisioned actually occurred. Until then, much of what differentiated the new from the old was technical. *Adoremus, Adorentimus* and *Tout mais pas la méduse,* both from 1947, while obviously unlike what Donati had painted previously, still retained several basic characteristics of the Mandragora canvases. They were improvised and haphazardly organized, depended on automatism for some of their more spectacular effects, and included forms as blatantly biomorphic as any he had painted in previous years. But most significant of all, their newfound geometric underpinnings, although as hard edged as any that would come later, served little, if any, solid structural purpose.

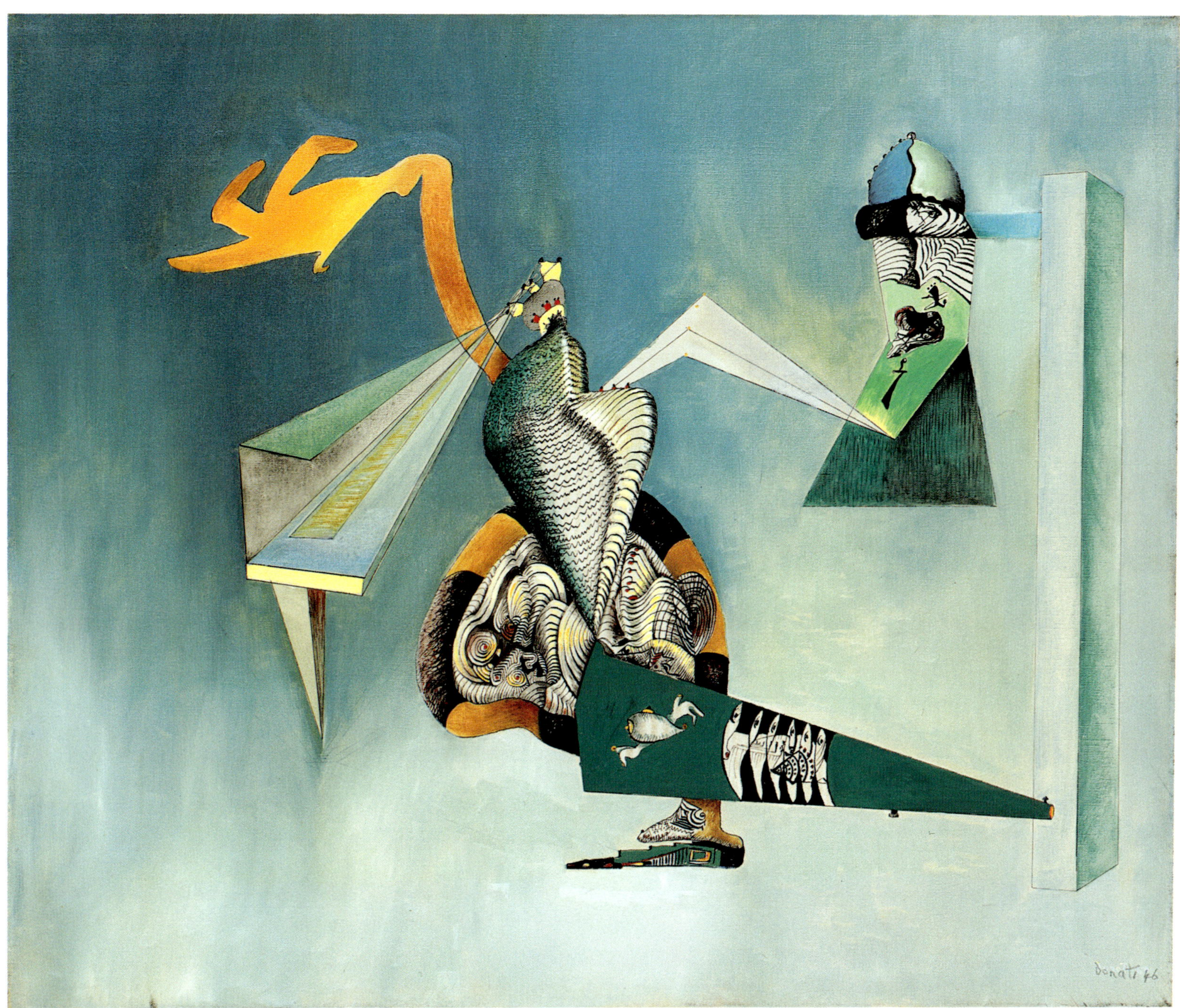

La méduse, l'araignée s'aimant

(The Jellyfish, the Spider Loving Each Other),
1946

Oil on canvas

25 × 30

Courtesy Virginia Zabriskie Gallery, New York

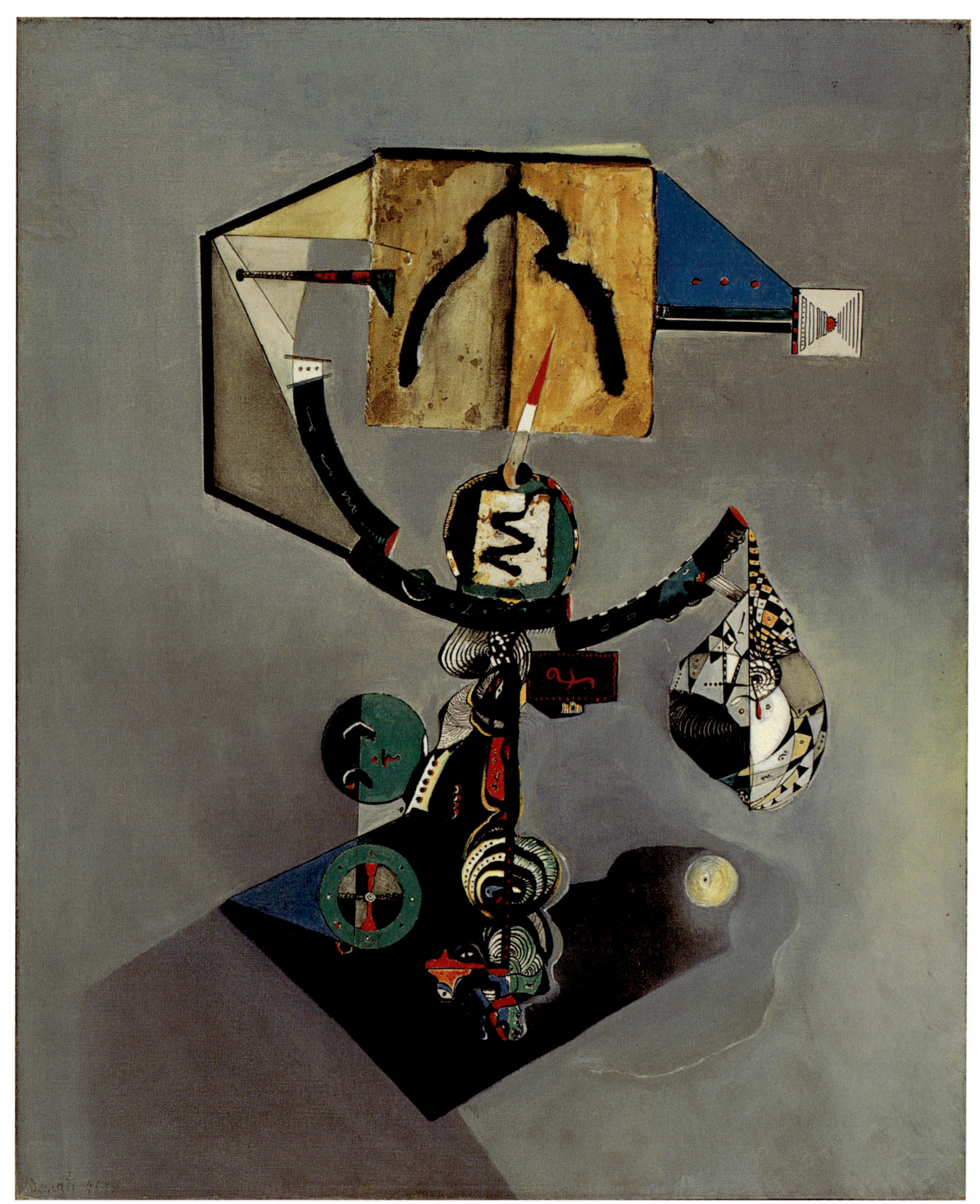

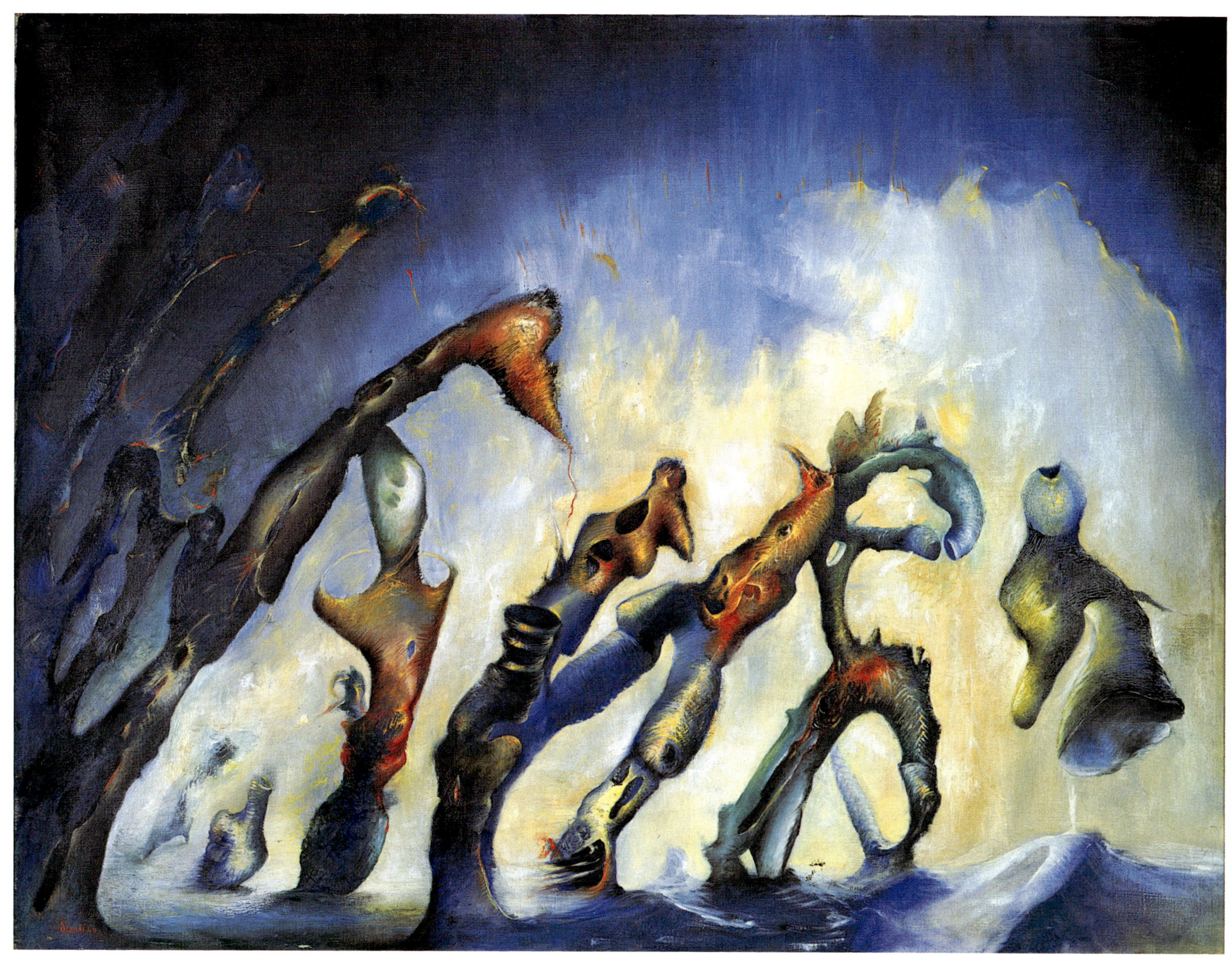

Exode (Exodus), 1946
Oil on canvas
30 × 40
Collection François Jolivet

Facing page
La prière de l'araignée
(The Spider's Prayer), 1946–47
Oil on canvas
24 × 20
Private collection

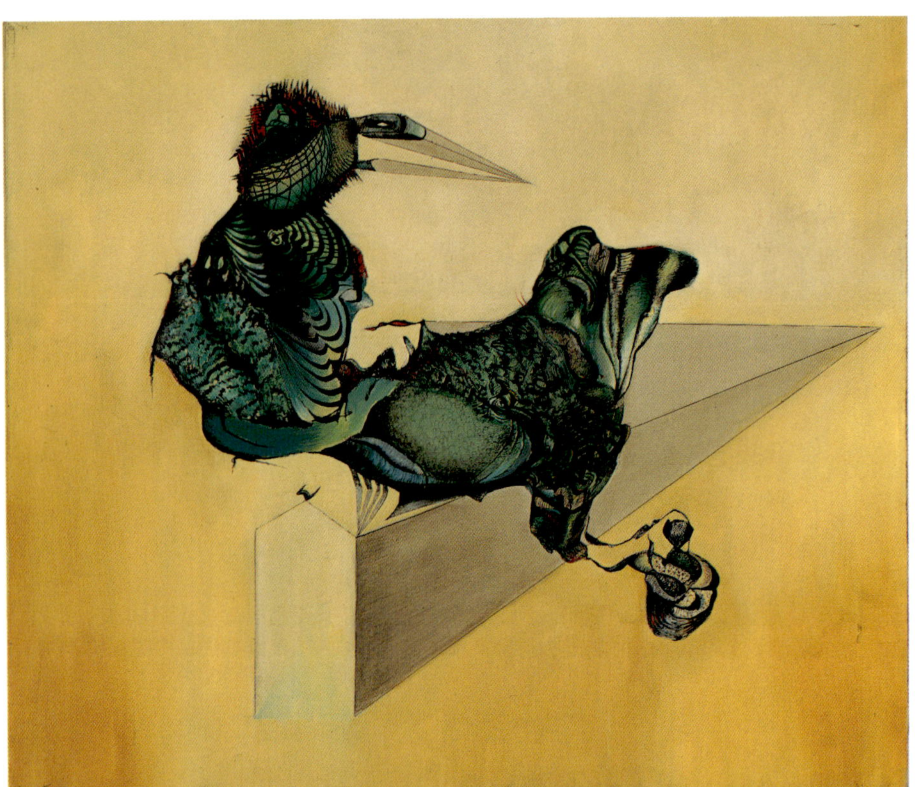

Adoremus, Adorentimus,
1947
Oil on canvas
25 × 29½
Private collection

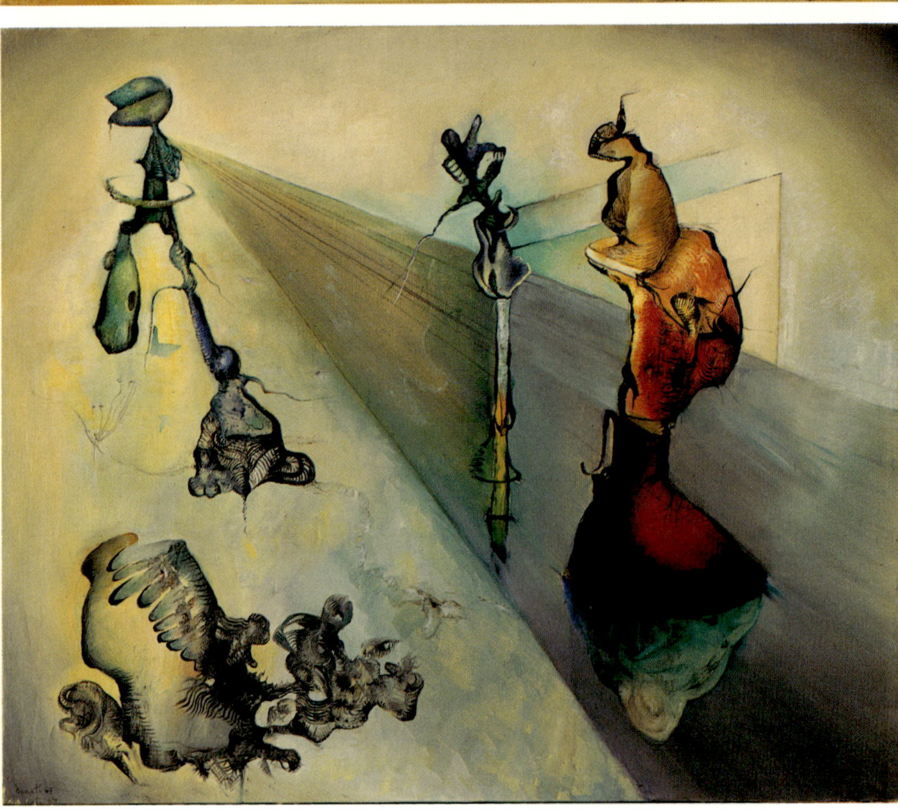

Tout mais pas la méduse
(Anything but Not the Jellyfish),
1947
Oil on canvas
25 × 29½
Courtesy Virginia Zabriskie
Gallery, New York

Technically, of course, the changes were obvious. But that was primarily a matter of substitution, of the replacement of organic forms with geometric ones, and the transformation of smudges and blobs of paint into straight lines and colored circles or squares. The technical devices undoubtedly were different, but the creative impulse that produced them was still largely the same.

All of that changed with *Champs électriques organisés par l'heure artificielle à longs prolongements de charge terrestre* (1947) and *Chambre à décompression* (1948). In them, the formal replaced the informal, and Donati's desire for greater creative control was finally realized. The latter painting, especially, demonstrated how successfully he had transformed his art. All that had been vague, soft, or romantic, or that had appeared undisciplined, was gone, and in their place Donati had fashioned a painted world that was crisp, clear, and uncompromisingly geometric.

Even more important, *Chambre à décompression* revealed a level of organizational planning far superior to any he had shown before. Every element of the painting, from its broadest areas of color to its tiniest textural details, appeared not only perfectly in place but also exquisitely in balance with everything else in the composition.

For Donati, past master of the unplanned and accidental in art, the degree of calculated structural sophistication realized in this work represented a profoundly significant step of far-reaching consequences. Only rarely in the future would his art be as exclusively intuitive and impulsive as it was before he attempted these paintings. And while he would seldom again produce anything as tightly controlled, he also would never forget the lessons learned during the process, as he put it, of "disciplining myself."

Yet while these later geometric canvases may have been compositionally clearer and structurally more sophisticated than what had preceded them, their

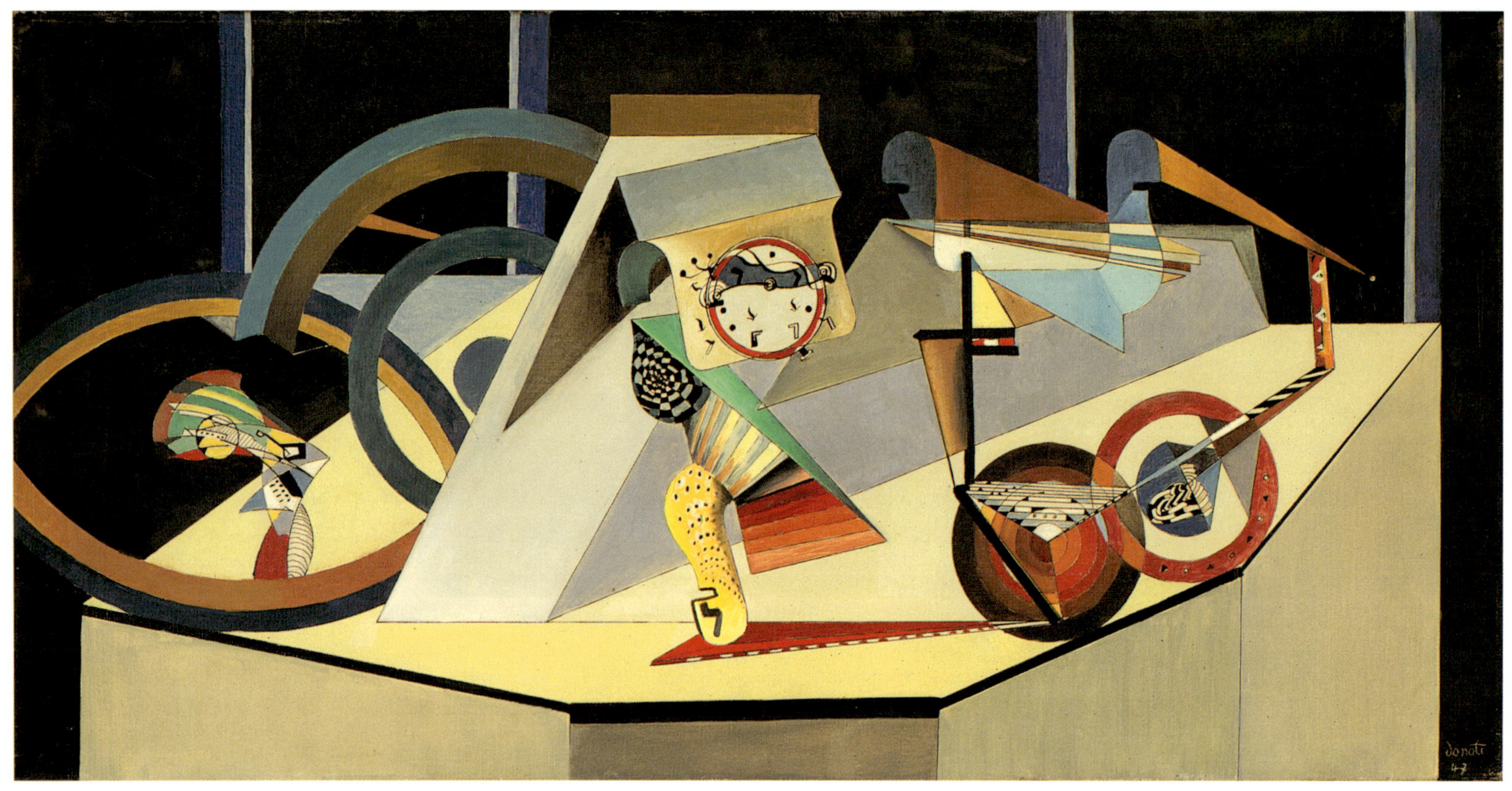

**Champs électriques organisés par l'heure
artificielle à longs prolongements de charge terrestre**

(Electrical Fields Organized by Artificial Time with Long
Extensions of Terrestrial Charge), 1947

Oil on canvas

15 × 30

Collection Mrs. Luigi Alemagna, Milan, Italy

Facing page

Chambre à décompression

(Decompression Chamber), 1948

Oil on canvas

36 × 30

Collection Mr. and Mrs. Stephen Owen, Jr.

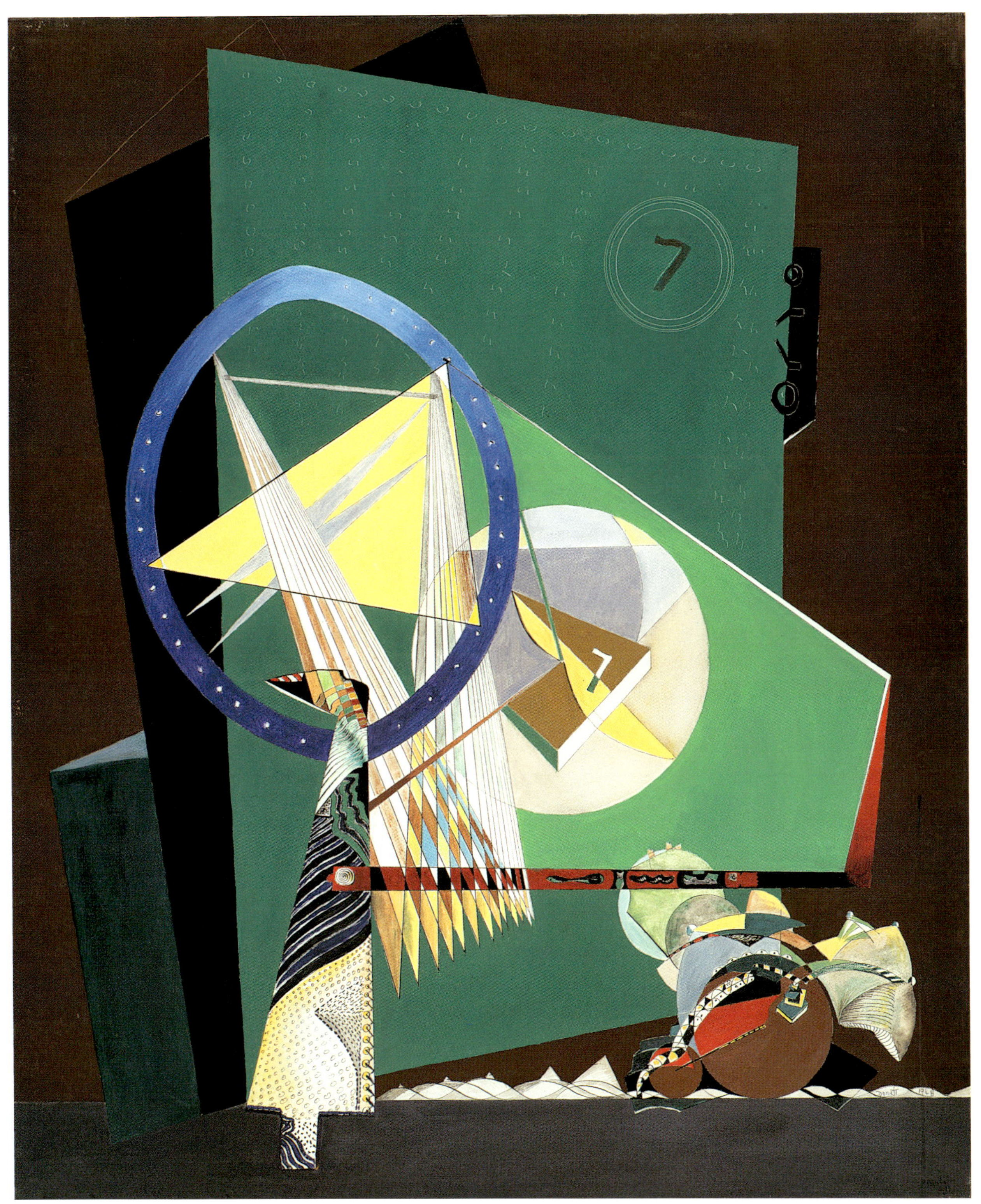

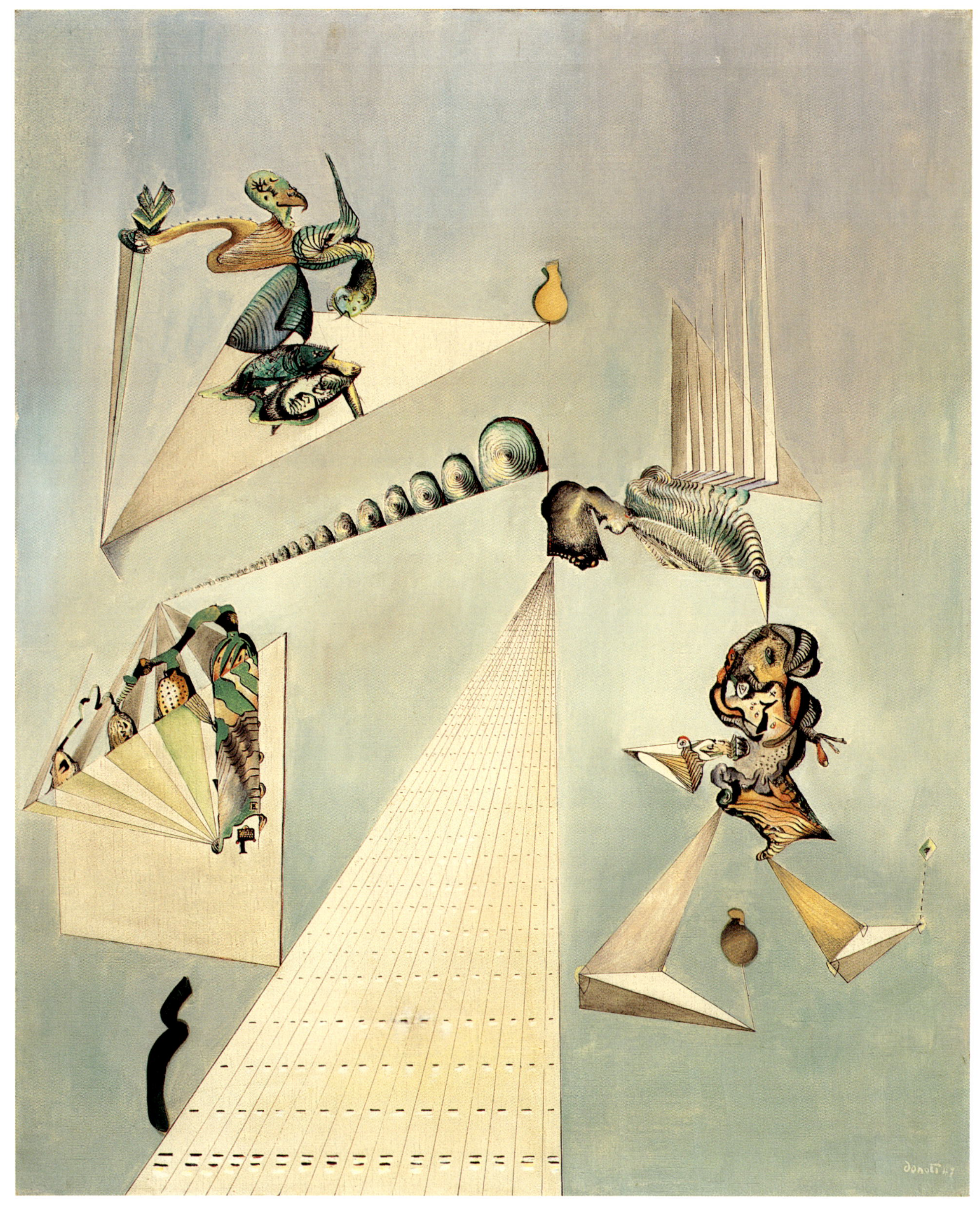

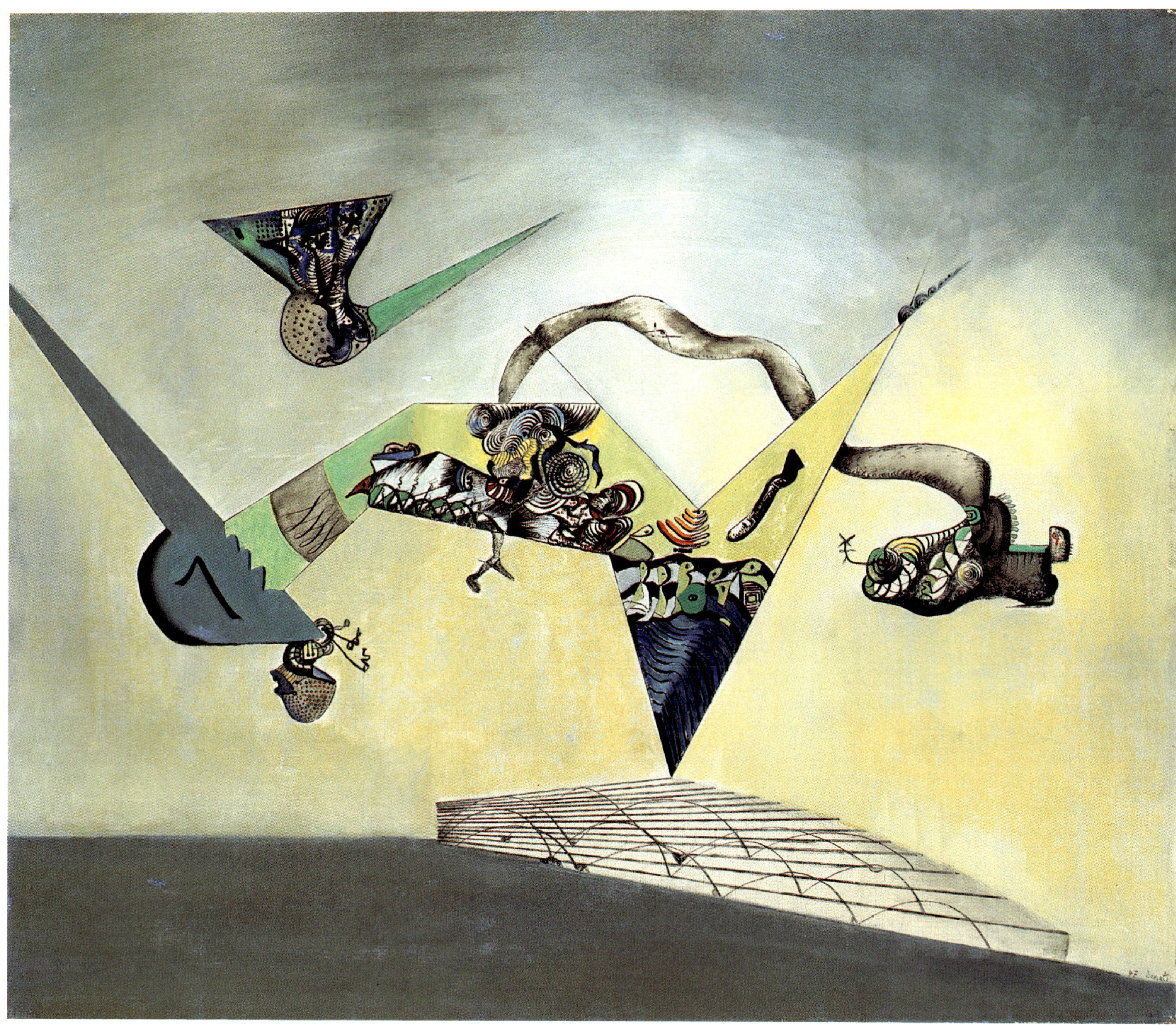

Médisance de l'air

(Scandal of the Air), 1947

Oil on canvas

25 × 29½

Courtesy Virginia Zabriskie Gallery,
New York

Facing page

Les cordes du vent

(The Ropes of the Wind), 1947

Oil on canvas

36 × 30

Collection Arturo Schwarz

49

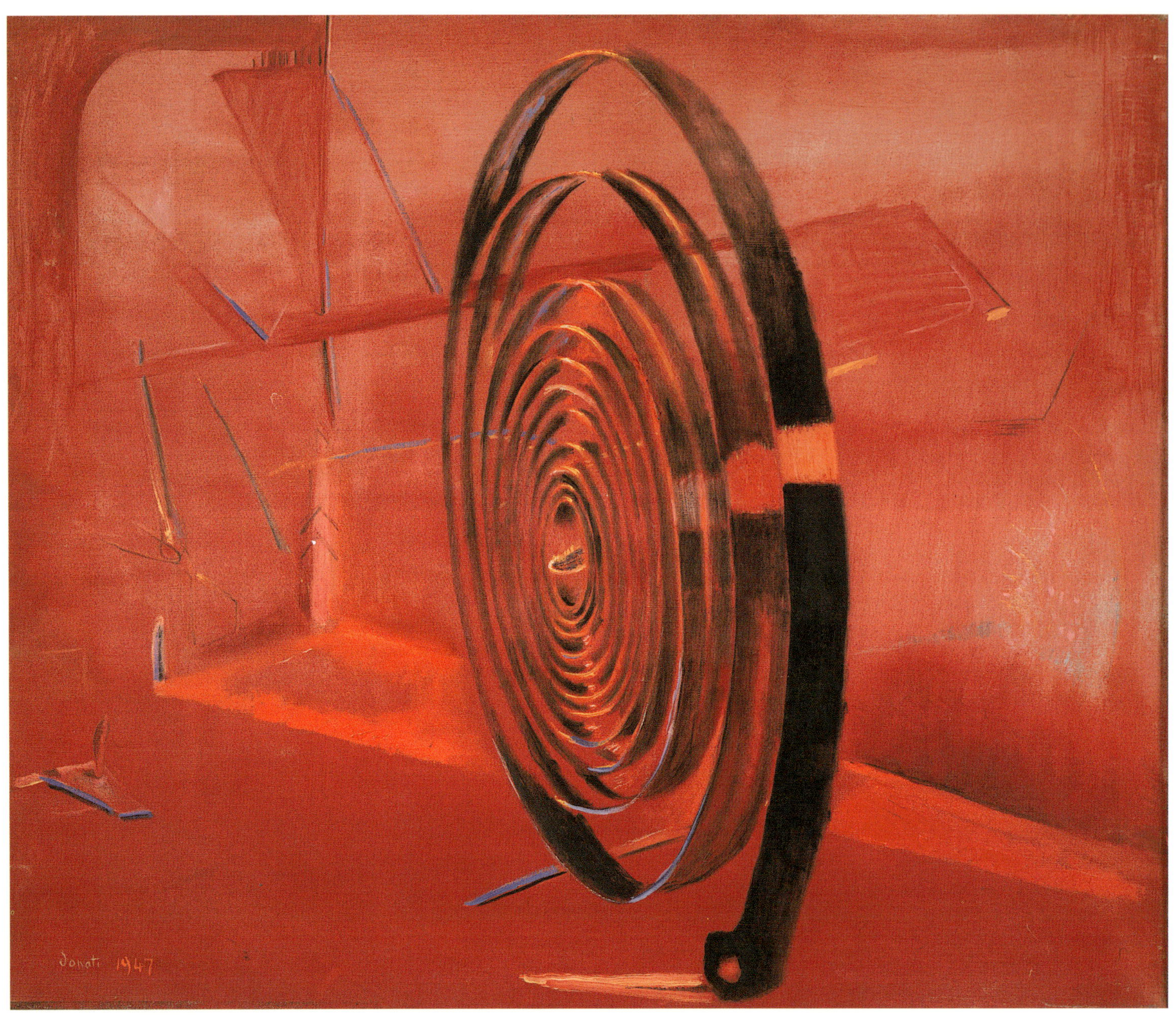

**Sfère roulante dans la
comète stable** (Sphere Rolling in
the Stable Comet), 1947
Oil on canvas
25 × 30
Private collection

Facing page
Soleil gris (Grey Sun), 1947
Oil on canvas
50 × 40
Private collection

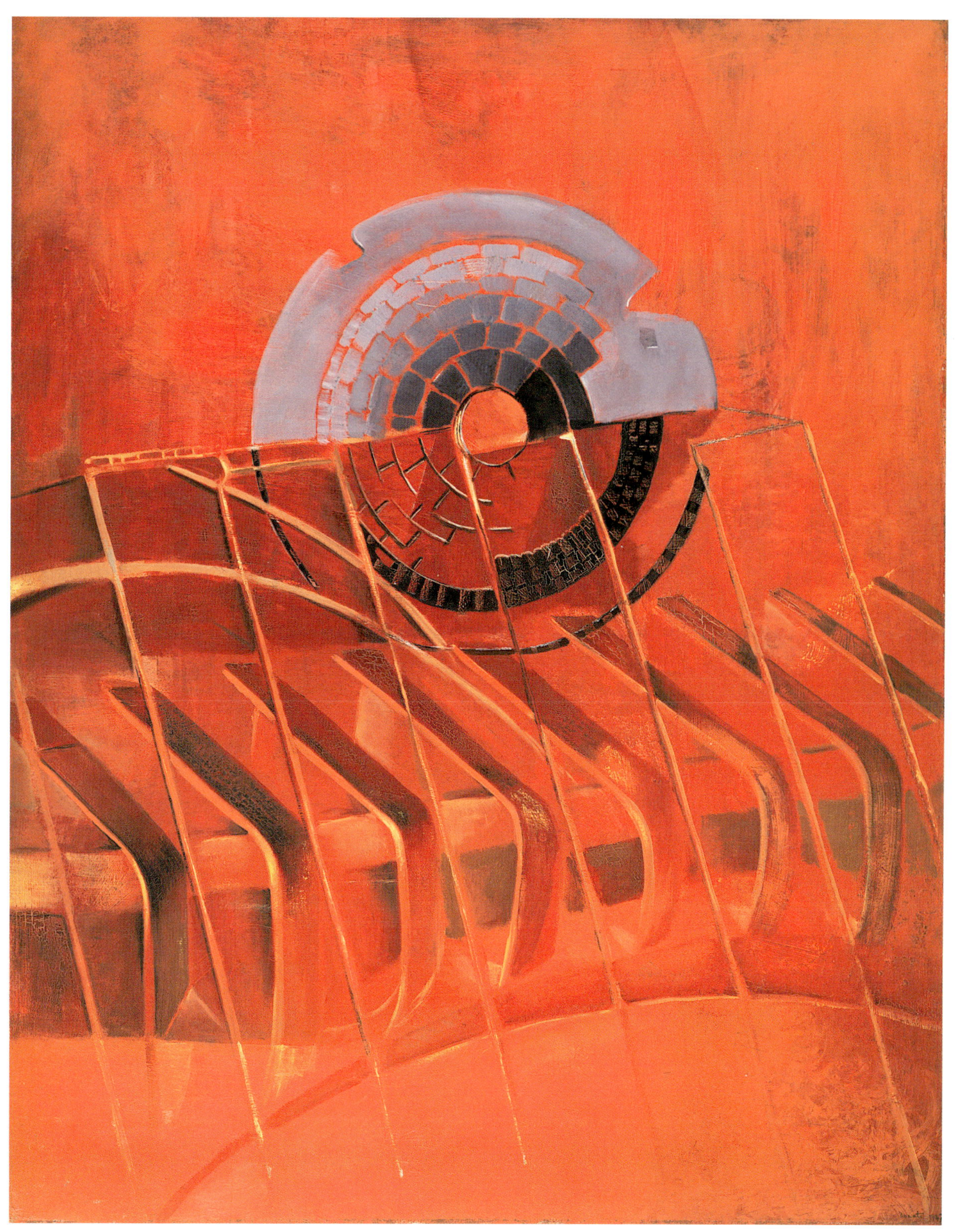

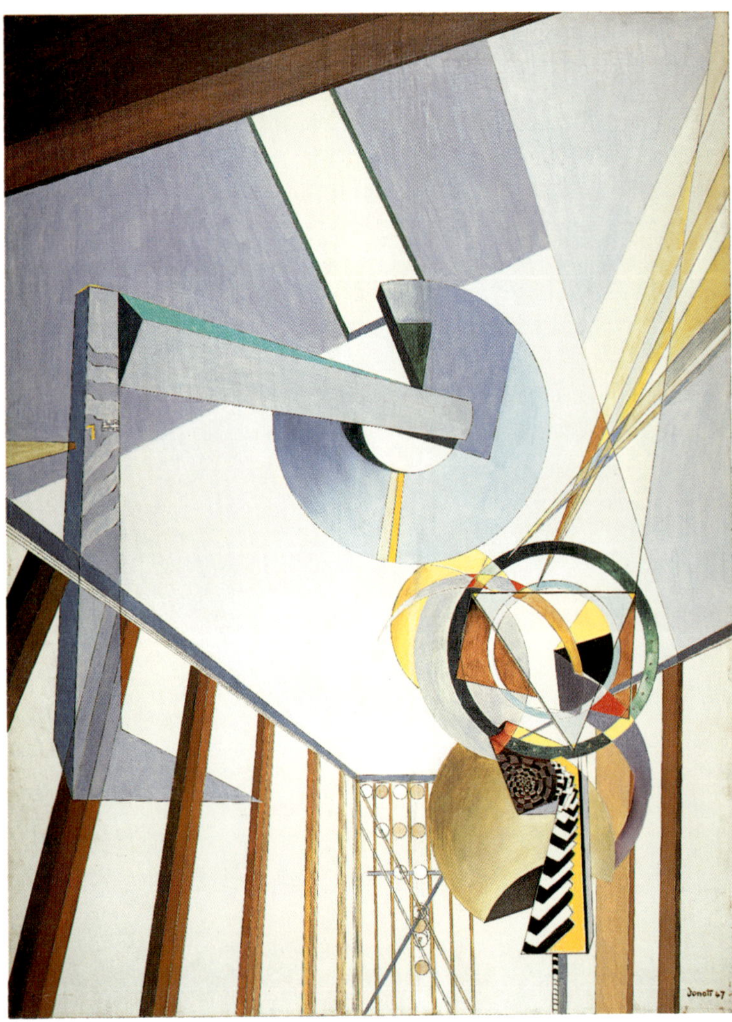

Tower of the Alchemist Seen from Below, 1947
Oil on canvas
40 × 30
Collection William Feick

Explosion du son (Explosion of Sound), 1947
Oil on canvas
110 × 80
Private collection

Plus loin, plus prêt (Farther, Nearer), 1947
Oil on canvas
30 × 25
Private collection

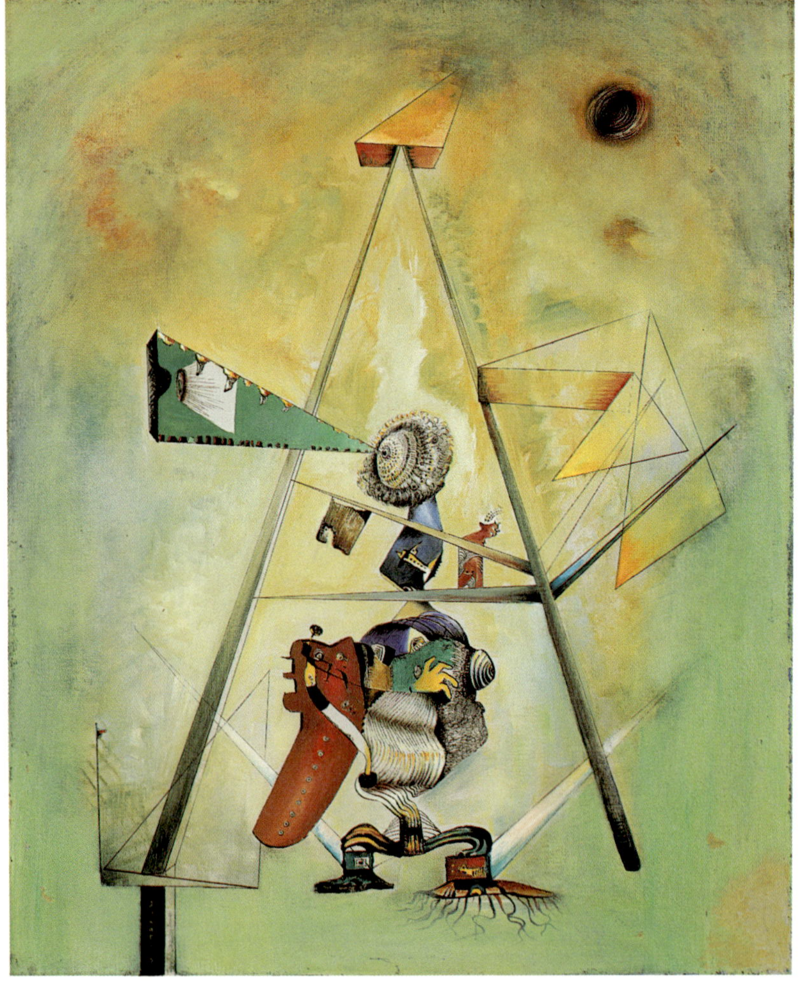

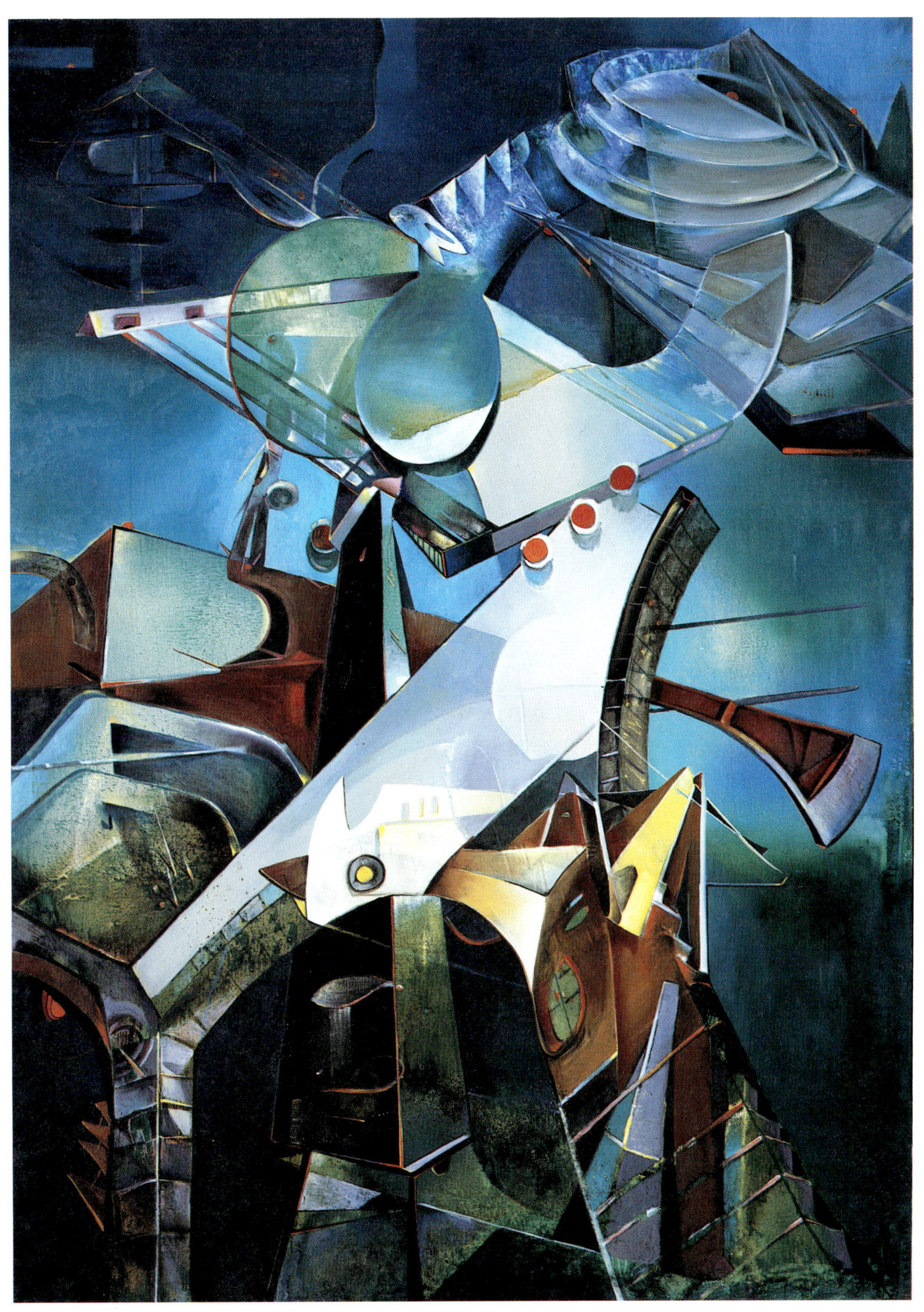

Facing page

**Creation of the Organic and
Mineral,** 1948
Oil on canvas
40 × 30
Collection Michael Dingman

Page 56

**Tower of the Alchemist:
Partie de l'ultrason**
(Springing from Ultrasound), 1947
Oil on canvas
97¹/₂ × 79¹/₂
Private collection

Page 57

**Tower of the Alchemist:
Creation of the Sun,** 1947
Oil on canvas
98 × 64¹/₂
Private collection

specific meanings remained as elusive as ever. The art historian Martica Sawin
hits the nail on the head: "Perspectives shift and cancel one another; transparent planes turn inexplicably opaque; tantalizing illusions of objectness are
swiftly nullified. Fragments of pattern and optical illusion alternately open or
close off the suggestion of spatial depth; exquisite little details of color draw the
eye like jewels. There is much that is suggestive and provocative, but the paintings remain singularly unyielding to the seeker of rational explanation."[9]

Donati himself is not very helpful in this matter, except to insist that interpretations of Surrealist paintings can never be exact; that such works are, by
nature, enigmatic and often almost as much a mystery to the artist who painted
them as to those who view them.

Taking that into account, it might be advisable, especially in the light of the
range and richness of Donati's production and the fact that the vast majority of
his paintings deal with the hidden, the magical, and the inexplicable, to take
him at his word and not insist on too rational an explanation. Certainly, any
attempt to probe for the deeper meanings of such complex works as *Creation
of the Organic and Mineral* (1948) and *Tower of the Alchemist: Partie de l'ultrason* (1947) will only result in frustration. Even the one real clue he presents,
the number 7, which appears in the former and in several other canvases of the
period, and which, according to the artist, represents the number of elements
required for the creation of life, leads at best to vague theories and inconclusive
interpretations. And should one look to the titles for help, it should be kept in
mind that it was Breton who gave so many of Donati's paintings their titles—and
then only after they had been completed.

On the other hand, *Tower of the Alchemist: Creation of the Sun* (1947) and
Chambre à pression osmotique (1948) point to something too easily overlooked: the extent to which a lively interest in formal invention for its own sake

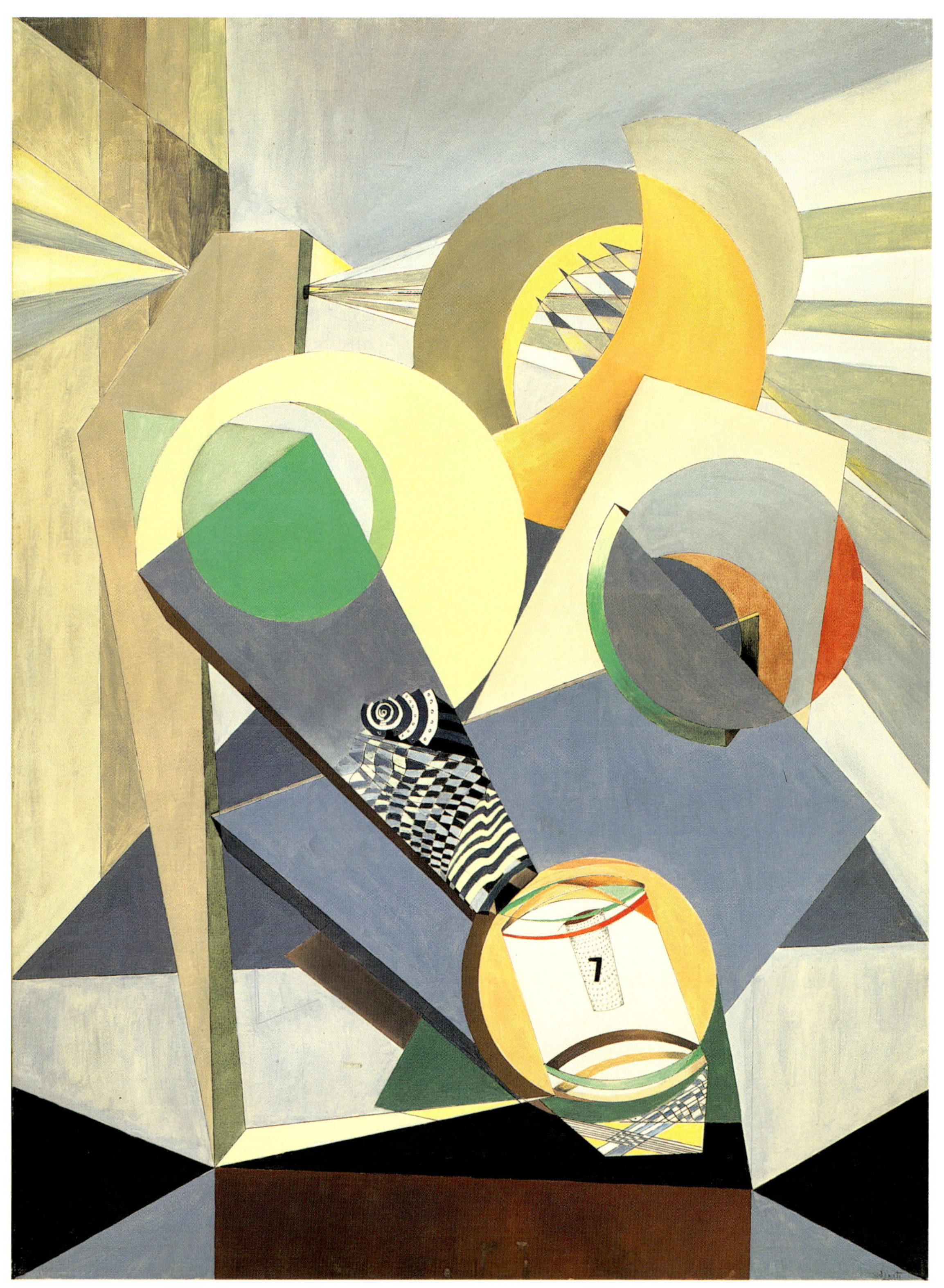

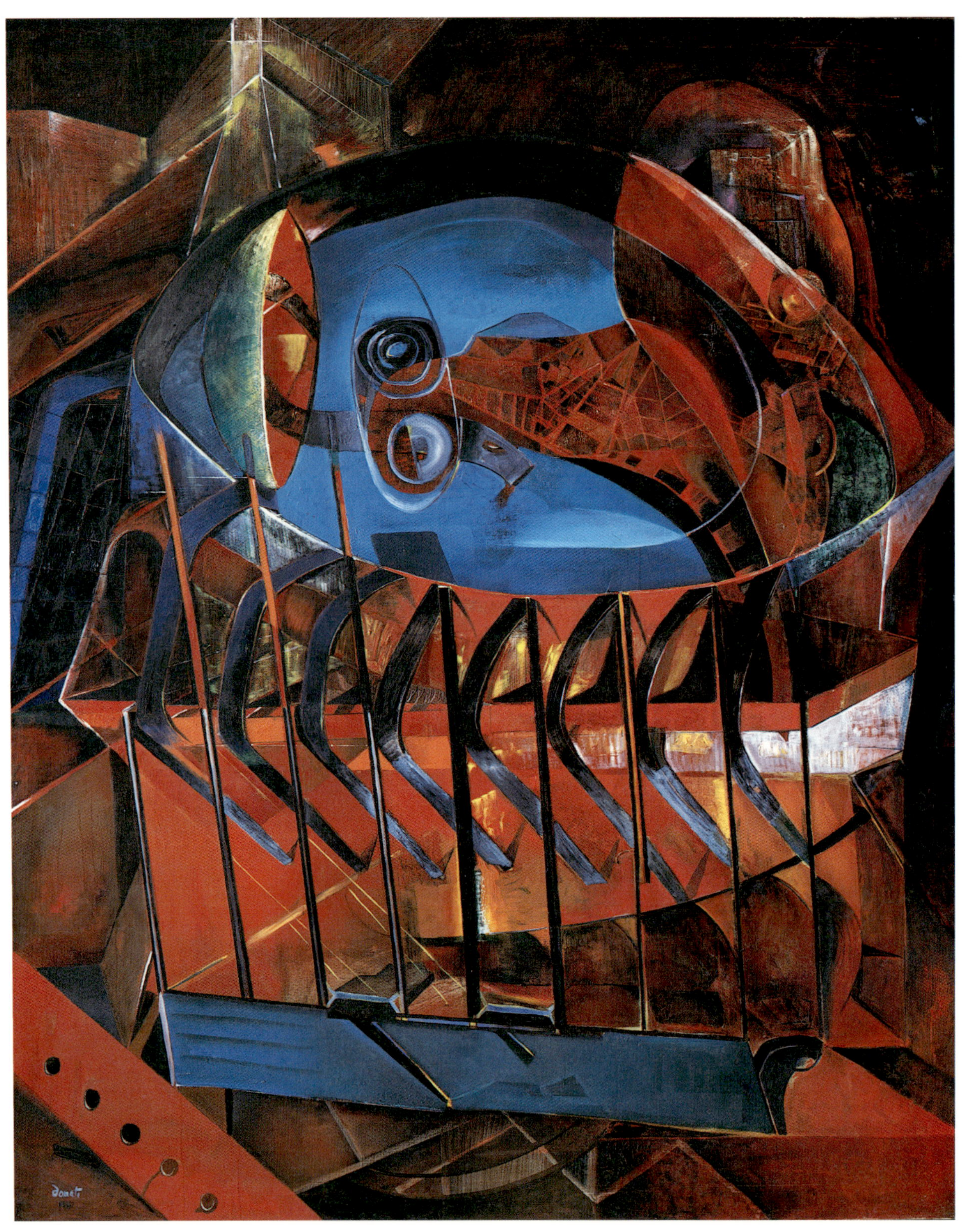

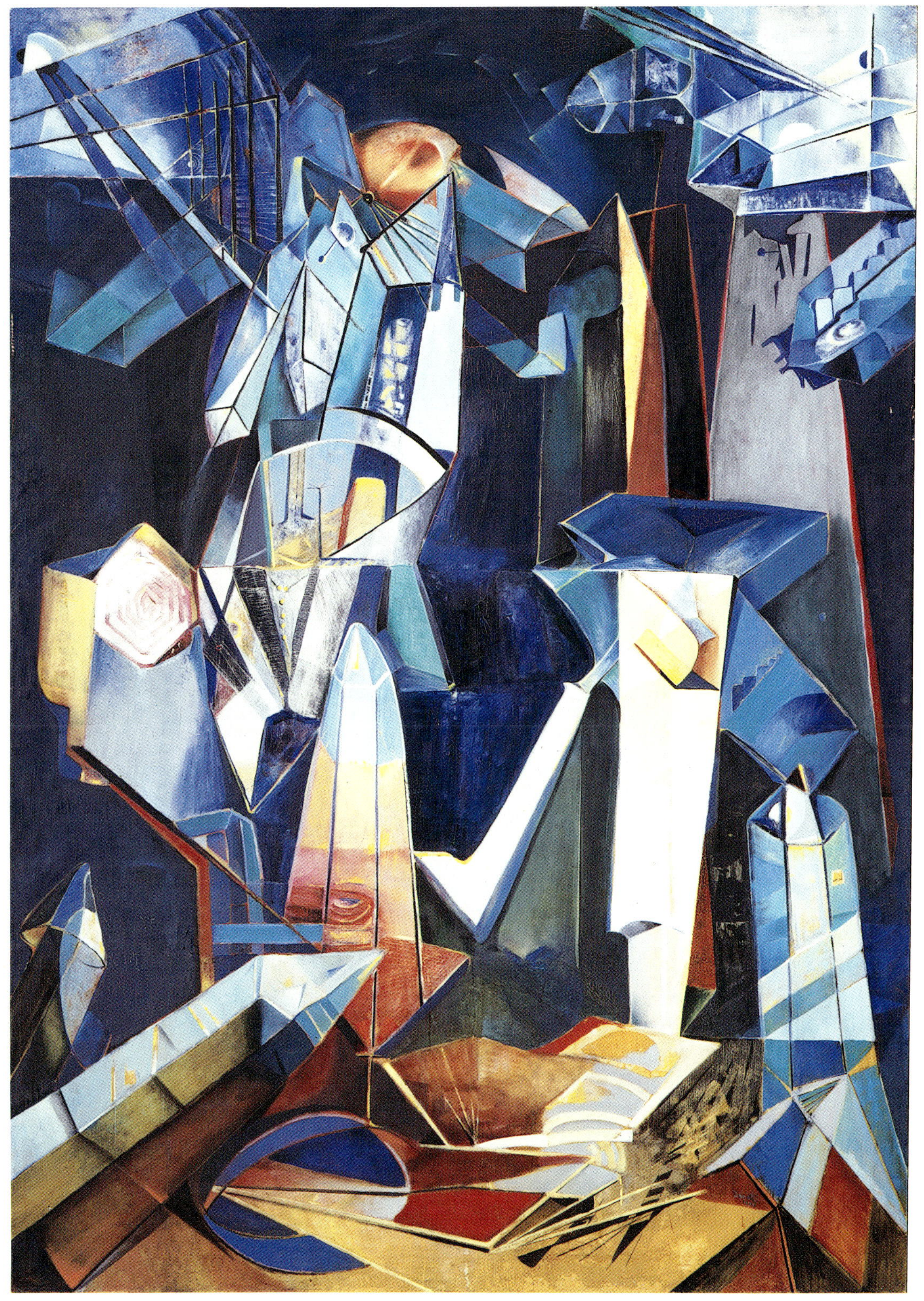

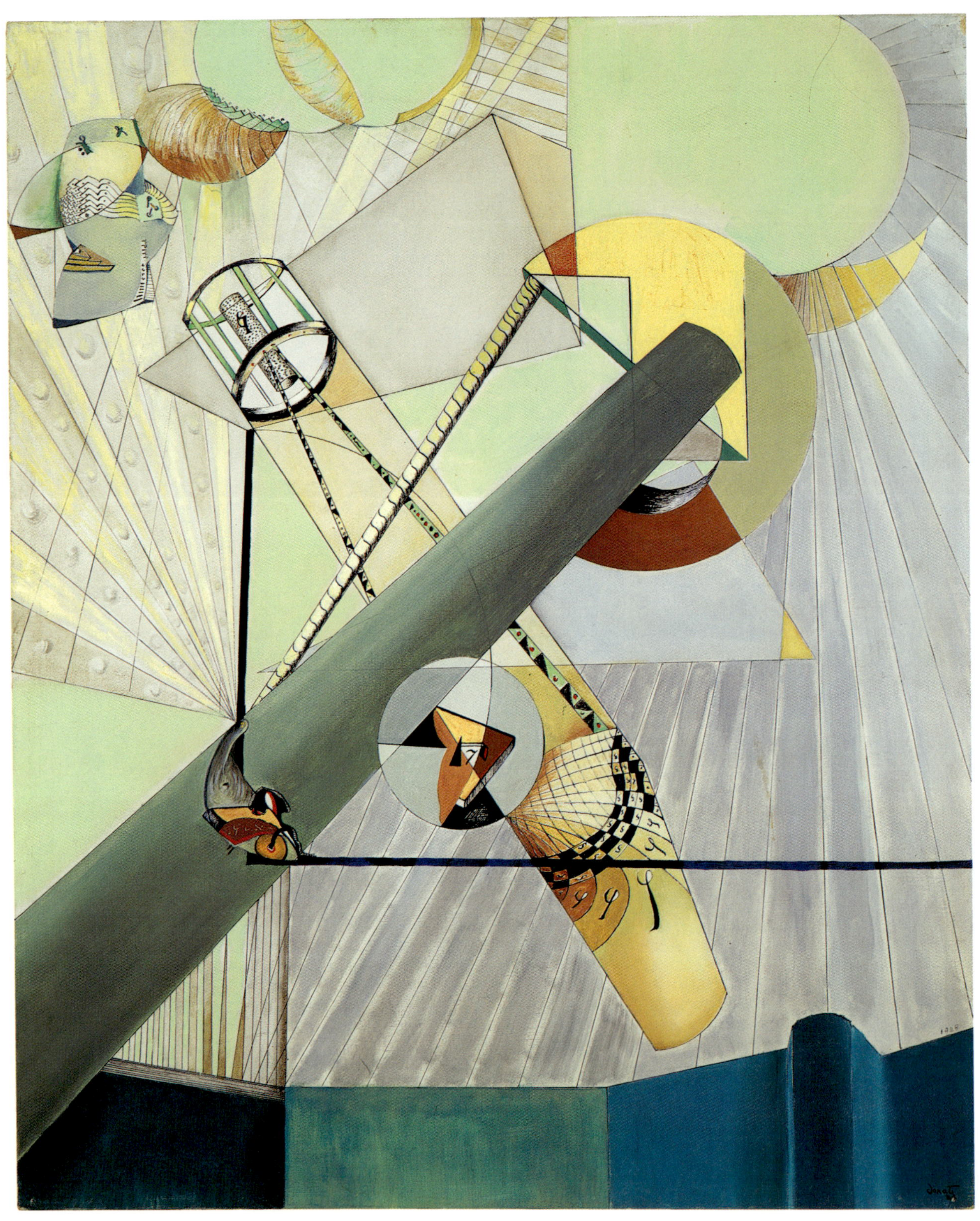

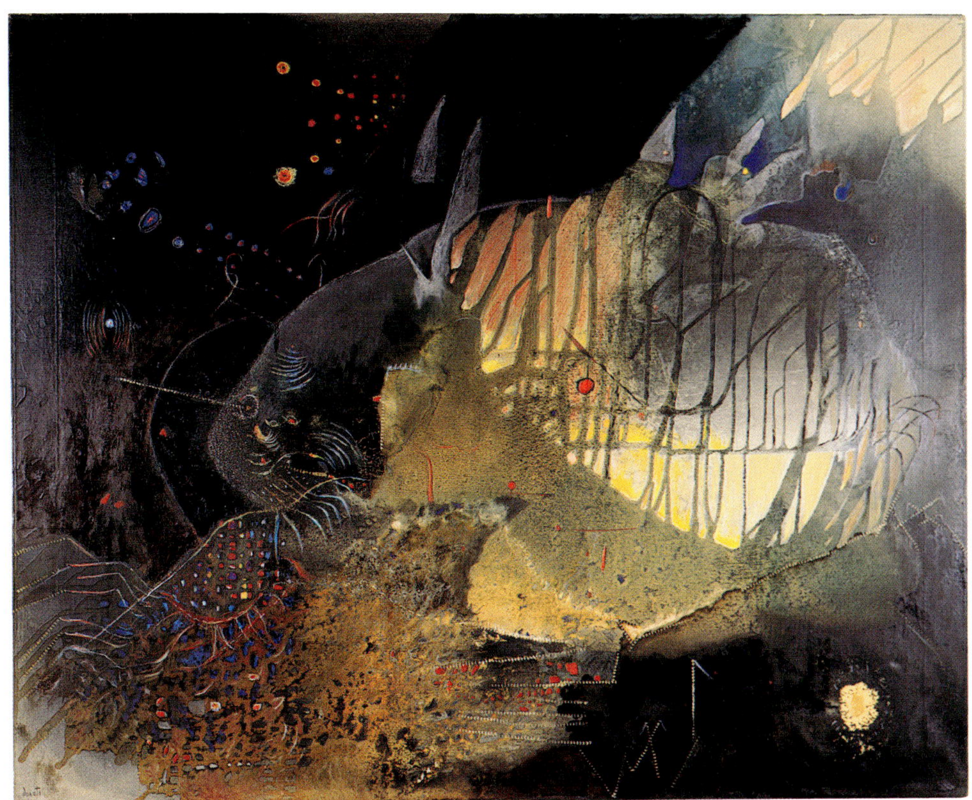

Time Exposure, 1948
Oil on canvas
40 × 50
Private collection

Courants intérieurs d'une cellule artificielle (Inner Workings of an Artificial Cell), 1948
Oil on canvas
25 × 30
Collection Alan Hruska

Facing page
Chambre à pression osmotique (Chamber of Osmotic Pressure), 1948
Oil on canvas
30 × 25
Private collection

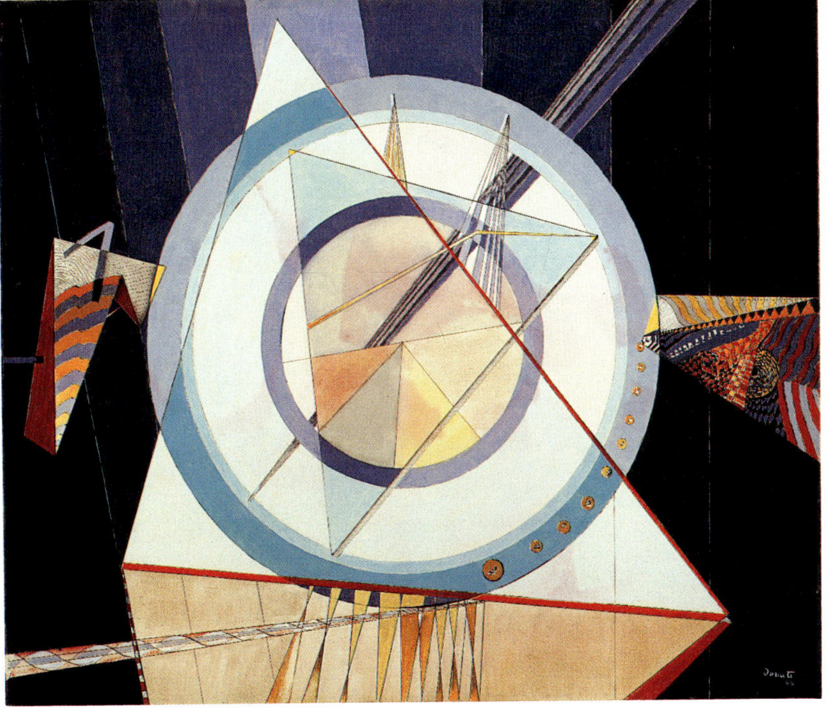

may have been a significant factor in the creation of many, if not all, of these 1947 and 1948 works. It seems entirely reasonable, at least to this writer, to assume that the painter who took such obvious delight in fashioning a biomorphic universe populated by vaguely Bosch-like objects and creatures in *Trouble-fête,* would, only a few short years later, take equal pleasure in inventing a fanciful mechanical world filled with a vast assortment of oddly intersecting and overlapping geometric forms and planes. How else can one make sense out of *Tower of the Alchemist: Creation of the Sun* if not by perceiving it, at least partially, as the result of a young and highly imaginative artist's stretching his inventive and organizational abilities to the limit? And how can one begin to understand *Chambre à pression osmotique* (even with its inclusion of the number 7, near the center of the canvas) without accepting at least the possibility that it was conceived largely *as* an enigma, *as* a puzzle with multiple interpretations, and not as a precise and carefully crafted visual metaphor for one or another of Donati's philosophical ideas?

Shortly after completing these pictures, Donati, exhausted and "fed up" after his extended period with geometric imagery, decided once again to reverse himself and to go off in another, this time more impulsive, direction. By the beginning of 1949 he was well on his way, with a number of gestural paintings that utilized a freely invented calligraphic approach. These Lettres, as this series would be known, were executed by means of free-flowing melted tar that hardened to the consistency of enamel. The resulting works ranged from simple "drips" and "hurlings" of paint on canvas—several actually resembled boldly handwritten letters—to complex images incorporating a variety of calligraphic and automatist techniques.

Concurrently, he was examining other ways to employ the element of chance in his work. Various approaches were investigated, but none appealed

to him so much as the one he devised to fashion a number of unusually spontaneous paintings. The method was simplicity itself. Paint was diluted with tur-
pentine and allowed to flow freely on the surface of unpainted canvas. While it
was still in motion, Donati manipulated the canvas, thereby inducing the
thinned-down paint to move more or less as he wished. Upon that surface,
then, he introduced any gestural devices he deemed appropriate. In the case of
The Voice of Silence (1949–50), that device took the form of a dark, cloudlike
shape moving aggressively from right to left against a watery backdrop. In *The
Ball* (1949), the manipulated, diluted paint and occasional drips and blobs
added up to a highly evocative futuristic image.

While the technique that produced these works may have been far from
new—several members of the then just-emerging New York School had already
experimented successfully with it—Donati added something that gave this manner of working a uniquely personal touch: a Surrealist's predilection for the
macabre and mysterious coupled with a draftsman's ability to use line for maximum effect.

The results were startling, especially when Donati brought all elements of this
approach—including the spatial—into play. For instance, *Spaziale 16* (1949),
while taking full advantage of the "drip, blob, and spatter" method used by
Jackson Pollock and Robert Motherwell, among others, went one dramatic step
further by employing these devices not against the kind of flat, implied space
that existed in Pollock's and Motherwell's canvases but within the infinite,
clearly defined atmospheric space also found in the works of such Surrealists as
Dalí and Tanguy.

Even when, as in *Spaziale 21* (1949–50), these dribblings and hurlings of
paint sit three-dimensionally atop the picture plane, and there is little, if any,
depthward spatial movement, the effect is still identifiably Surrealist. No mem-

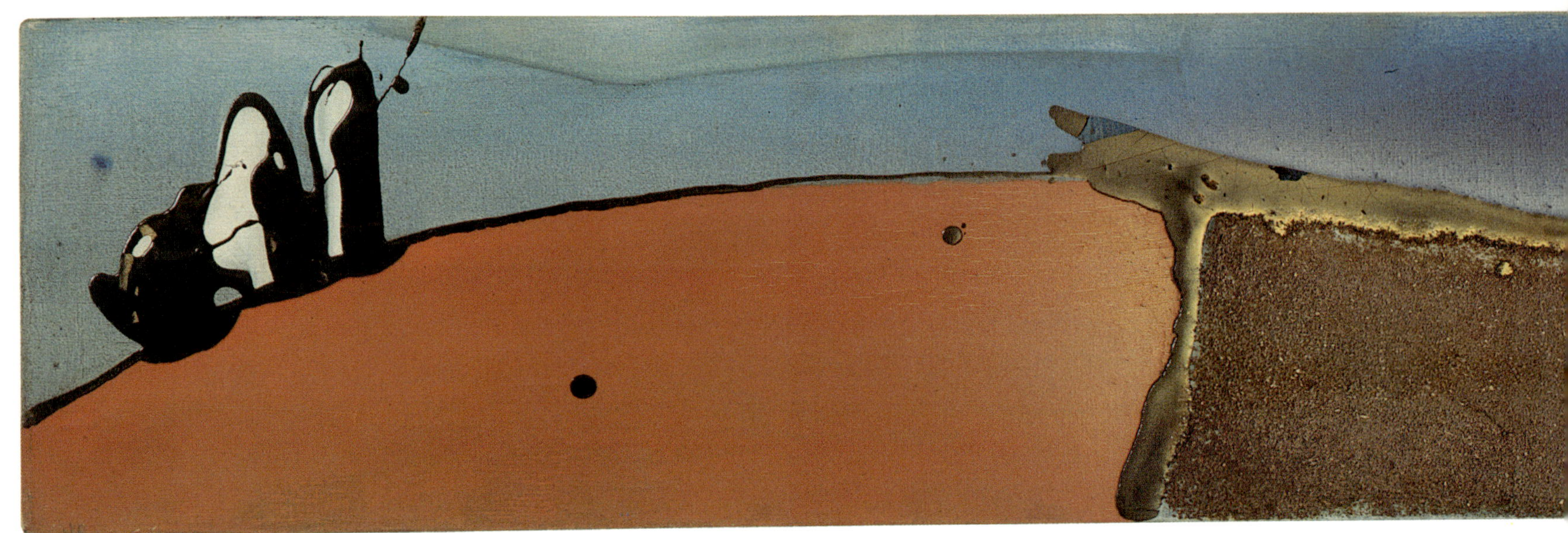

The Ball, 1949
Oil on canvas
8 × 50
Private collection

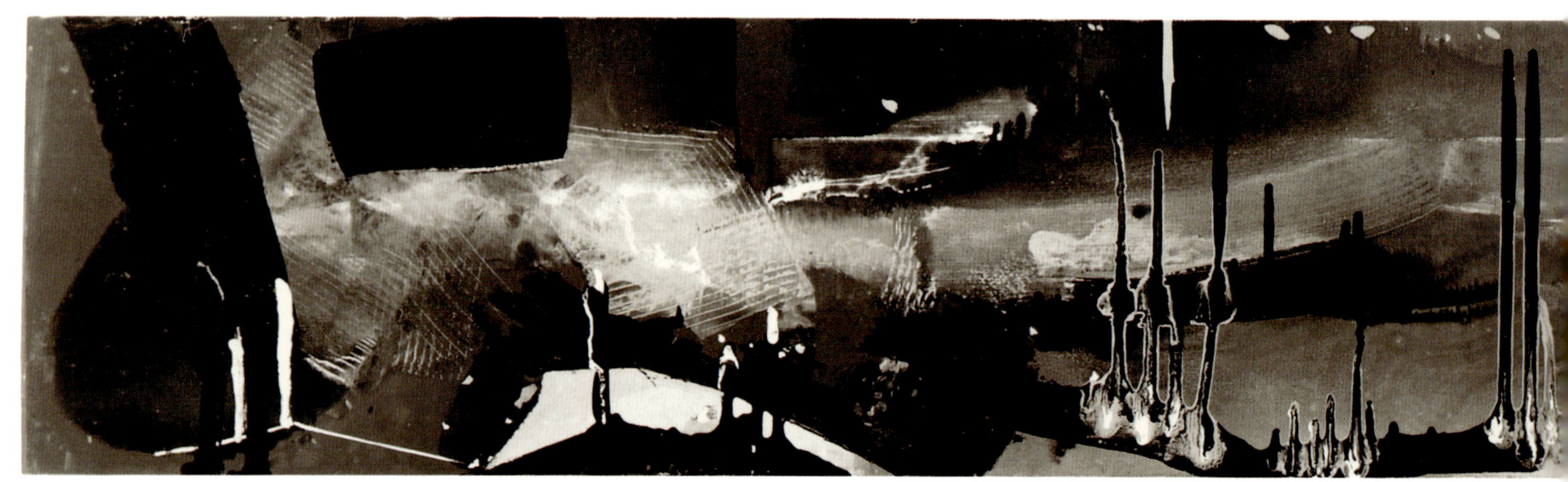

3rd Shift, 1949
Oil on canvas
10 × 64
Private collection

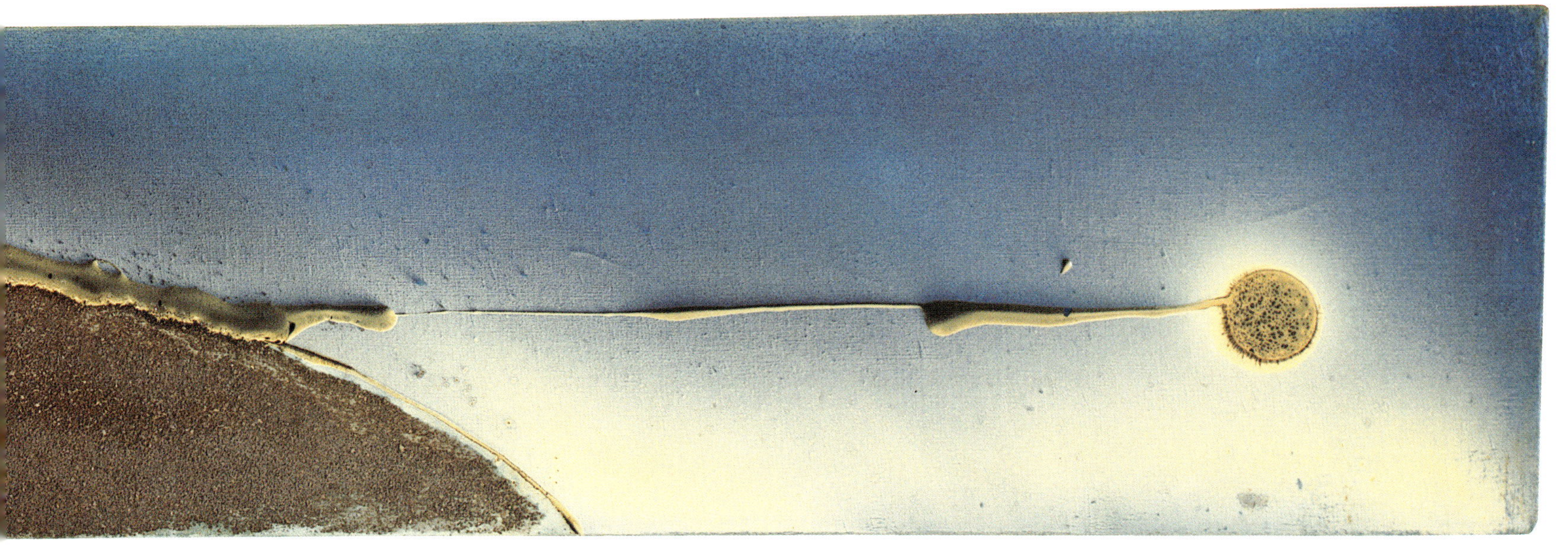

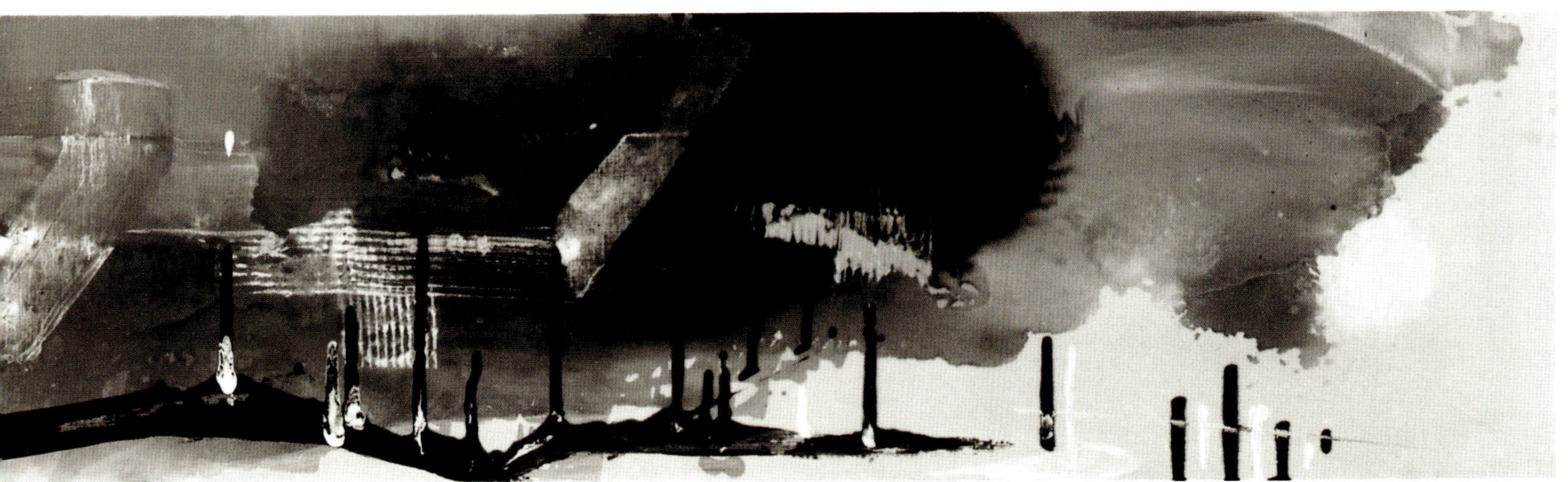

64

E N R I C O

D O N A T I

ber of the New York School, certainly not Pollock or Motherwell, would have produced an Abstract Expressionist painting in which gestural devices functioned more as loosely related surface objects than as tightly interlocking compositional components. And yet that is precisely the role these devices played—and to very good effect—in several of Donati's canvases of this period.

Now, while this approach may have run counter to that practiced by most of his contemporaries, it served Donati well, for it permitted him to explore a challenging new direction without having to sacrifice his Surrealist sensibilities. In that respect, one could say of him, "Once a Surrealist, always a Surrealist"—a sentiment, at least in regard to himself, with which he is in total agreement.

Still, effective as that method was, Donati soon felt the need to explore other possibilities as well. To a certain extent, this was due to professional concerns. With most of his Surrealist friends back in Europe and the movement itself all but dead, Donati found himself in a somewhat difficult position. His reputation as one of Surrealism's younger stars, and the fact that he was still seen by some as a wartime expatriate, threatened to isolate him from his more ambitious contemporaries at a time when American painting was starting to flex its muscles and to assume a leadership role in world art.

He need not have worried, for it was at this time that he stumbled across a novel approach to painting that not only satisfied his creative objectives but also helped revitalize his reputation.

He began exploring this approach in 1950 when he discovered that dirt removed from vacuum cleaners and combined with pigment and glue before being applied in thick layers to canvas produced opaque wooly surfaces ideal for the dense blacks, luminous greys, and occasional whites he was now using almost exclusively in his paintings. Donati was pleased with the results, especially when he realized that these dark, slightly ominous works consisting

Facing page
The Voice of Silence, 1949–50
Oil on canvas
30 × 25
Private collection

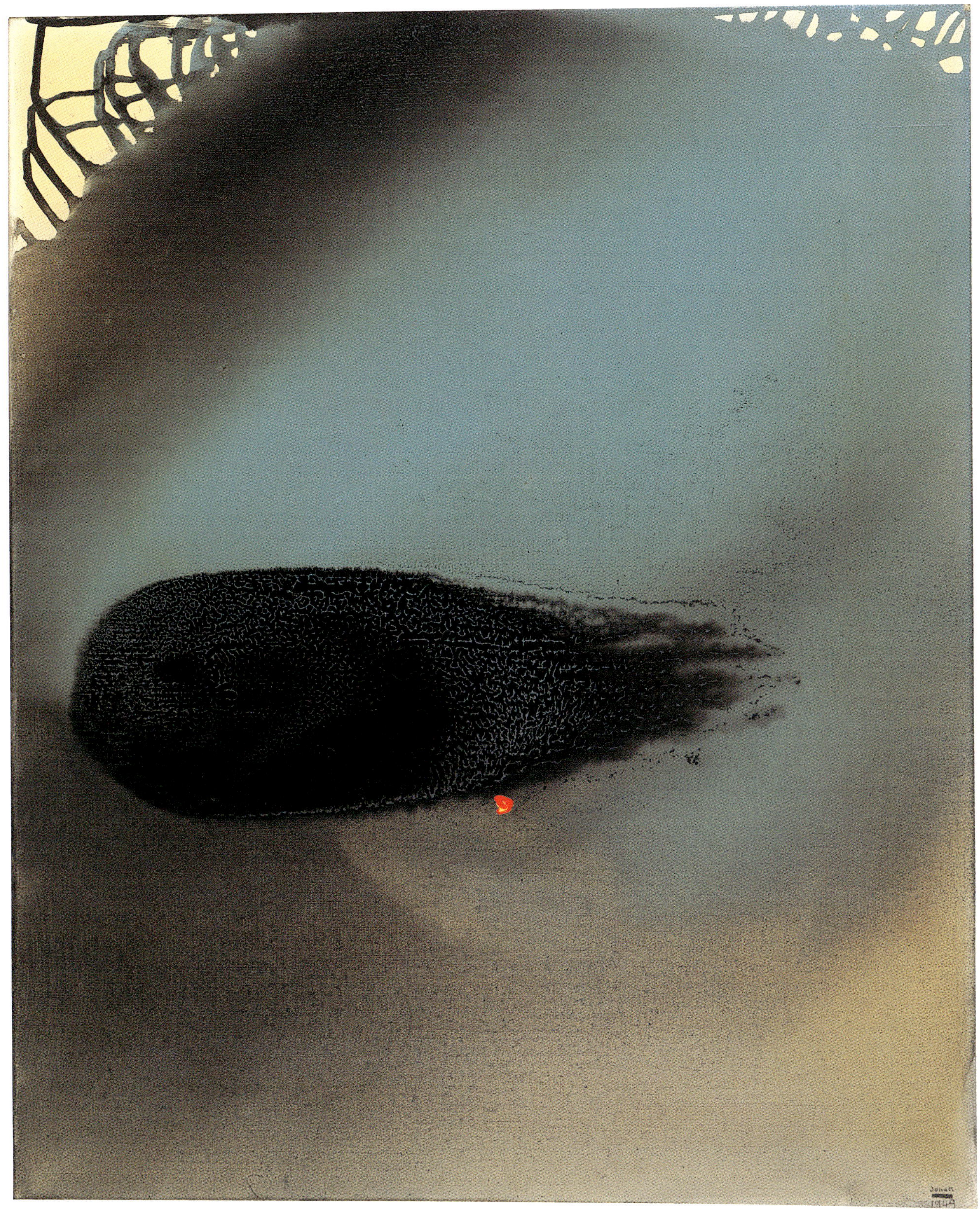

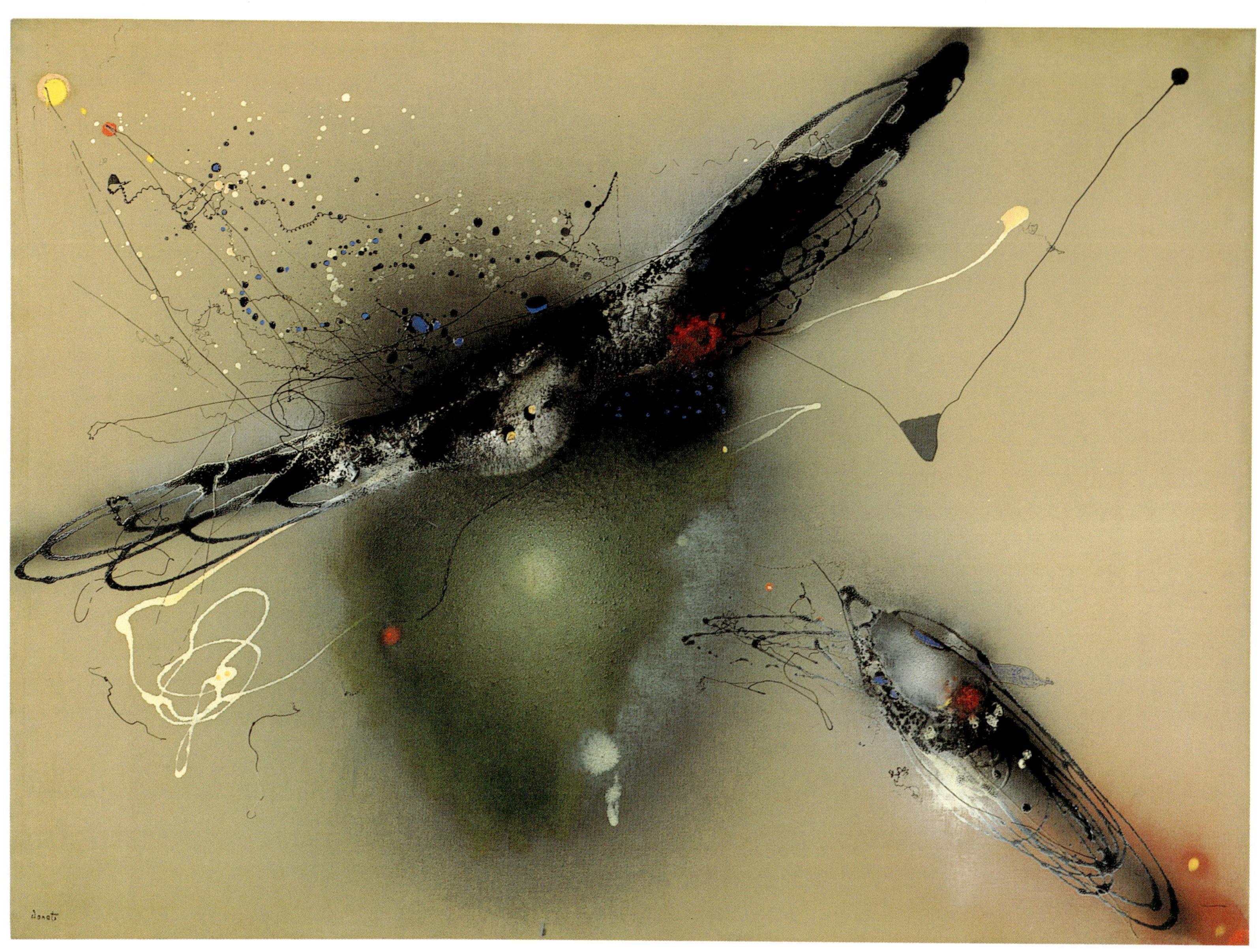

Spaziale 16,
1949
Oil on canvas
36 × 50
Private collection

Facing page
Spaziale 21, 1949–50
Oil on canvas
30 × 26
Private collection

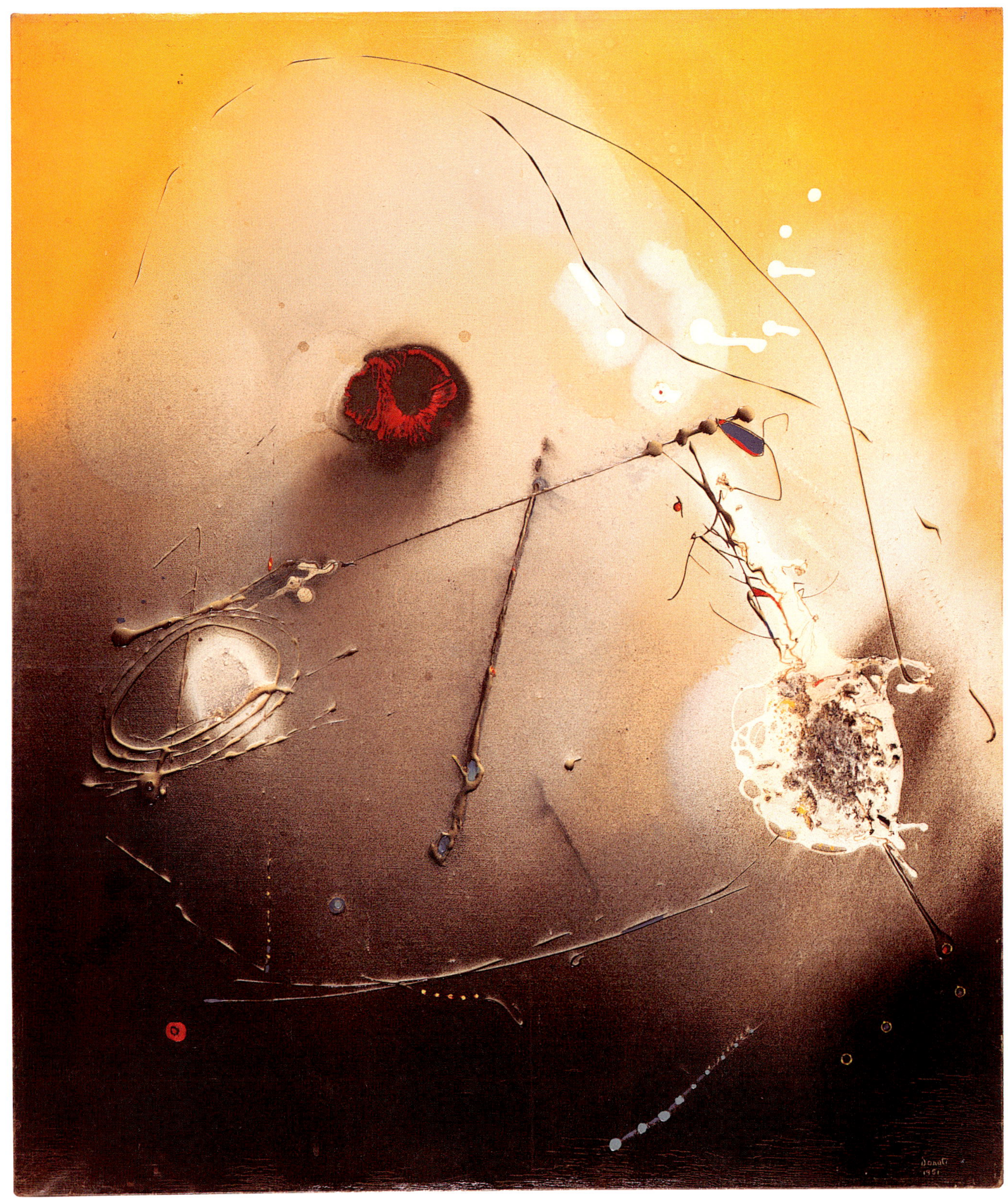

entirely of a few bulky, richly textured, semigeometric forms suggested nothing so much as vast dream landscapes or, more specifically, barren lunar surfaces.

In a purely formal sense, these Moonscapes, as Marcel Duchamp named the new series when several of the works were first shown in the early 1950s, shared some of the vision and more than a few of the characteristics of work produced during this period by a number of America's finest avant-garde painters. (Mark Rothko, in particular, springs to mind, as do Franz Kline and Ad Reinhardt.) Donati, however, had acquired this vision and had developed these characteristics for his art independently, without any concession to the vision or art of others.

And so, quietly and on his own terms, Donati entered the mainstream of American art. One of his first acts was to join the Betty Parsons Gallery in New York, then undoubtedly one of the best places in the world for a member of the avant-garde to show his work. There he exhibited alongside such gallery regulars as Pollock, Rothko, Barnett Newman, Richard Pousette-Dart, and Theodoros Stamos, all founding members and leading lights of the New York School. Obviously, his timing was once again superb. With hardly any greater effort than it had taken a few years earlier to become a Surrealist star, he now found himself accepted into equally exalted company by individuals whose critical opinions were respected throughout the international art community.

Even so, when his Moonscapes were first exhibited at the Parsons gallery, they took many by surprise. The viewing public and art professionals alike were not prepared for such roughly textured, pitch-black, grey-and-white abstractions, especially ones that resonated with vaguely ominous otherworldly qualities. The art historian Martica Sawin recalls entering the gallery in the early 1950s and finding the walls hung with "darkish canvases that appeared to be afflicted with a hairy form of mold."[10] The museum curator and writer Peter Selz remembers

Facing page

Black Ice, 1951–52

Mixed media on canvas

70 × 70

Private collection

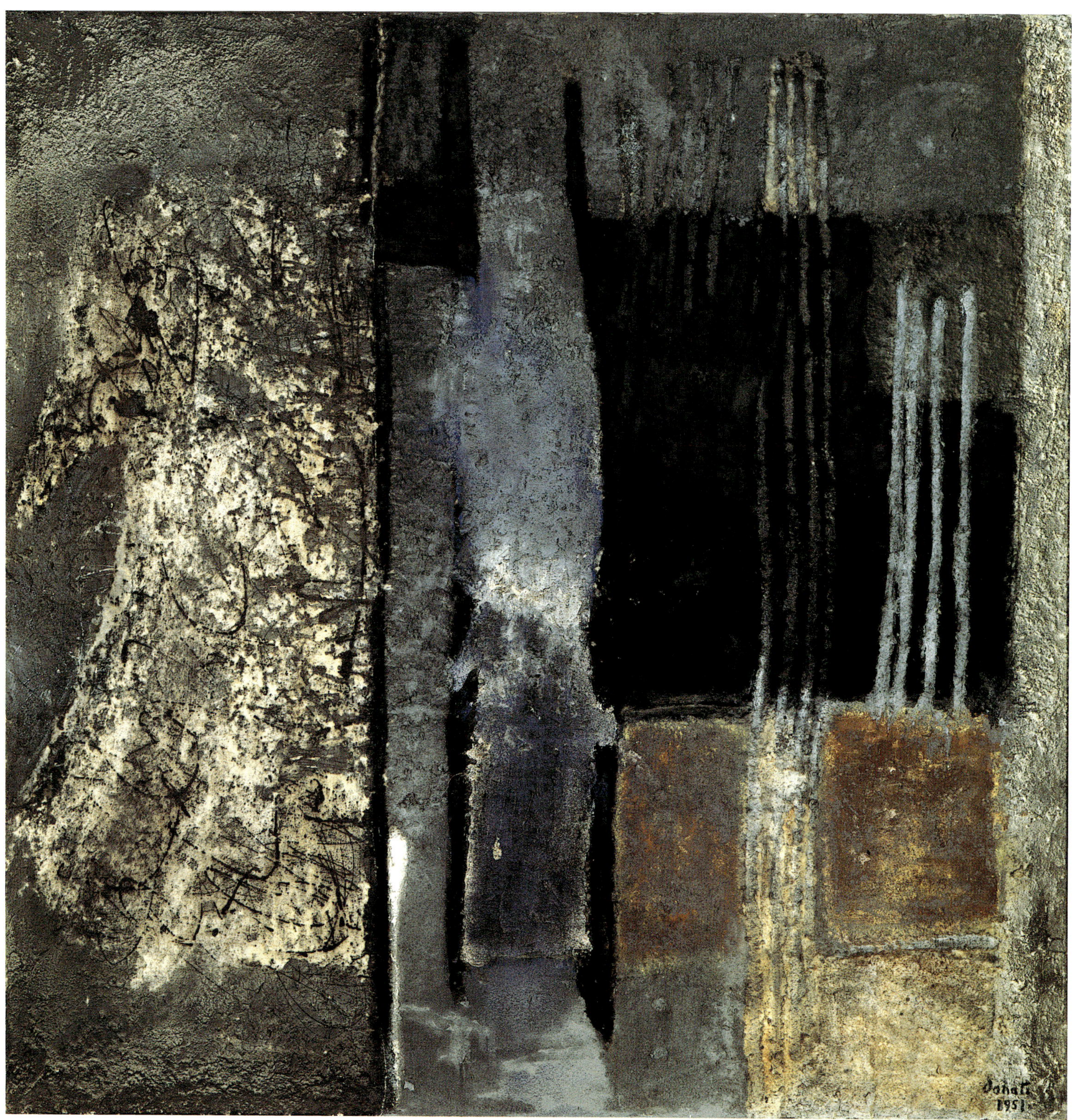
Donati
1951

that Donati's *Moonscapes* "suggested arid lava fields" as well as "the faces of old, battered walls."[11] And the present writer will never forget his own disbelief that anyone could have achieved such totally opaque, startlingly wooly blacks, or could have played them so effectively against the dark grey forms adjacent to them.

An excellent introduction to the Moonscape series is *4 Greys and Black*. Painted in 1953 and very small—it is roughly one foot square—it demonstrates Donati's newfound technique at its most basic and unsophisticated. No reproduction, of course, can do it justice. Its velvety blacks and richly textured surfaces must be seen in the original to be fully understood and appreciated.

That same year's *Black and 3 Whites* and *Composition in Grey with Dot* are much larger and more fully developed compositionally. In both works, rough-edged, semigeometric forms and striations combine with a narrow range of heavily encrusted surfaces to create the rugged, austere effect that led Duchamp to name the series as he did. Both paintings, furthermore, are devoid of color and succeed or fail entirely on the interrelationships of their textures and tones.

That would soon change. Color, as anyone familiar with Donati's art could have predicted, reasserted itself. Not dramatically at first—indeed, the earliest indication of its return occurred in the mid-1950s with the introduction of subdued earth colors to several of the Moonscape paintings—but inexorably and with the certainty that it never again would be absent from his palette.

Other changes, some resulting from Donati's greater mastery of his new technique, but most reflecting a clarification of his long-range objectives, were also taking place at that time. The most obvious change had to do with texture, the rougher and thicker the better, and with the numerous ways it could be utilized to give a more solidly physical, almost bas-relief look to his work. Another change concerned monumentality and formal grandeur—occasionally even

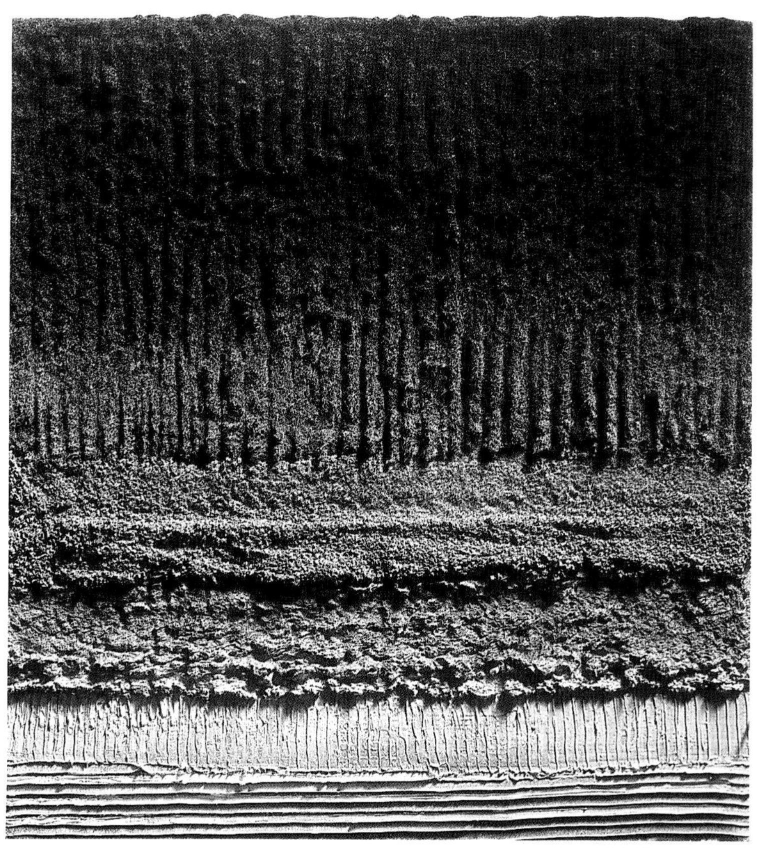

4 Greys and Black, 1953
Mixed media on canvas
12 × 13
Private collection

**Composition in Grey
with Dot,** 1953
Oil on canvas
50 × 70
Private collection

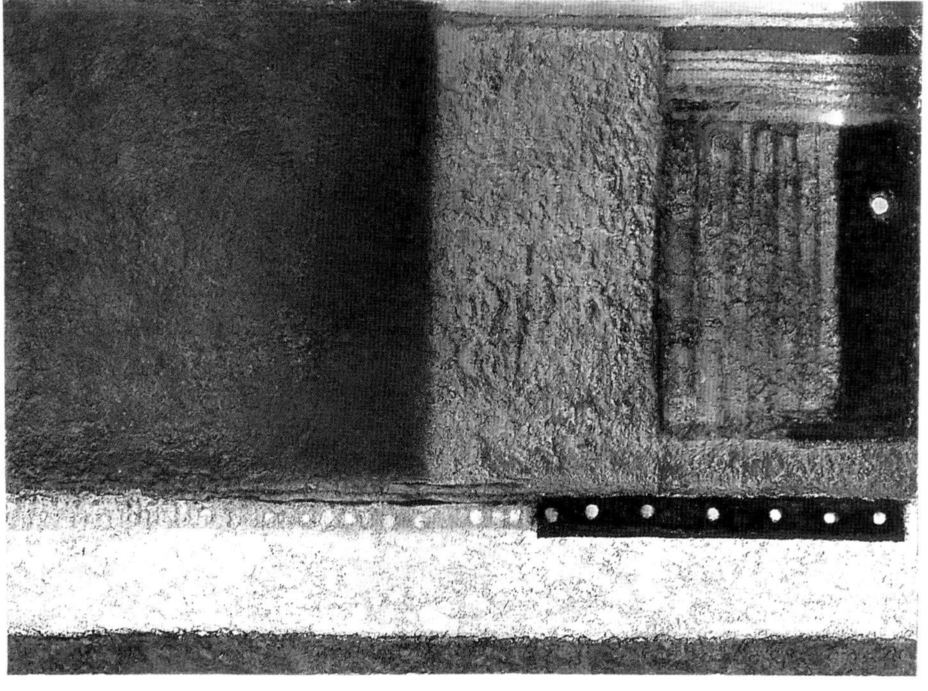

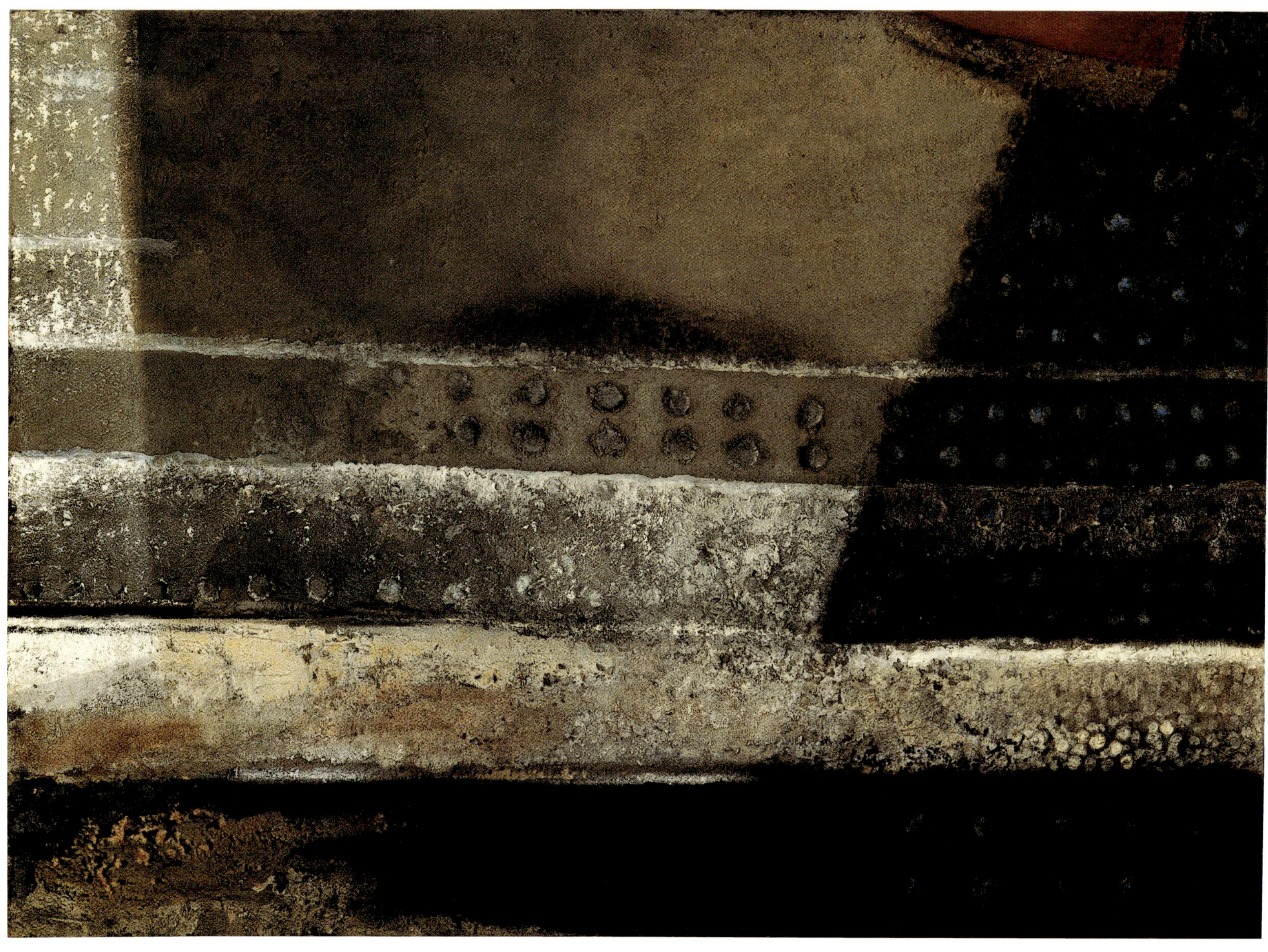

**Moonscape Black and
Terracotta,** 1952
Oil on canvas
50 × 70
Private collection

Facing page
Black and 3 Whites, 1953
Mixed media on canvas
70 × 70
Collection Musées royaux des
Beaux-Arts de Belgique, Brussels

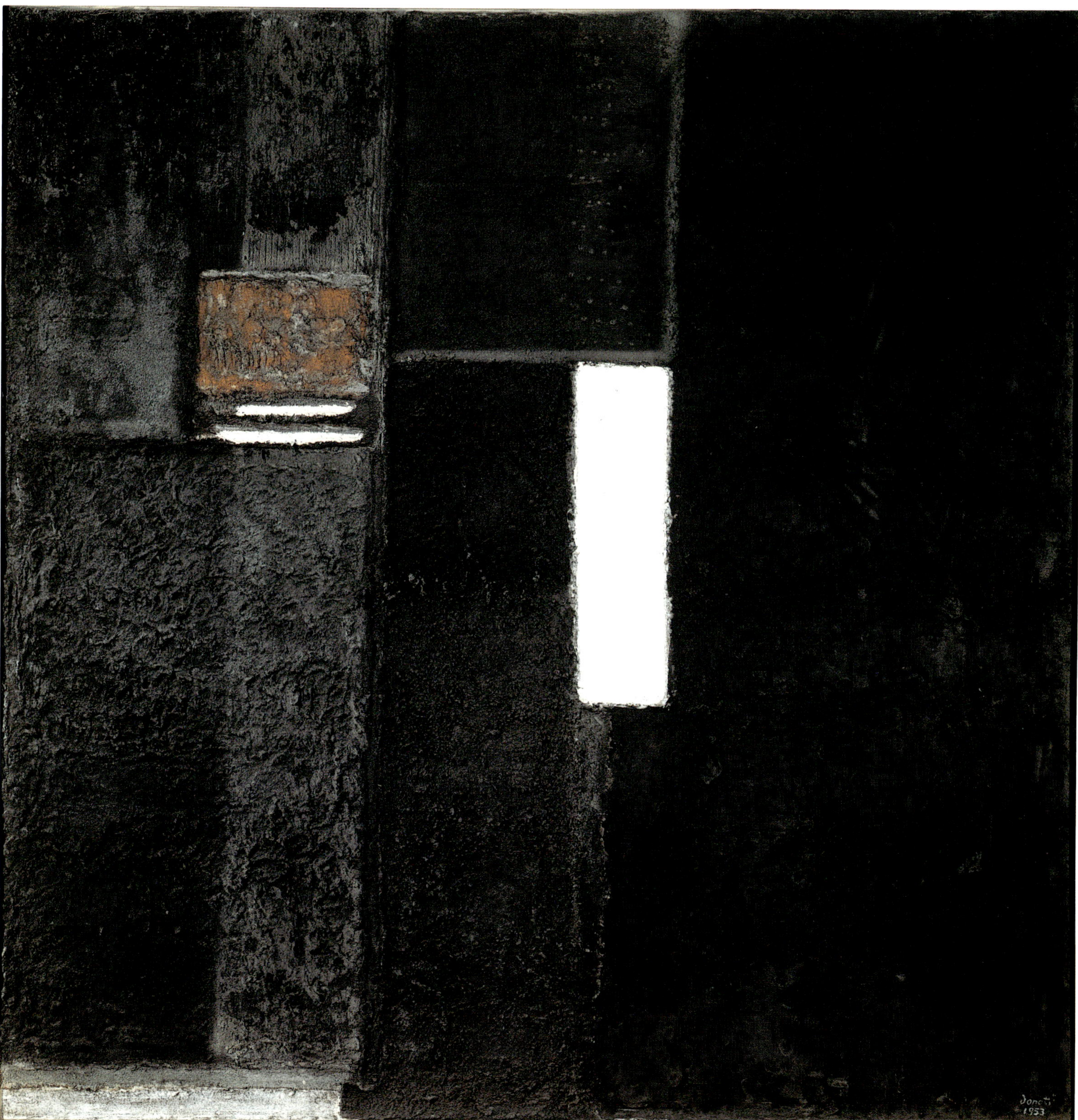

Donati
1953

Black and Black, 1954
Mixed media on canvas
30 × 24
Private collection

White to Black, 1953
Mixed media on canvas
70 × 70
Private collection

Threshold to White, 1953
Oil on canvas
70 × 50
Courtesy Louis Newman Galleries,
Beverly Hills, California

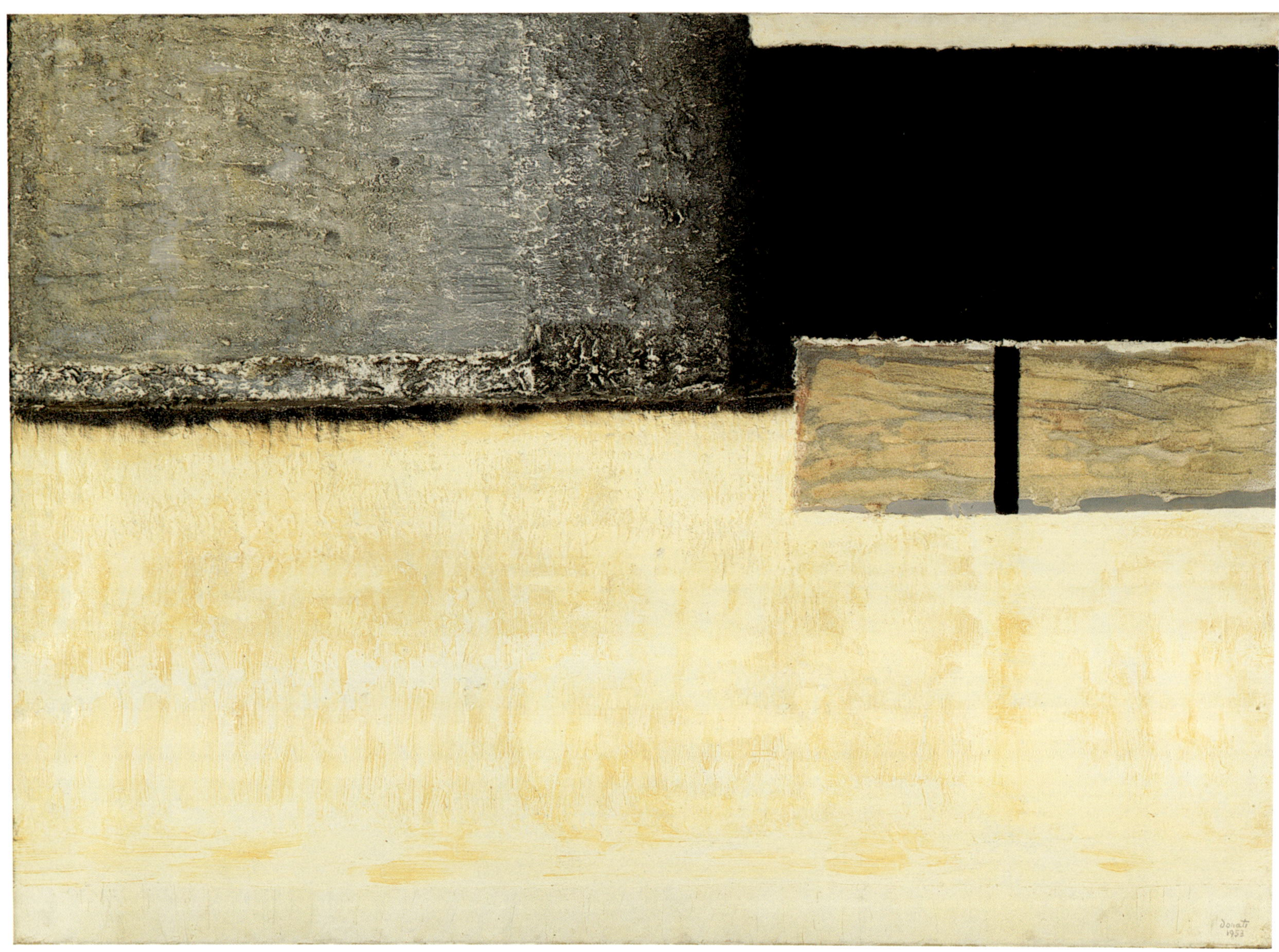

White to White, 1953

Mixed media on canvas

50 × 70

Collection Valerie Barnard-Webster,
Del Mar, California

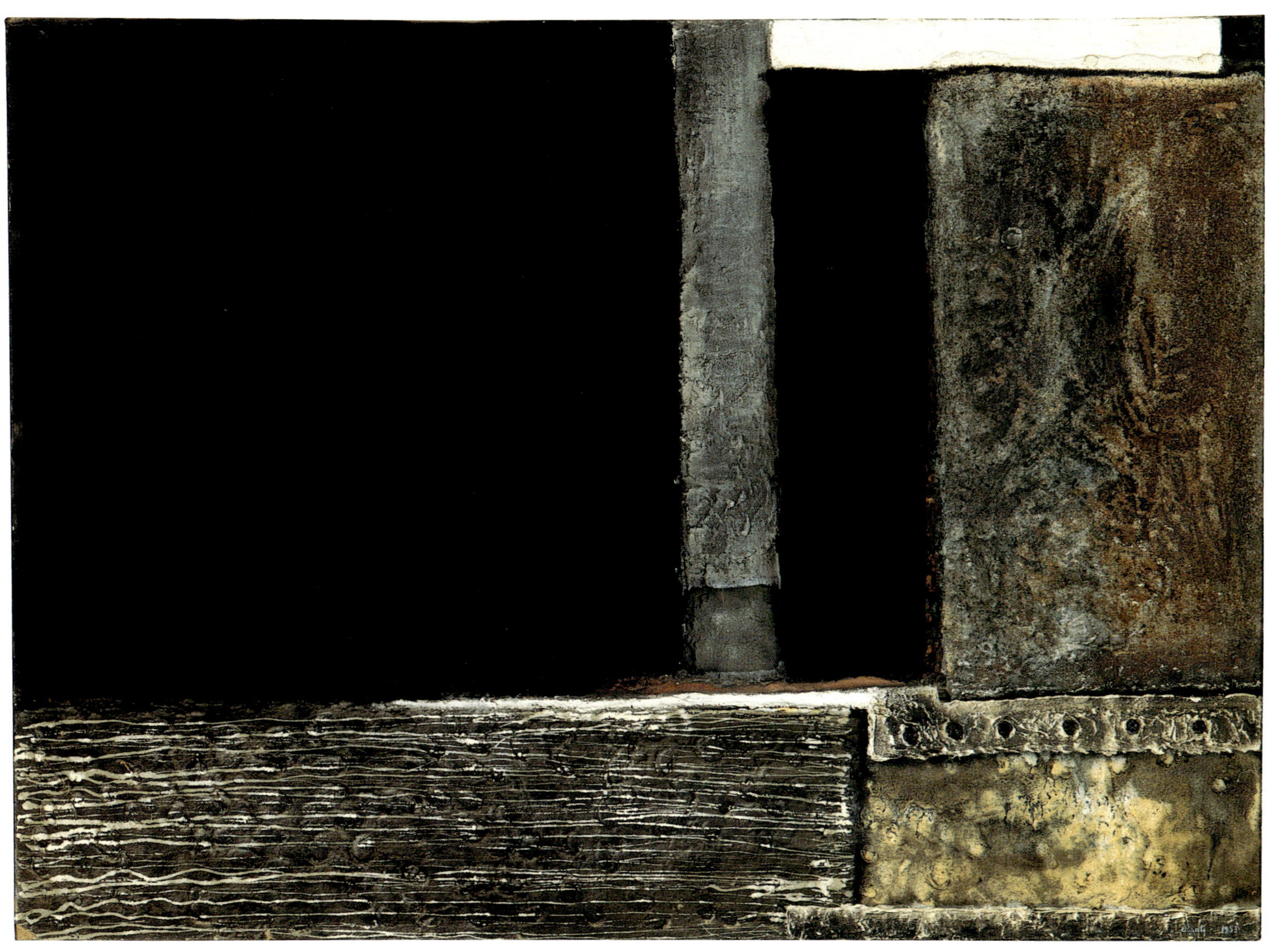

Black and Two White Lines,
1953
Mixed media on canvas
50 × 70
Private collection

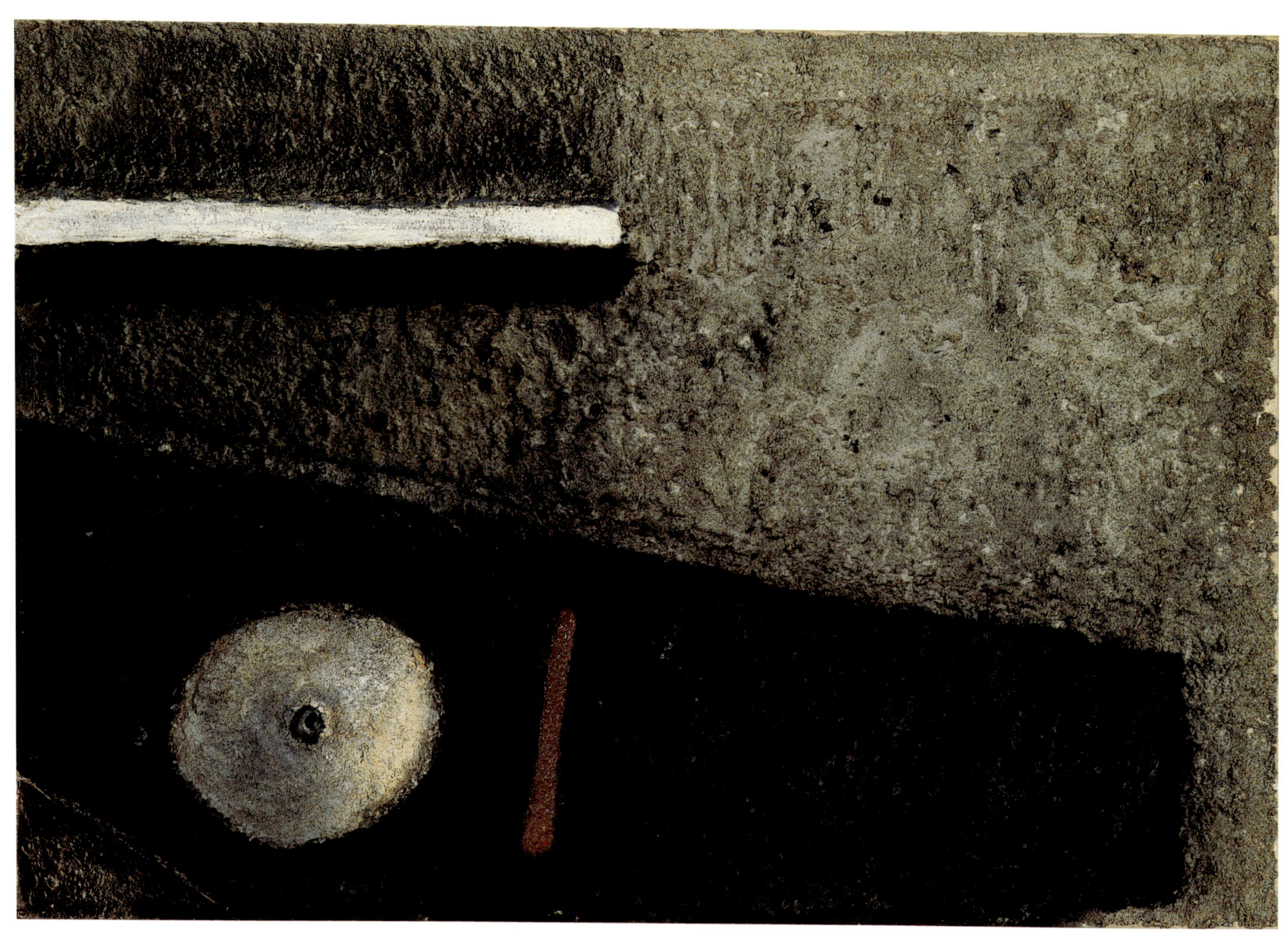

Lunar Fish, 1953
Oil on canvas
35 × 50
Private collection

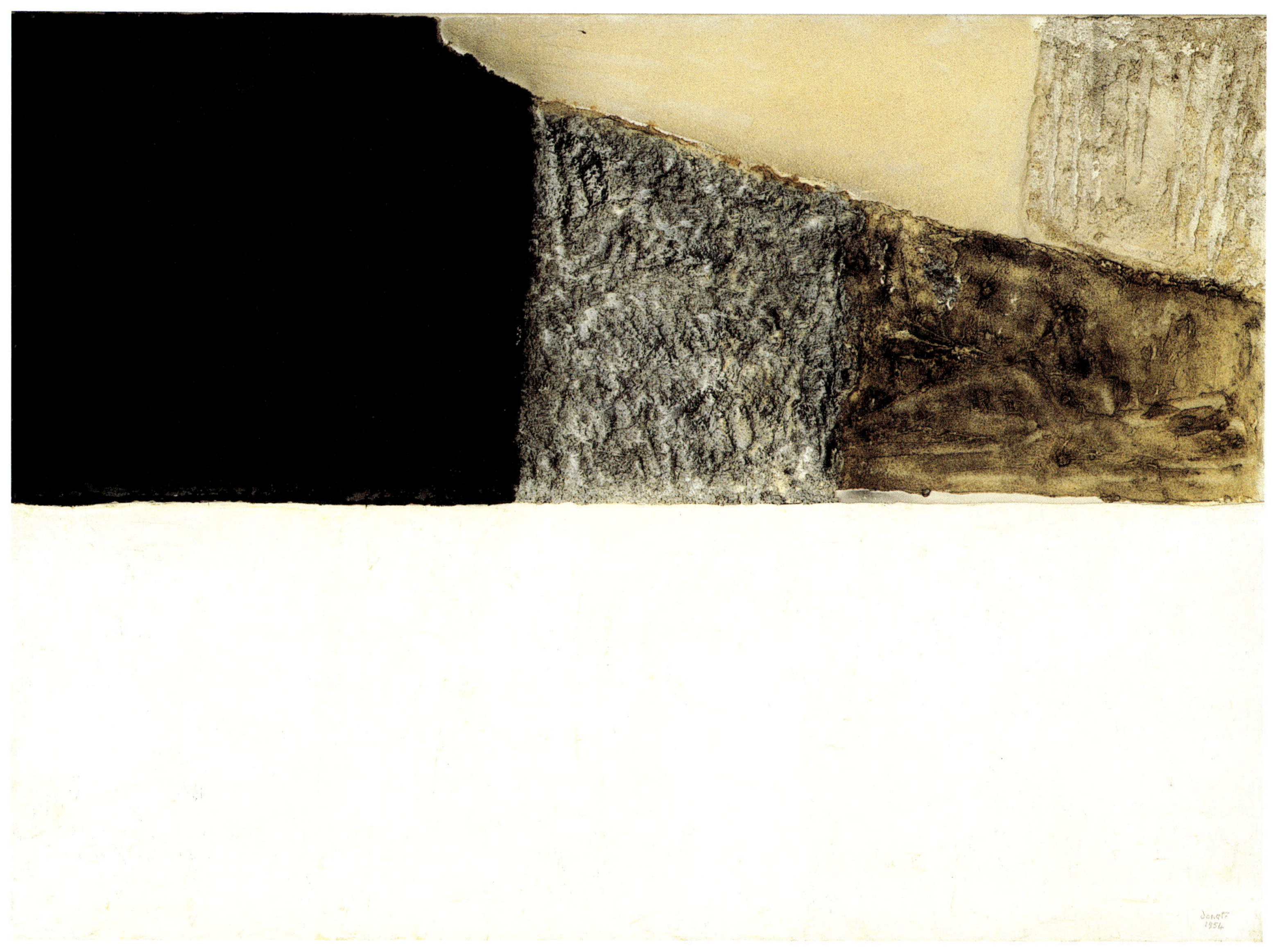

White to Grey, 1954
Oil on canvas
50 × 70
Private collection

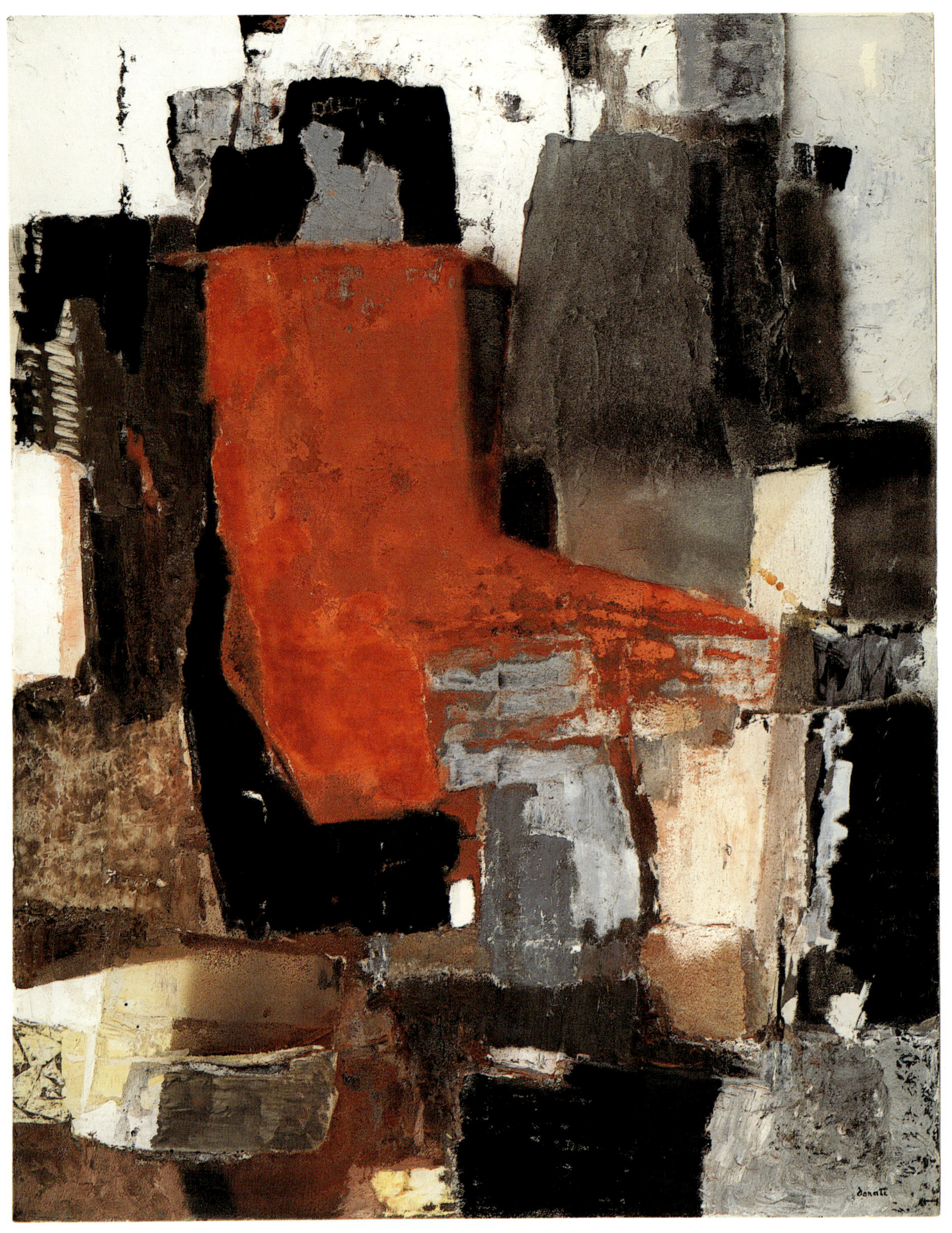

sheer size—and how best to fashion complex, tightly interlocking compositions whose dignity and authority would echo the art of ancient civilizations. Finally, there was the matter of color and its return, first (as noted) in muted earth tones but then, gradually, as richer and more varied hues until it was once again playing a dominant role in Donati's art.

By 1957 these changes were sufficiently realized for Donati to begin exhibiting some of the results. Searching around for a title for his new series, he settled on *Sargon,* after Sargon II (reigned 722–705 B.C.), the Assyrian warrior king who had massive bas-reliefs commemorating his triumphs carved into the mountains of the Tigris valley.

Of all Donati's paintings, past or present, those of the Sargon series are the least immediately identifiable as his. Not only are they more purely—even exclusively—painterly in their approach than is typical of Donati, but they are also devoid of anything that could be described as even vaguely Surrealist in attitude or sensibility.

For instance, only its title gives any indication that *Gore et Mandra* (1957) was painted by Donati, and even then, it does so only if one recognizes the wordplay pertaining to the mandragora or mandrake root that occupied so crucial a role during his Surrealist period. One looks in vain for the deeply interior, provocative, even fanciful touches that normally indicate the presence of Donati's hand in a painting's execution. What one finds instead is a brilliant demonstration of painterly prowess, a highly professional performance that does credit to his talent and skills but that reveals little of what is most unique and valuable in Donati's art—his ability to create images resonating with intimations that some of life's most deeply hidden secrets and most tantalizing mysteries are accessible through art.

Facing page
Kabara II, 1956
Mixed media on canvas
58 × 48
Solomon R. Guggenheim Museum,
New York

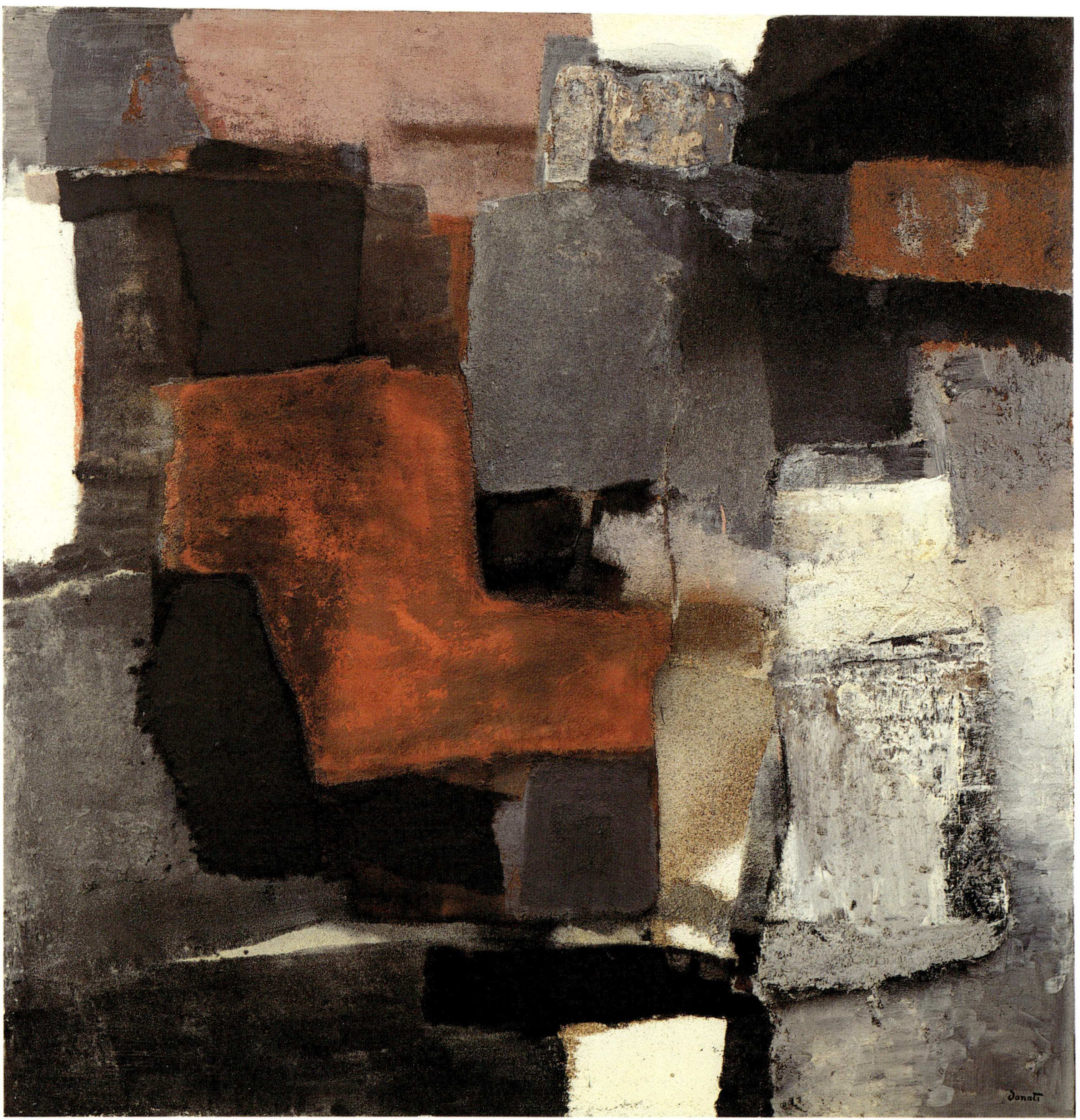

donati

And what is true of *Gore et Mandra* is equally true of *Coincidence Point* (1958), *Exodus* (1958) (which is very nearly twelve feet wide), *From Body to Soul* (1957), and the vast majority of the Sargon paintings Donati exhibited at the Betty Parsons Gallery in 1957, 1959, and 1960. All are remarkable, and all give clear evidence of Donati's excellence as a painter, but none cuts to the core of his creativity to disclose what is most special about him or his talent.

Obviously, Donati was also aware of this fact, for it was at this point in his career that he finally took advantage of an event that had occurred a decade earlier to redefine what was important to him as an artist and to set his work on the course from which it would never again significantly deviate.

In 1949 on a beach at Dover, Donati picked up a small smooth stone that caused an "odd vibration" to pass through him. His suspicion that it contained a fossil was verified by Tanguy, who also showed him how to open it without doing any damage. Donati resisted doing so, however, because he feared that what he found inside would too closely resemble what he recently had been painting out of his unconscious. Nevertheless, he kept the stone until, in 1960, following Tanguy's advice, he tapped its edges and opened it.

The fossil he discovered within the stone did indeed strongly resemble some of his personal imagery. Not surprisingly, this was an unsettling but oddly exhilarating experience.

Donati immediately set about trying to discover not only the reason for the similarity between the fossil's form and the images he had created but also the significance of that similarity. Although the fossil and all it implied had long fascinated him, he had never before fully realized its effect on his creative imagination. "Once again," he states, "I was in touch with the cycle of creation, destruction, and rebirth." Holding the halves of the stone in his hands, he under-

Facing page
Gore et Mandra, 1957
Oil on canvas
60 × 60
Collection Whitney Museum of
American Art, New York

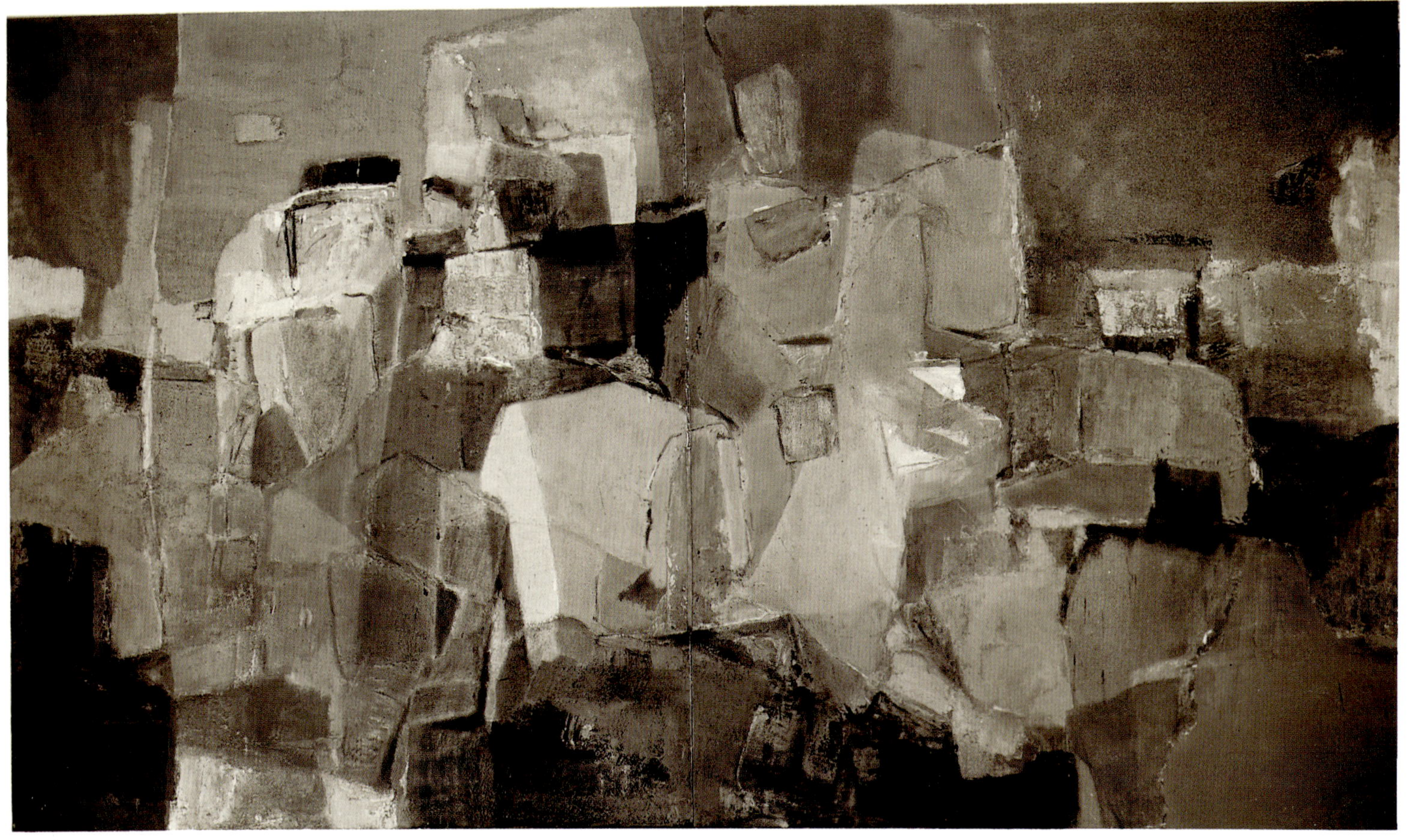

Exodus, 1958

Oil on canvas with sand

86 × 140

Washington University Gallery of Art,
St. Louis, Missouri. Gift of Mr. and
Mrs. Morton D. May, 1960

Facing page

Coincidence Point, 1958

Oil on canvas

75 × 60

Permanent Collection,
MIT–List Visual Arts Center,
Cambridge, Massachusetts

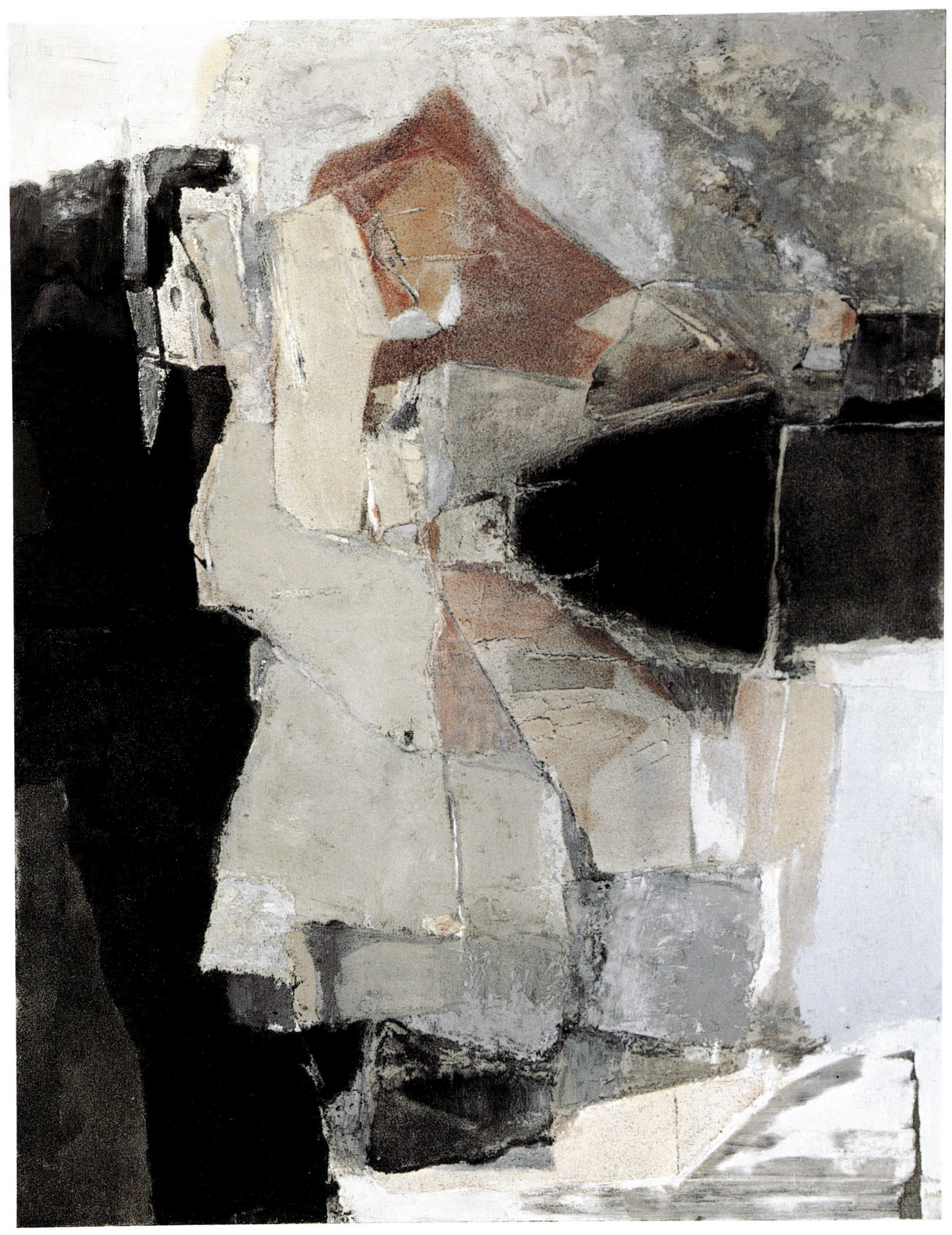

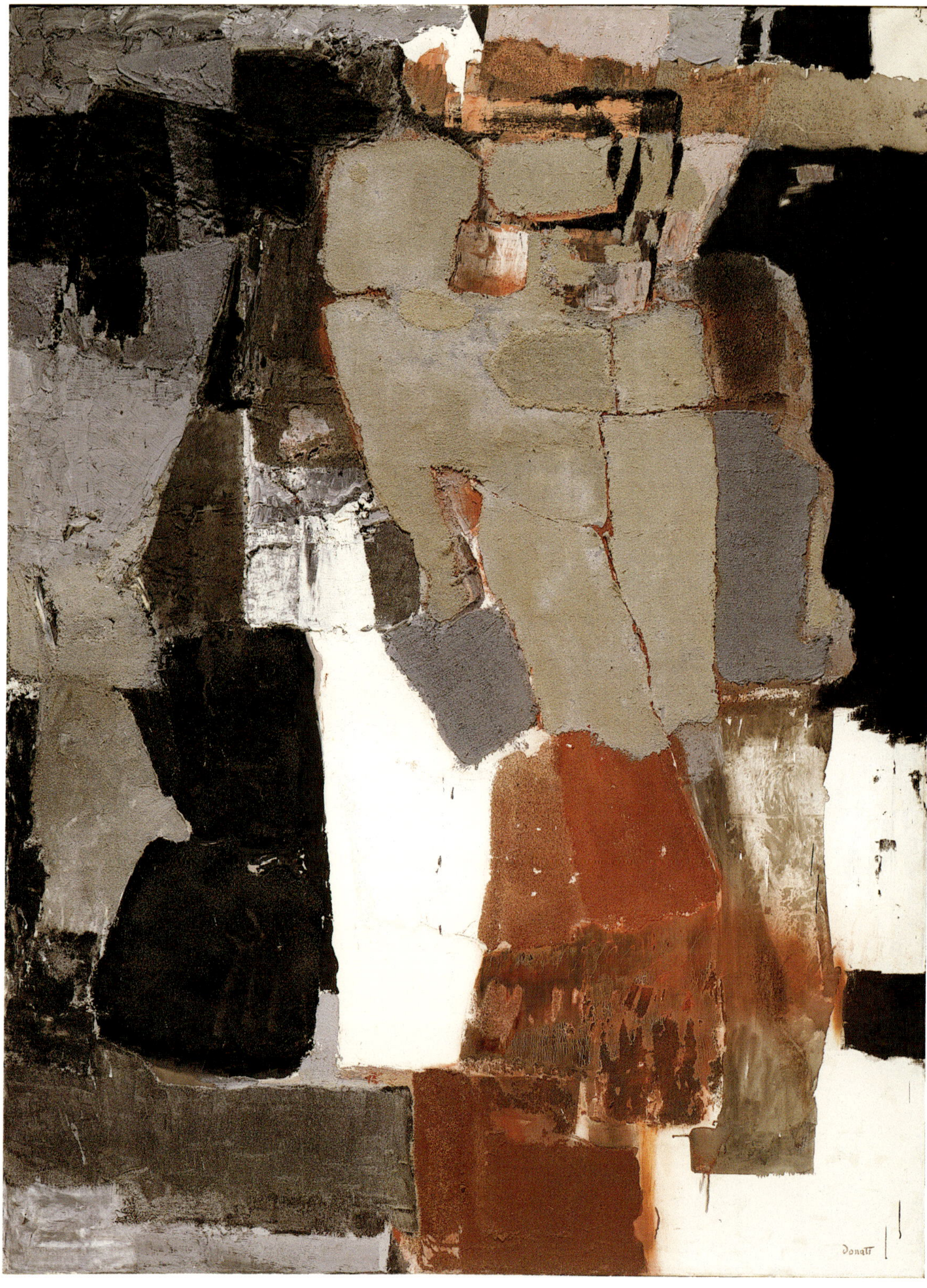

From Body to Soul, 1957

Oil on canvas

80 × 60

The Detroit Institute of Arts,
Founders Society Purchase, Friends
of Modern Art Fund

Facing page

Habbaku Dancers, 1958

Oil and sand on canvas

80 × 70

Collection Albright-Knox Art Gallery,
Buffalo, New York, Gift of Seymour
H. Knox

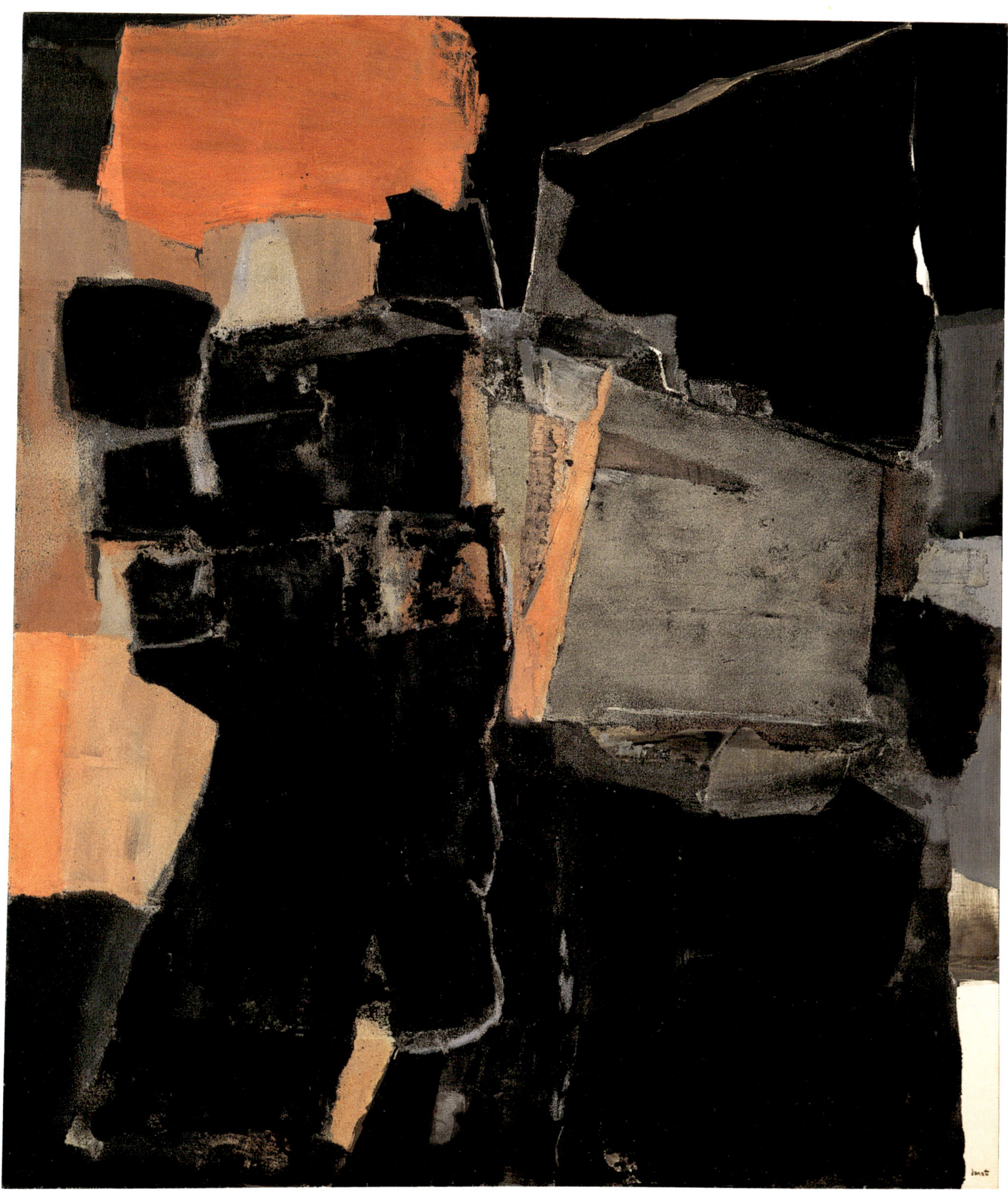

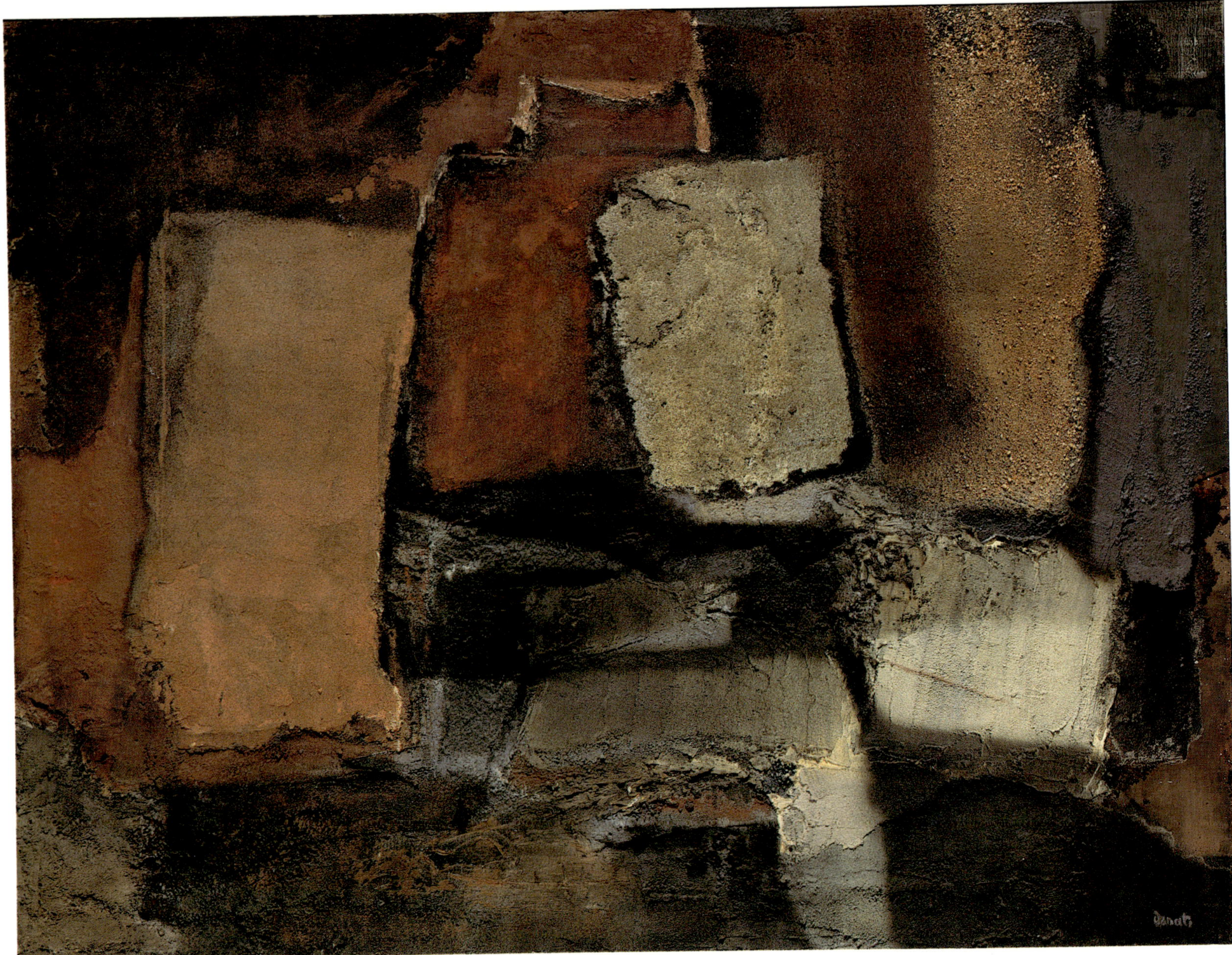

Akki, Creator of Waters

(from the Sargon series), 1958

Oil and granulated quartz on canvas

54 × 72

Hirshhorn Museum and Sculpture
Garden, Smithsonian Institution.
Gift of Edwin Weisl, Jr., 1980

stood finally the depth of the fossil's hold on him, and that it "had always been my true myth and metaphor, my guide from the very beginning of my career."

Impelled to put his thoughts into more concrete form, he wrote: "There is a Latin word 'incubus' which I roughly describe in terms of a hammer which keeps tapping at your head. . . . You become aware of the knock but not of its significance. In order to find the source you must connect and relate various clues and fleeting insights. My incubus developed from a fossil. . . . The fossil has an incredibly animated inside form . . . and carries the whole cycle of creation within it. Nature has destroyed the life it once was and has reincarnated it in a new life that will have perpetual existence. . . . To me, the fossil contains within itself all the mystery, power and indestructibility of life."[12]

These words, written as much for himself as for others, were meant not only to clarify the role the fossil had played in his life but also to help lay the groundwork for the work that was to come.

As such, they succeeded beautifully. Within a year, the monumental complexities of the Sargon series had been replaced by simple, rigidly frontal compositions of, at most, two or three richly colored, sand-textured geometric forms of vaguely geological or archaeological origin. Some of these forms were plain, others were incised with what appeared to be ancient, partially eroded inscriptions, and others revealed what might be fossil fragments.

With these simple, blatantly physical, and provocatively iconic images of mysterious and indeterminate ancestry, Donati finally and fully came into his own. Changes in his art would occur in future years, but they would be more in the nature of variations on a theme than of significant shifts in direction.

Among the first of these heavily encrusted, ancient-looking canvases to appear was *Imperial Seal.* Painted in 1961, this large, still somewhat transitional painting was also one of the first to be exhibited at New York's Staempfli Gallery

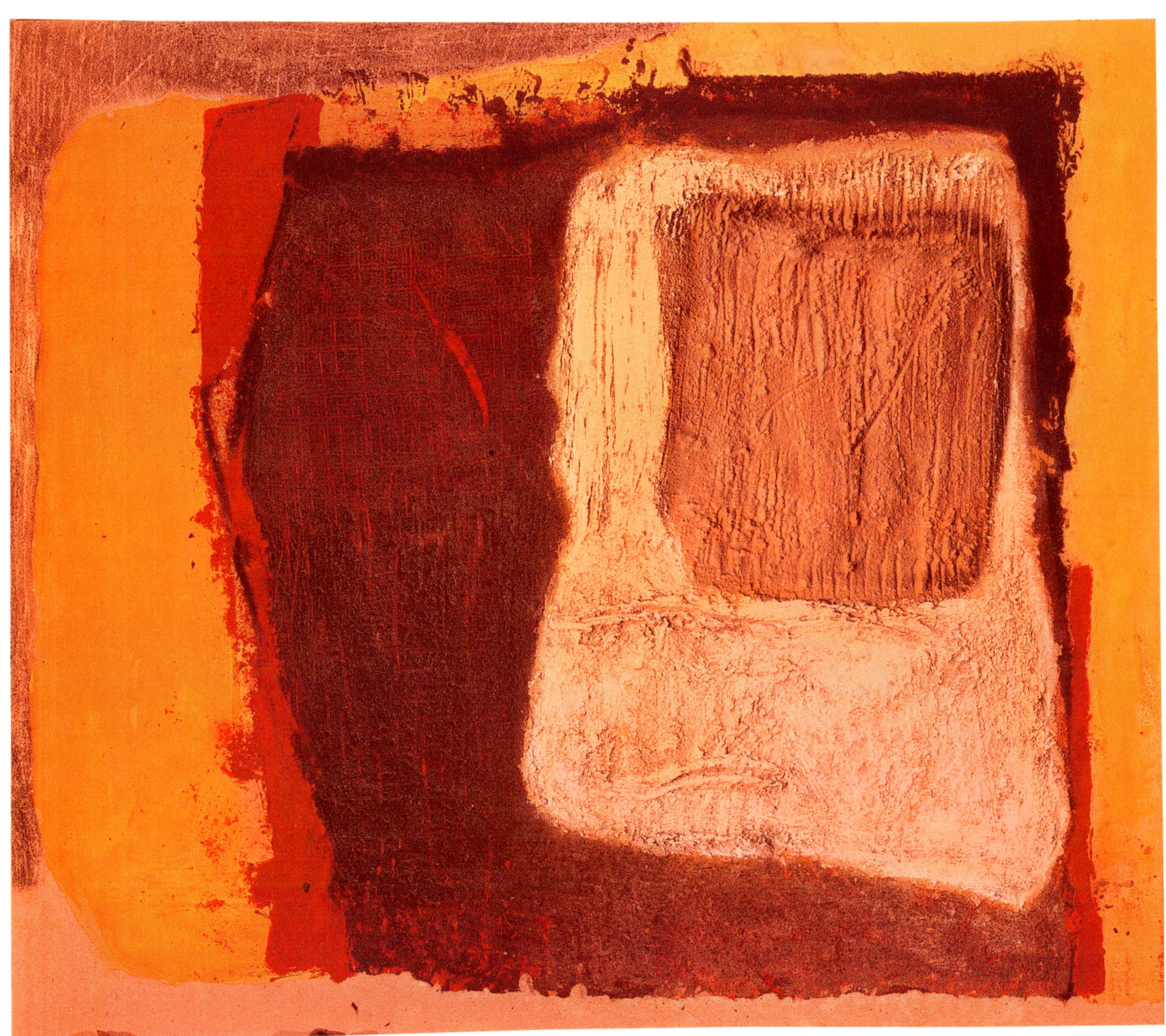

Imperial Seal, 1961

Mixed media on canvas

72 × 84

Collection James Robison

shortly after Donati joined its ranks in 1962. Other pictures of this original group, including *Eannatoum's Victory Wall* (1961) and *The Undeciphered* (1961), while also rather tentative in execution and direction, did achieve a kind of rugged grandeur primarily because of their simplicity and judicious use of color.

Inscription 4026 B.C. (1962) was even more successful. It was the single work of this period that best foreshadowed what was to follow. Almost everything that defines a mature Donati work of art is present in this painting, from the granular impasto technique he developed to the manner in which he was able to imply the existence of wondrous and mysterious things within or just beneath the surface of his canvases.

It is all there: the severely frontal, roughly textured slablike form set squarely against a flat, single-color (in this case, red) background; the suggestion that the central shape is old beyond time and the conveyor of ancient wisdom—if one were only capable of deciphering the fragment of the inscription that remains; and the nagging certainty that, no matter how long or how deeply one might study this image, its meaning will forever elude precise interpretation.

To these must be added one other characteristic of a mature Donati painting: the high degree of aesthetic pleasure it is capable of inducing in the viewer.

The last trait is of particular significance to Donati since he is a firm believer in the strategic importance of pleasure in the creation of a work of art. Not everyone's art, of course, and not as an end in itself, but as a means of charming the viewers of his paintings on one level in order to engage them more profoundly on another.

To succeed at that strategy, Donati had to develop a highly sophisticated tactical approach. This he did by discovering and then perfecting an imagery that not only touched the deepest wellsprings of his own being but that could also touch those of others through provocative symbolic and metaphoric refer-

Following pages

Ennatoum's Victory Wall,
1961
Mixed media on canvas
60 × 50
Collection Fleur Cowles, London

The Undeciphered
(from the Fossil series), 1961
Mixed media on canvas
70 × 80
Collection Rockefeller University,
New York

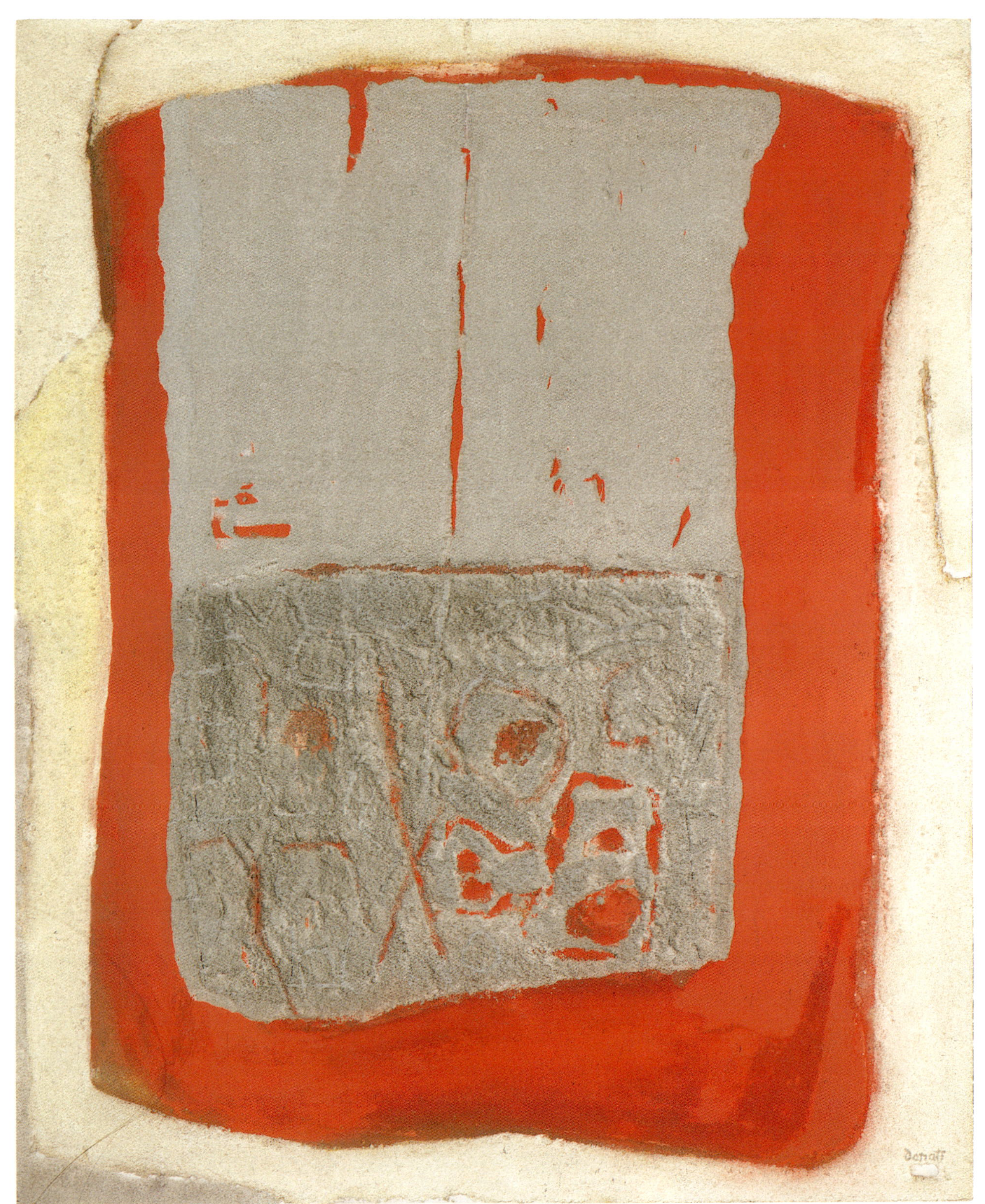
Donati

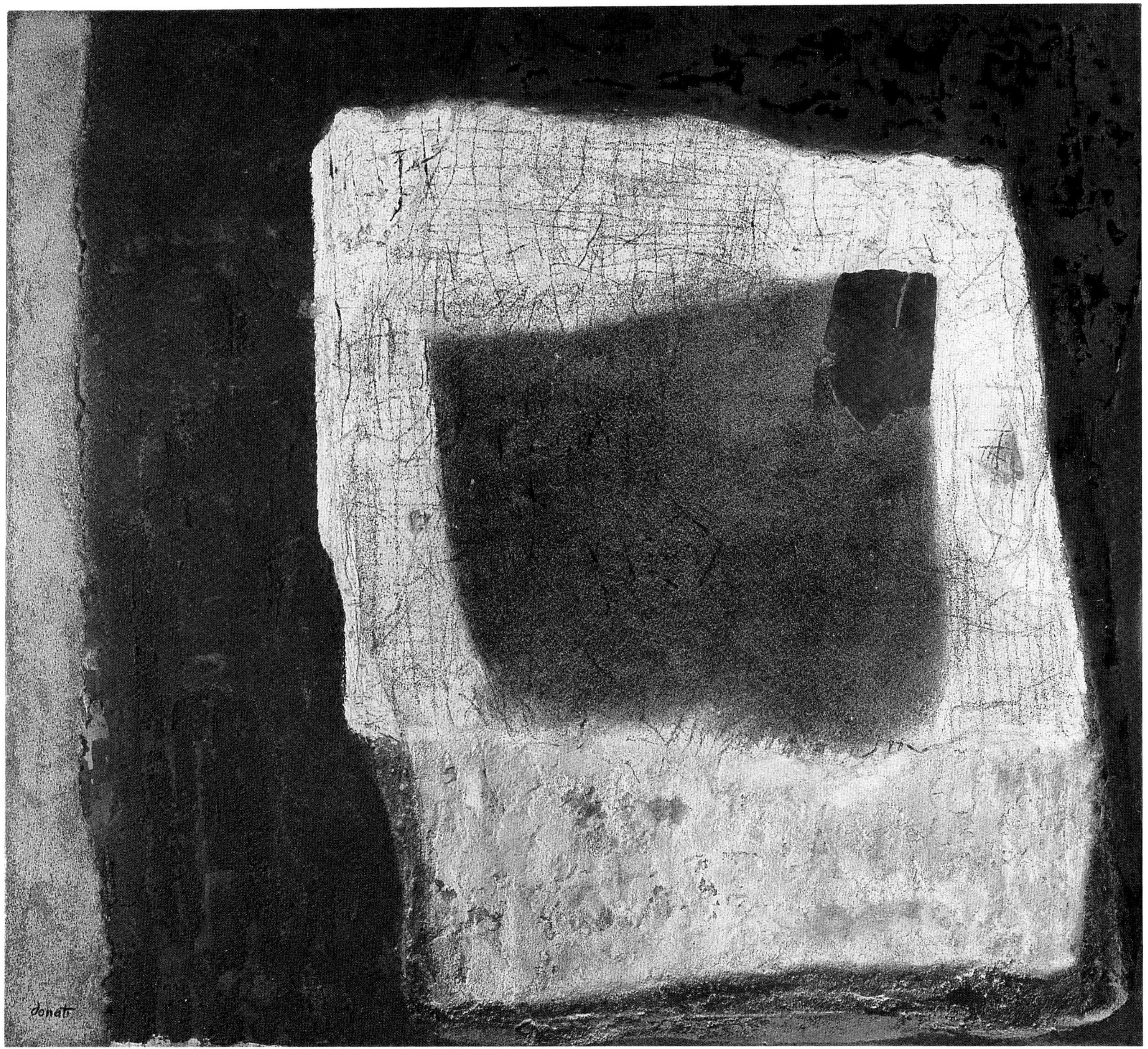

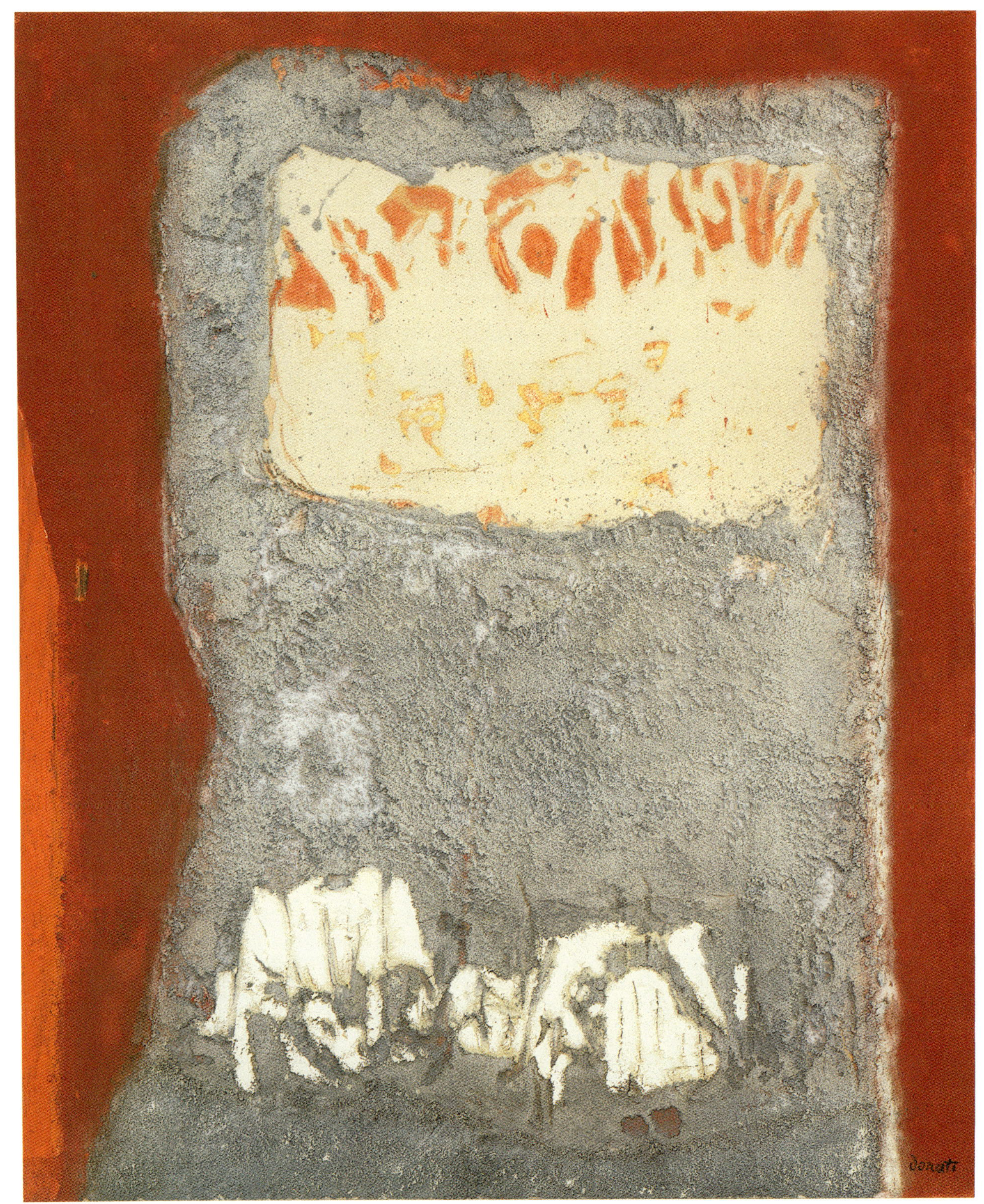

donati

ences to long-buried and half-forgotten geological and archaeological realities and myths.

Thus, glimpses of partially exposed fossils and fragments of age-old, undecipherable commemorative tablets came to dominate his art. But that was not enough. In order to make his canvases both as compelling and moving as possible, he also introduced a personalized touch of painterly magic.

In this he was only being true to his Surrealist roots. Ernst, Duchamp, Tanguy, Dalí, and the other members of the movement were also painterly magicians, past masters at seducing the eye and inflaming the imagination for carefully calculated results. Each had his special talent—Ernst for paradox, Duchamp for diversionary tactics, Tanguy for spatial illusion, and Dalí for Old Master techniques—and all used them as effectively as any magician wielded his magic wand.

Donati's forte was the utilization of color and texture for maximum pleasurable effect. In this he was without peer among the Surrealists and almost, one must add, among his contemporaries in general.

If one delights in ravishing color and rich, sensuous surfaces, especially in conjunction with evocative images, Donati is the artist to seek out. And the best place to start is with the work he began immediately after his encounter with the fossil.

Since the Fossil series, which occupied him for the greater part of the 1960s, owed so much of its success to its remarkable fusion of color and texture, a discussion of Donati's technical processes at that time might be in order. No reproduction, no matter how superb, can adequately convey the richly tactile nature of these paintings. And small wonder, considering how much material went into their production. To begin with, generous portions of ground quartz were mixed with paint and medium. This mixture was then molded and

Facing page
Inscription 4026 B.C., 1962
Oil and sand on canvas
60 × 50
The Museum of Modern Art, New York. Gift of Mr. and Mrs. Gilbert W. Kahn

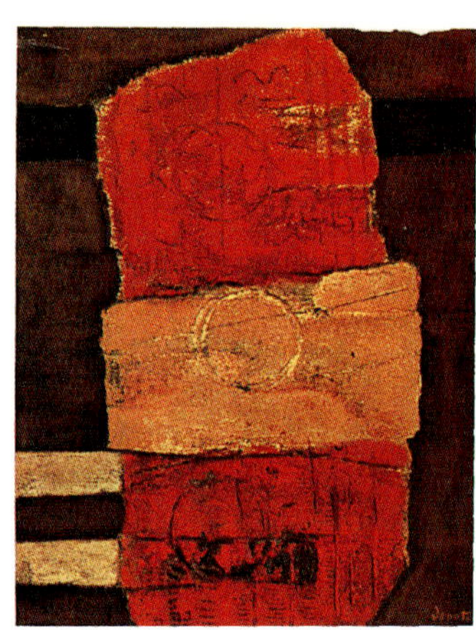

Red-Yellow Fossil (from the
Fossil series), 1964
38 × 30
Mixed media on canvas
Private collection

troweled onto the canvas until it was up to an inch thick. While the mixture was drying, the surface was incised, gouged, or pitted to suit Donati's purposes. At times this mixture was so heavily applied that the results resembled bas-reliefs or mounds of calcified rock more than paintings. At other times, thick paint and thin washes were juxtaposed to create more purely painterly effects.

And should there be any doubt, color—rich, pure, and vibrant—also played a highly significant role in these paintings' pleasurable impact. One need only glance at *The Great Stone* (1965) and *Red-Yellow Fossil* (1964) for proof. In both, color and texture combined to fashion a wonderfully tantalizing, seamless whole so physically real and coloristically alive that one is tempted to reach out to touch it.

With the Fossil series, then, Donati entered the most integrated and long-lasting phase of his career. Nothing he had produced before had so successfully fused what he wanted to say with the best and most effective way to say it. And nothing had been both so simple in form and so open-ended in its range of possibilities.

Not only was Donati's art moving ahead briskly, but his personal life was taking a new turn as well. He remarried in 1965, and a few years later his wife, Del, gave birth to their only daughter, Alyssa. On the professional front, things also could not have been better. In addition to his regular one-man shows at the Staempfli Gallery, he had exhibitions during the 1960s in Brussels, Munich, Detroit, Cambridge, and Washington, D.C. And just as important, major museums and private collectors decided with increasing frequency during this period that they had to own at least one of his paintings.

In between, he served as a visiting lecturer at Yale University; as a member of that school's Council for Arts and Architecture; and as a juror for the Fulbright Scholarship Program.

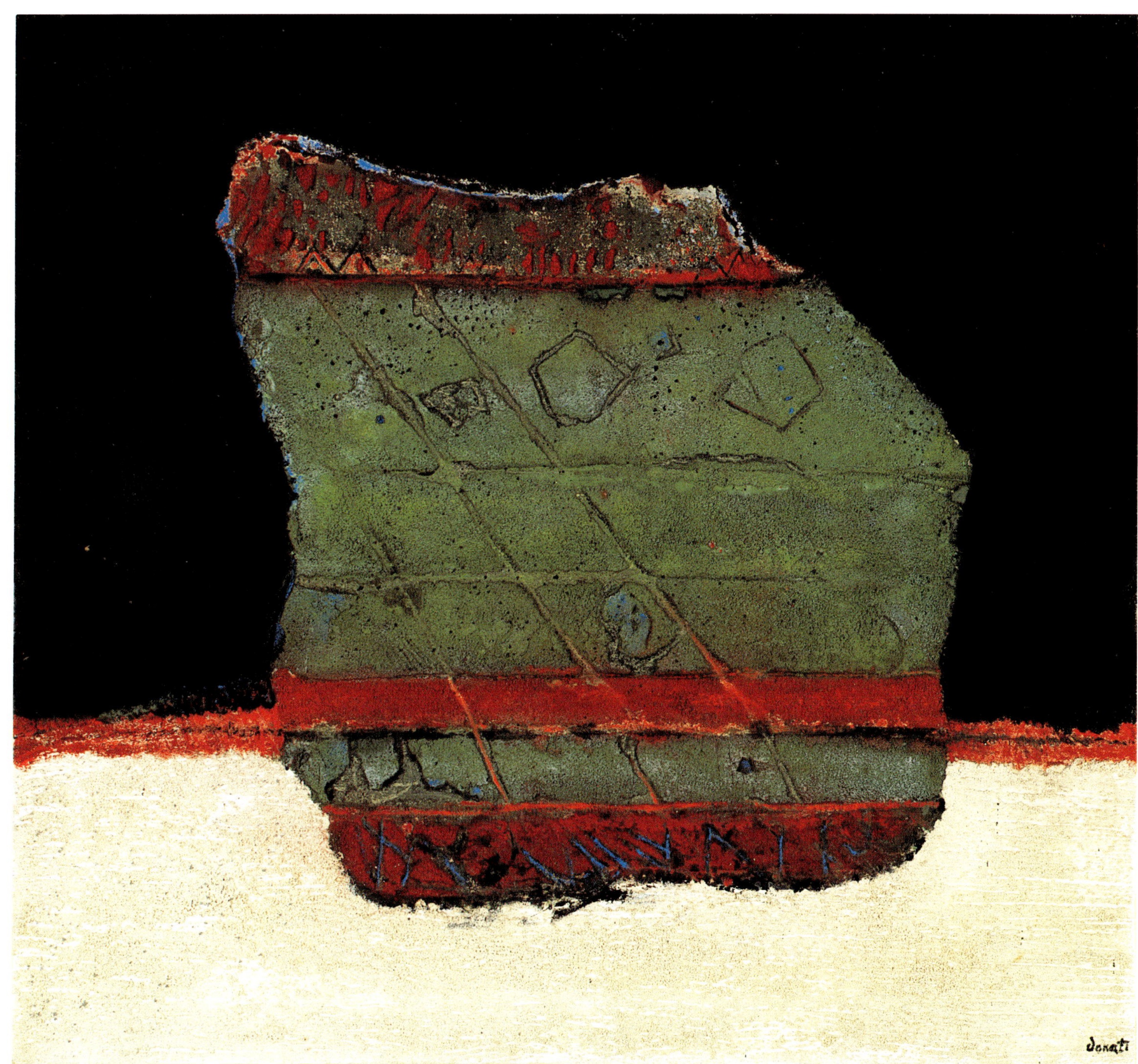

The Great Stone, 1965
Mixed media on canvas
39 × 43
Private collection

Nothing, however, could keep him from painting, and he did so as conscientiously and fruitfully as ever. The end of the 1960s and most of the 1970s saw a succession of intriguing variations on his primary theme, including a number of paintings that dramatized rock forms in subtly Surrealistic ways. And then these, in turn, led to another group of canvases that had a significant impact on what he would produce in the 1980s.

The paintings of the Coptic Wall series are among the most austere and difficult of his creations. At first glance they seem simple enough: Two broad, irregularly shaped bands of rough-textured stone or plaster surfaces are separated, in most cases vertically, by a much narrower band of what appears to be sky. But one cannot be certain. Is it really sky? In most instances it is. Nothing else could be so atmospherically blue. But in others of the series the identity of this feature is less clear. In *Coptic Wall X* (1978–1979), for example, the narrow band is red. In *Coptic Wall XXVI* (1980) it is both yellowish and streaked and is entirely nonatmospheric in appearance.

These differences can be reconciled if one understands that the series is primarily about sections of massive adjacent forms interacting subtly with one another. But no matter what form these bands take, it is important to remember that the paintings themselves are sectional close-ups of large masonry surfaces. In this light, Donati's next creative move becomes more readily comprehensible.

Perhaps the best way to put that move into perspective is to point out that the later (1980–81) canvases of the Coptic Wall series represent a gradual "pulling back" from a "close-up" to a more distant viewing position. In *Moonscape 81* (1981), for instance, Donati had already pulled back sufficiently to paint all of one masonry form and a sizable portion of the other. And by 1983, in *The Walls of Thebes*, the process was complete and the viewer once again was presented with totally self-contained images.

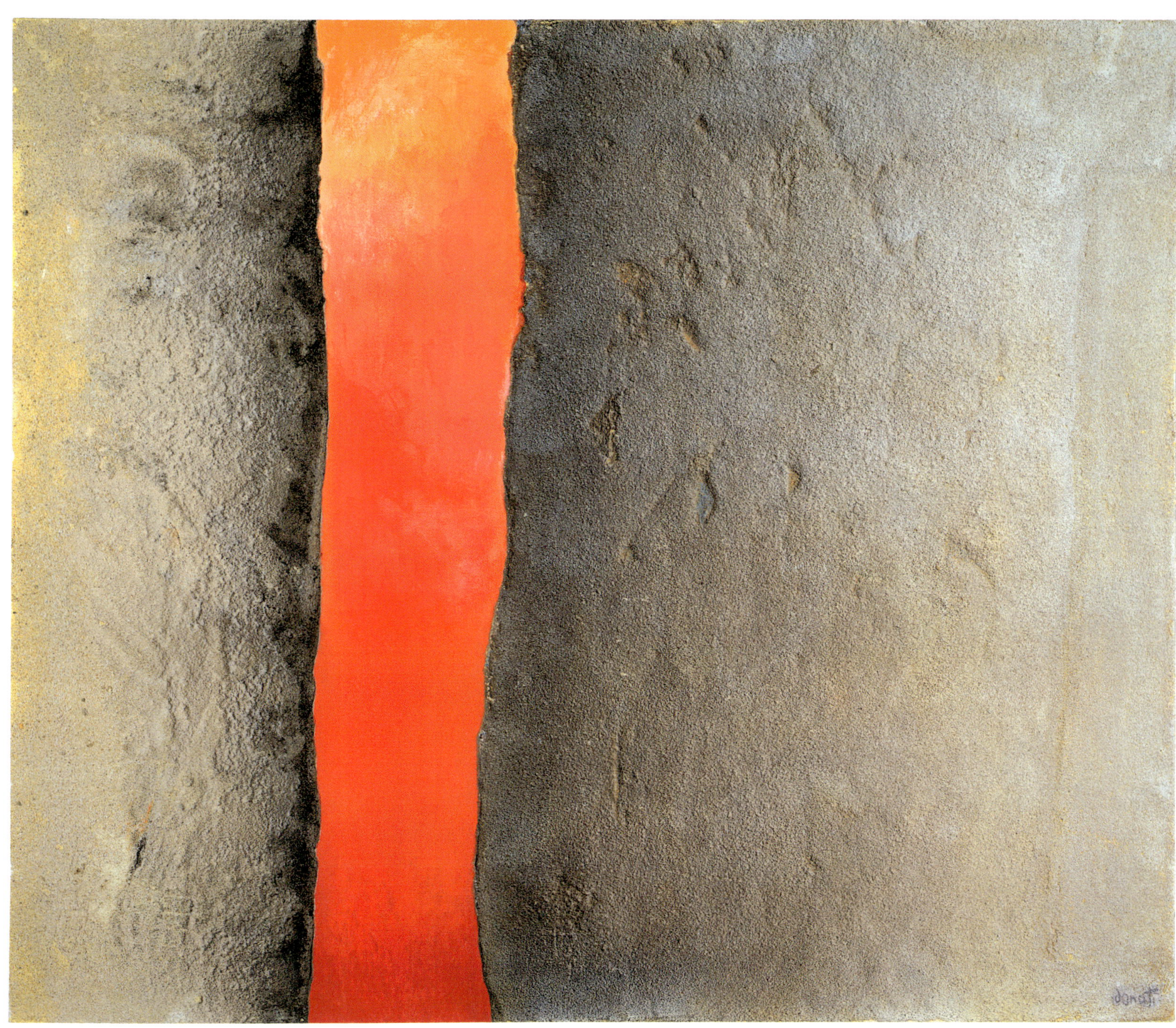

Coptic Wall X, 1978–79
Mixed media on canvas
40 × 48
Private collection

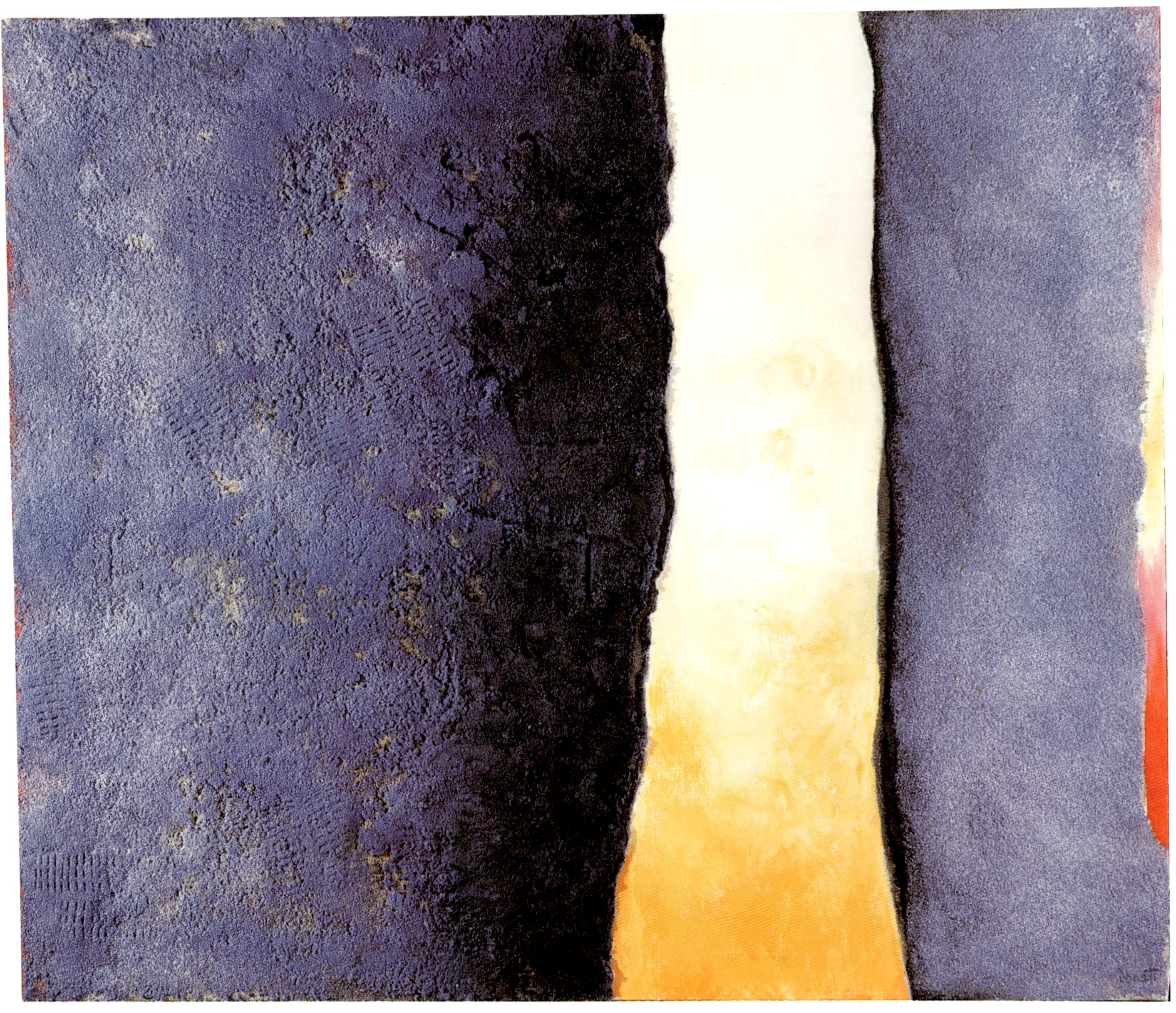

2 Blues and Orange, 1979
Mixed media on canvas
40 × 48
Private collection

Facing page
Coptic Wall XXVI, 1980
Mixed media on canvas
42 × 48
Private collection

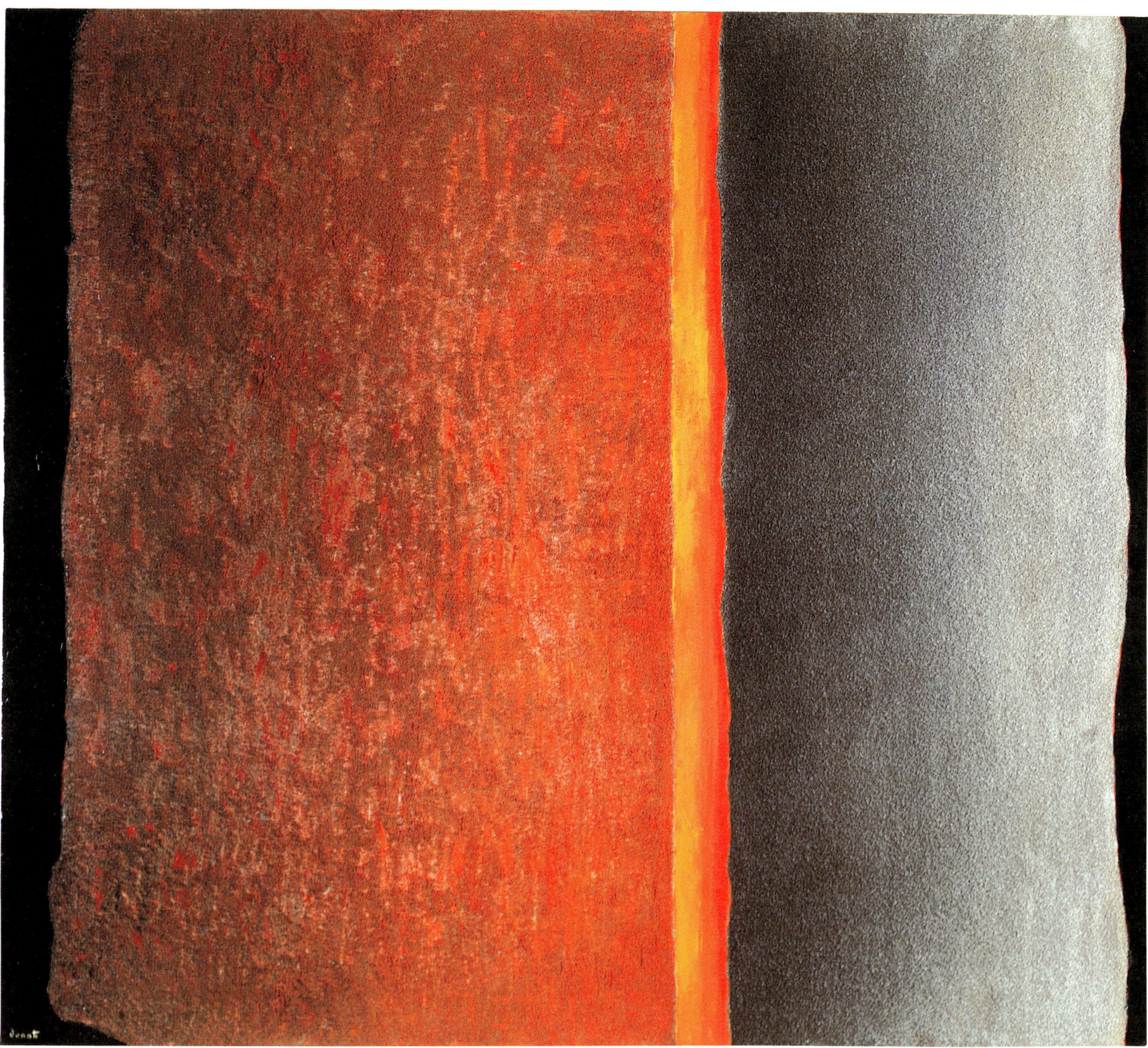

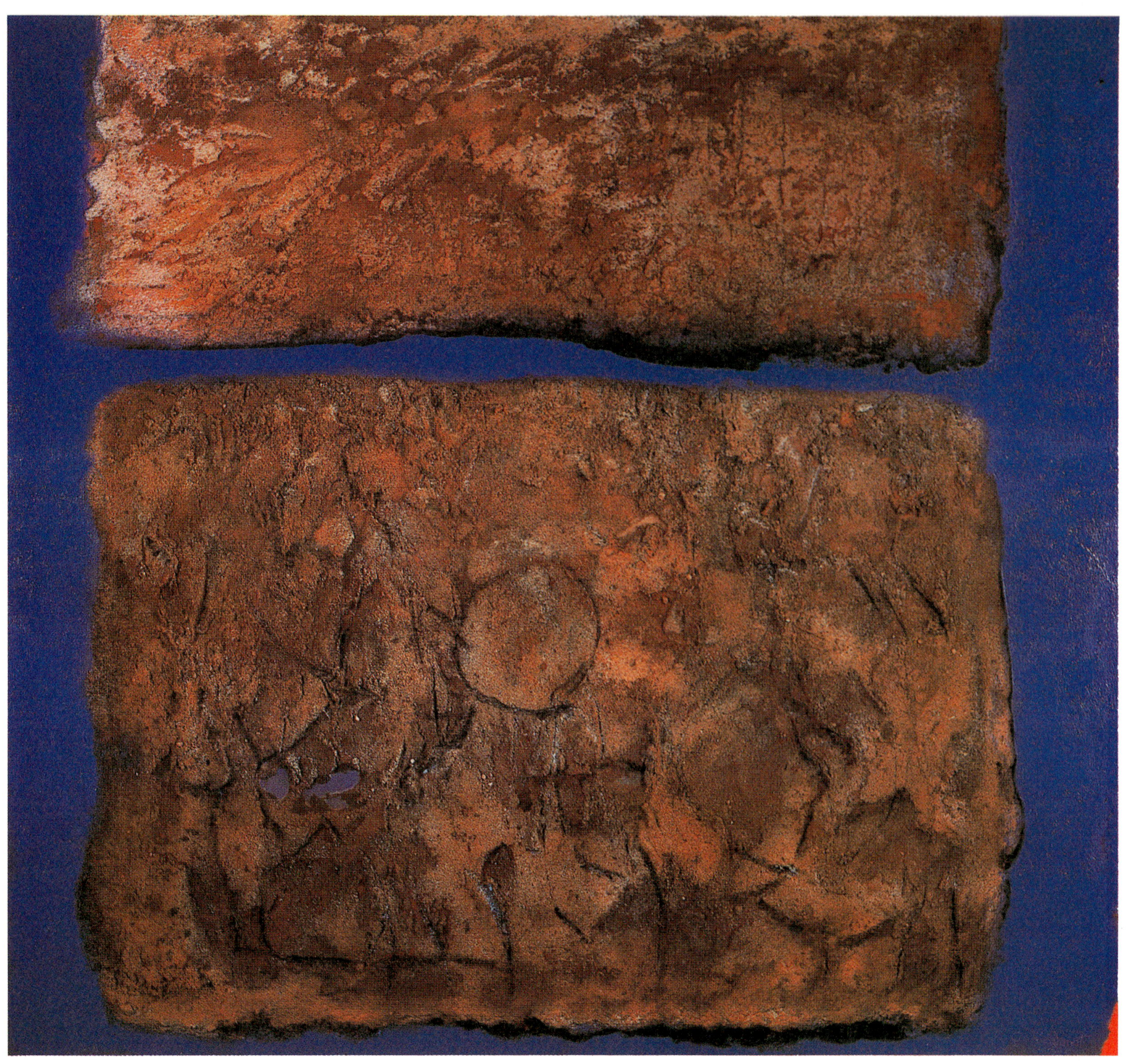

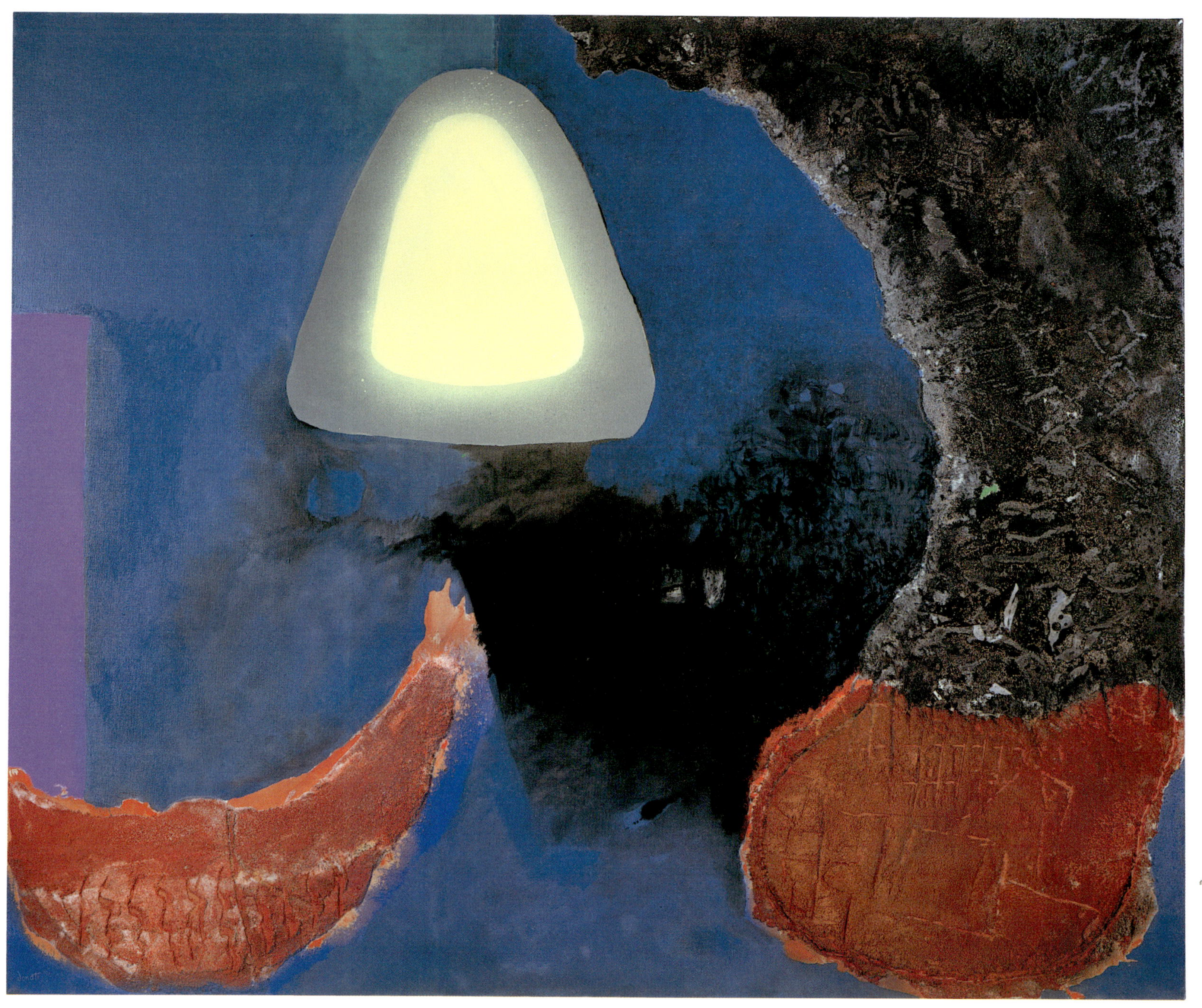

Facing page ·

Moonscape 81, 1981
Mixed media on canvas
39 × 43
Private collection

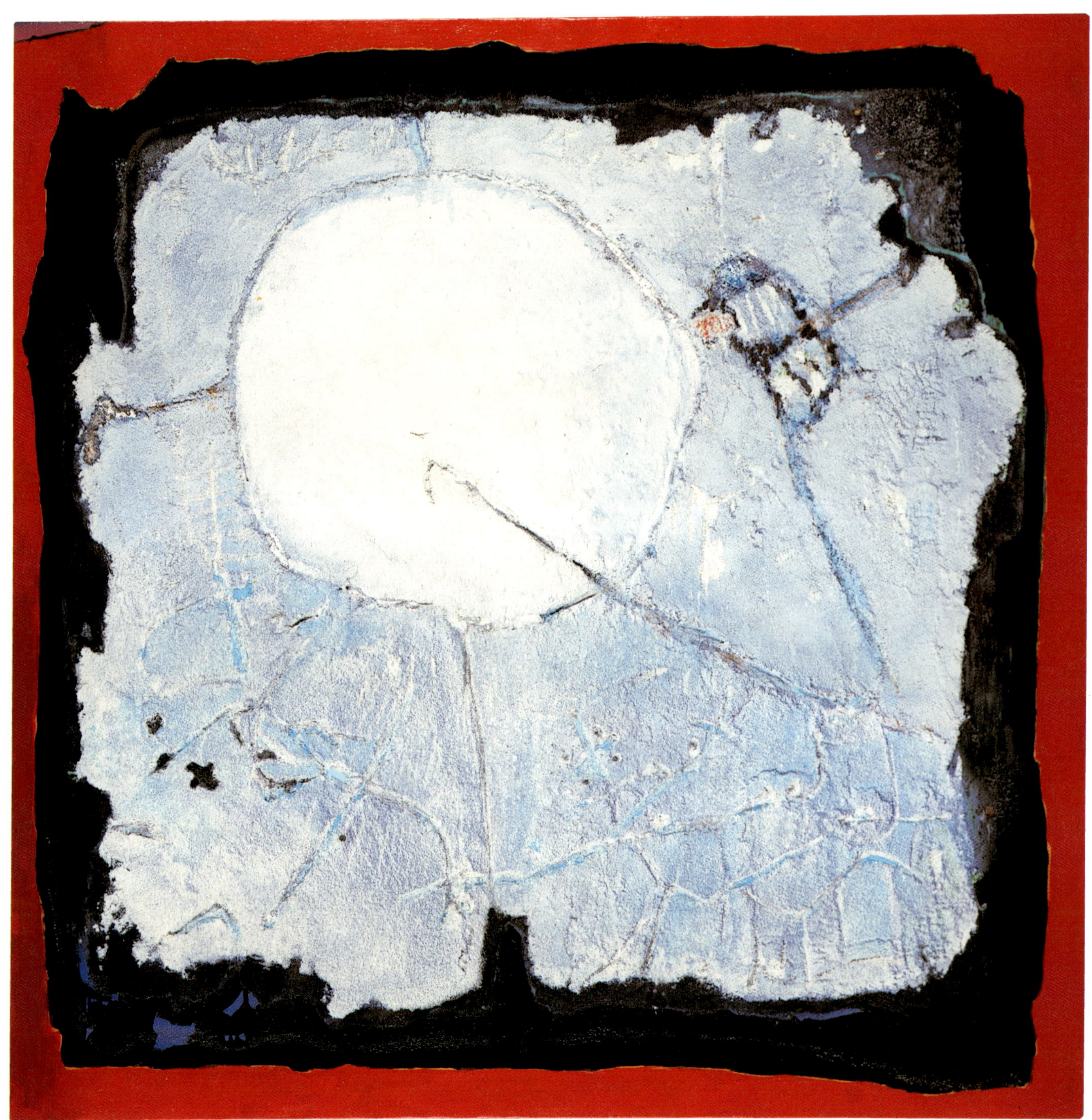

Oasis Middle Nile, 1982
Mixed media on canvas
50 × 50
Private collection

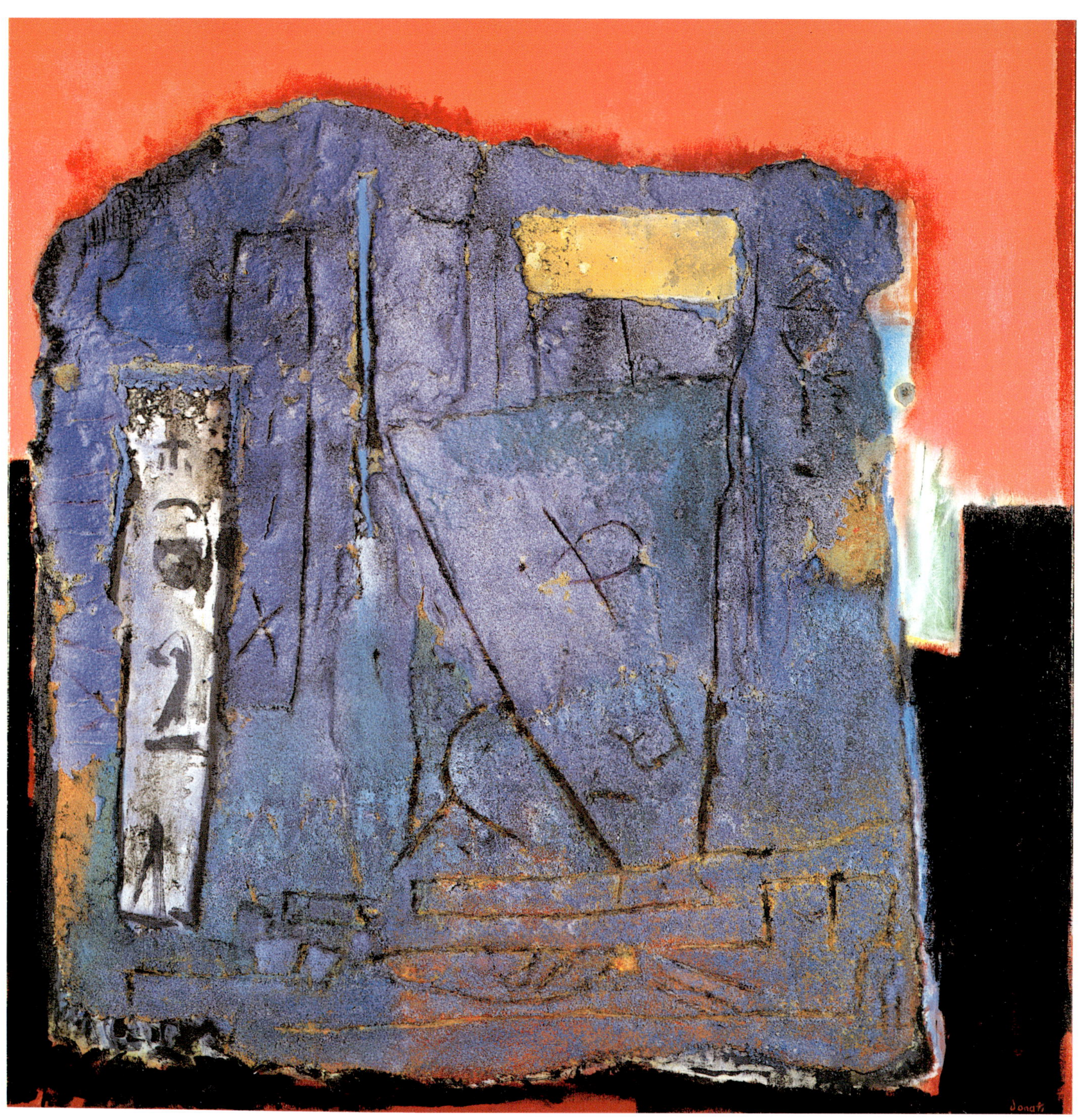

The Walls of Thebes, 1983
Mixed media on canvas
50 × 50
Collection James Robison

Not only were these paintings more dramatic, but they were also brighter and richer in color and more sumptuous and varied in texture. More important, they resonated with deeper emotion. In this regard, *The Walls of Thebes* represents Donati at his best, both as artist/poet with something valuable to share and as painter/magician with the best and most appropriate means needed to share it.

Interestingly, for all its enhanced color, more tantalizing surfaces, and greater depth, *The Walls of Thebes* remains as enigmatic and impossible to interpret precisely as any of his previous works. If anything, this painting and most of those that followed during the remainder of the decade and well into the 1990s were even more enigmatic than the paintings of earlier periods.

Even so, it is possible at times to sense one is drawing close to the hidden core, the secret, of Donati's art—only to be diverted at the last minute and sent off in another direction. *The Walls of Thebes* has provided this writer with such a moment, as have several later canvases, including two from 1991, *Anybody Can Figure It . . .* and *Composition '91.*

Unfortunately, unlike the small smooth stone found on the beach at Dover, Donati's paintings cannot be tapped open to reveal what lies inside. Since they exist as carefully distilled, skillfully dissembled, and handsomely packaged embodiments of his deepest and most private feelings, insights, and intuitions, they must remain forever "untapped" and "unrevealed," a constant source of speculation and enchantment but never of resolution or clarification.

In short, Donati's art is both "fossil" *and* "stone" fused into an indivisible whole. Only by keeping it so can he fashion successful pictorial metaphors for the mystery of the eternal cycle of life, death, and regeneration that has animated his work since its inception. To do otherwise, to provide answers and interpretations, would be to deny the "magical," regenerative nature of that cycle.

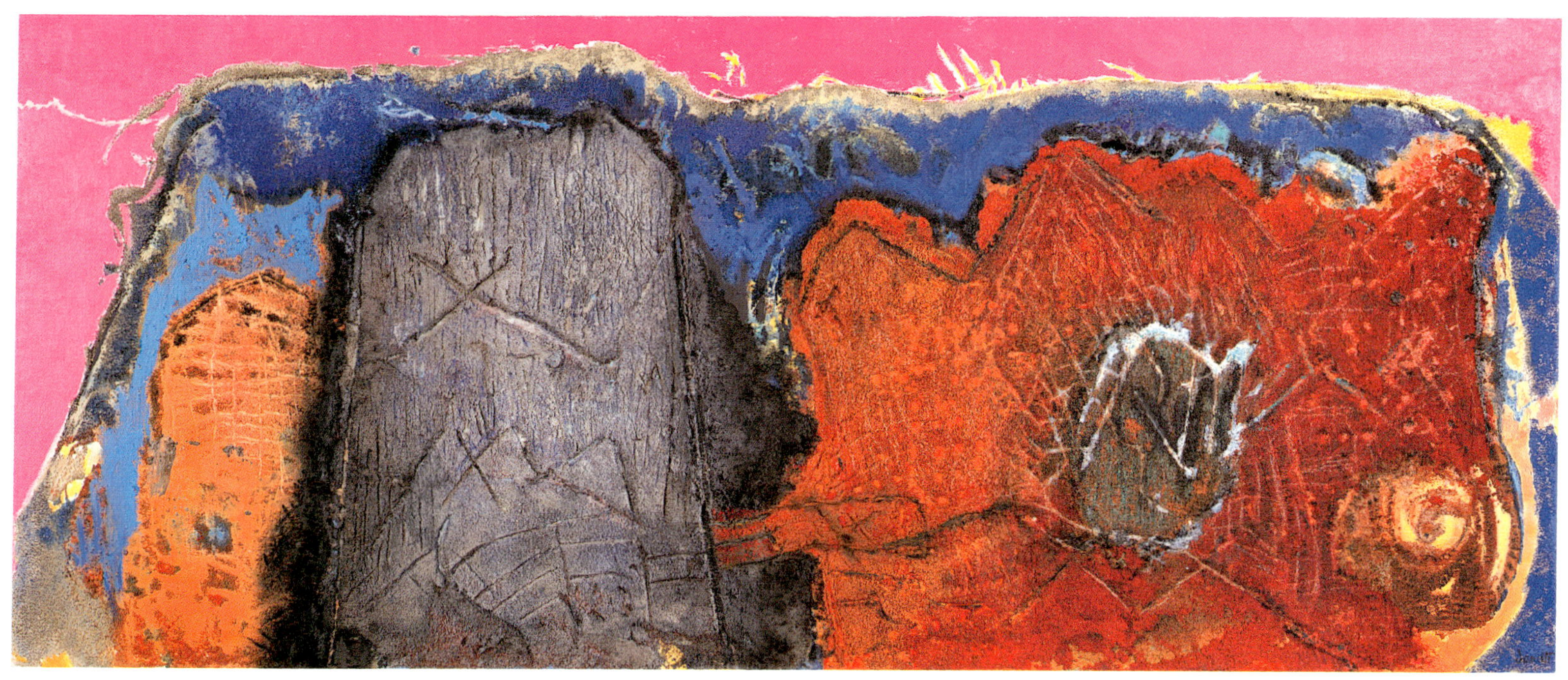

Les oreilles du monde

(The Ears of the World), 1984

Mixed media on canvas

32 × 78

Private collection

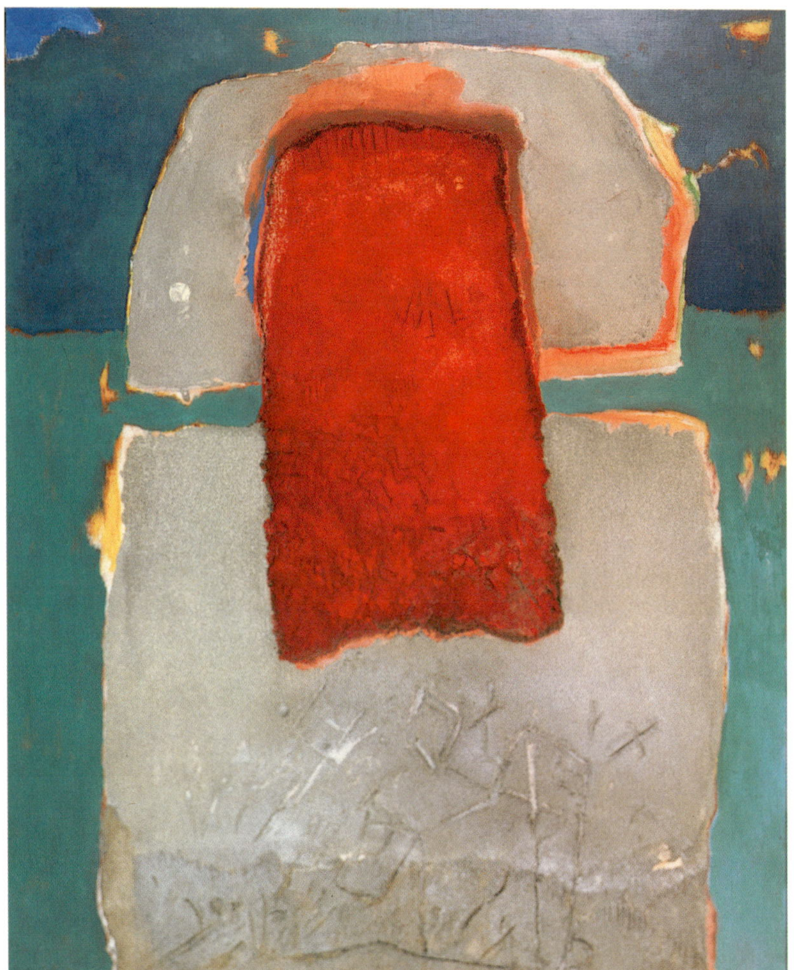

Emperor's Hat, 1988
Mixed media on canvas
60 × 50
Collection Eleanor R. Baldwin

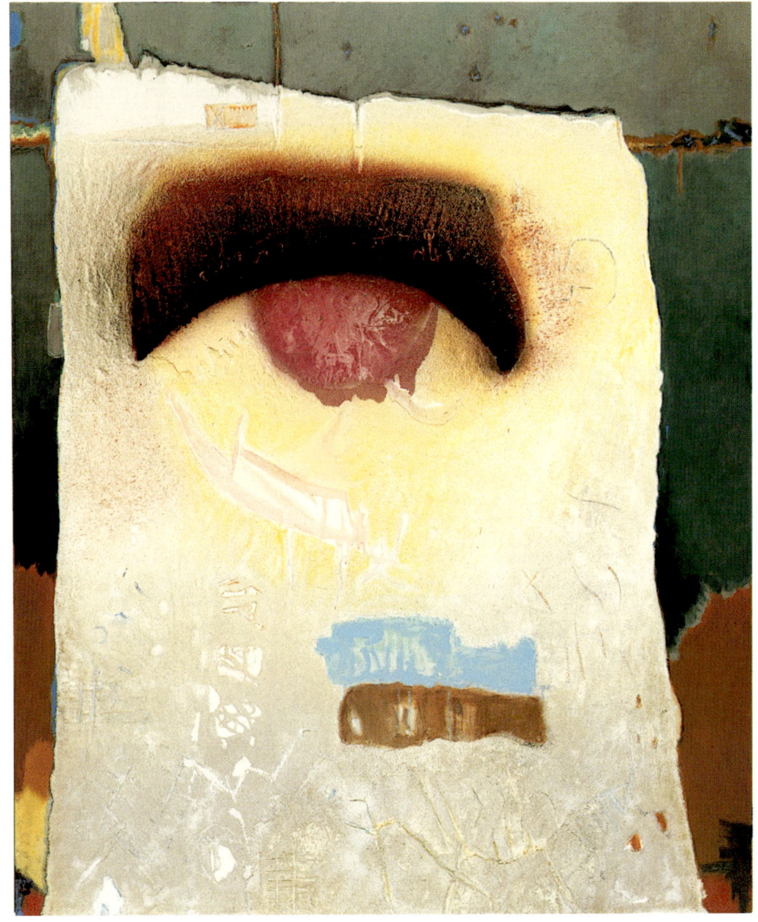

Pompeian Wall, 1986
Mixed media on canvas
60 × 50
Courtesy Louis Newman Galleries,
Beverly Hills, California

What has always fascinated Donati and lain at the center of his art is the inexplicable nature of life. As such, he sees more truth in wonder than in certainty, in a questioning attitude than in dogma, and, most particularly, in an art that provokes and confounds than in one that details and defines.

No greater proof of this attitude can be found than in the canvases he produced from 1983 onward. In image after image, mystery and enchantment increasingly take center stage. In *Yesterday and Today* (1983) runic and hieroglyphic inscriptions add a touch of magic to a partially exposed, richly colored fossilized area. And in *Anybody Can Figure It . . . ,* blue and red forms leap upward against a yellow sky much as the legendary phoenix must have thrust itself into the heavens.

Even *Composition (1990)* (1990), a haphazardly arrayed assemblage of five flat, irregularly shaped stones of various sizes and hues, scores handsomely, thanks primarily to its daring juxtaposition of color and texture. There is little that is directly appealing about this composition. Its color, except for one deep glowing red, is unexceptional, and its textures show little of the scarring and pitting that attract attention elsewhere. And yet, in Donati's hands, it all comes together brilliantly. Few of his paintings are more palpably, physically alive than this one, and none makes one wonder more if rocks and stones might not have lives of their own.

One of his favorite technical devices, and one that did much to create the impression of great age that characterized so much of his work during the 1980s, is a deceptively simple one. Different colors are layered over partly or completely hardened mounds of ground quartz that have been mixed with pigment and medium. Then, when the paint has dried, selected portions of the surface are carefully scraped away to reveal glimpses of the colors underneath.

Following pages
Yesterday and Today, 1983
60 × 50
Mixed media on canvas
Private collection

Anybody Can Figure It . . . ,
1991
Mixed media on canvas
60 × 60
Collection Robert Orell and Linda Lenck

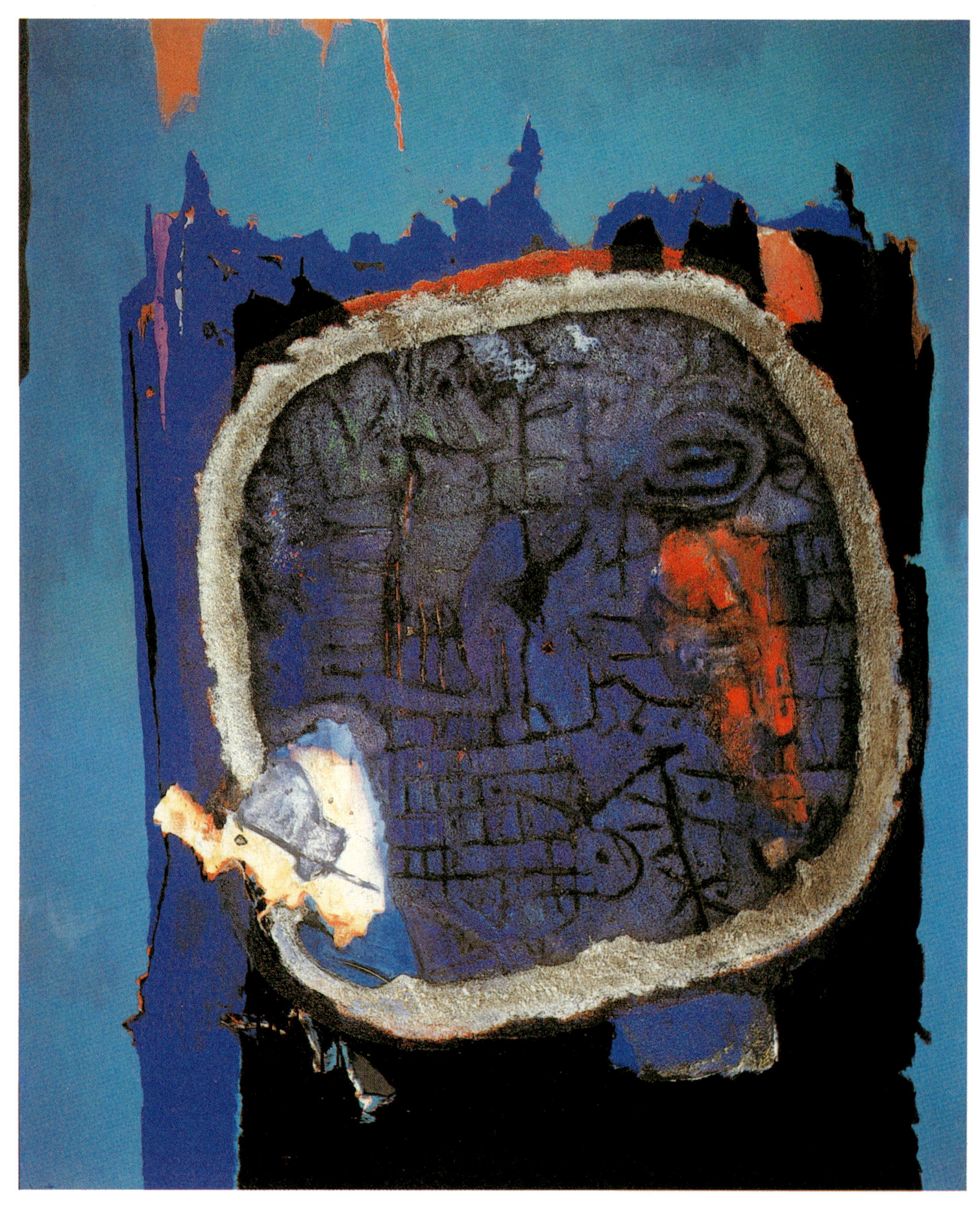

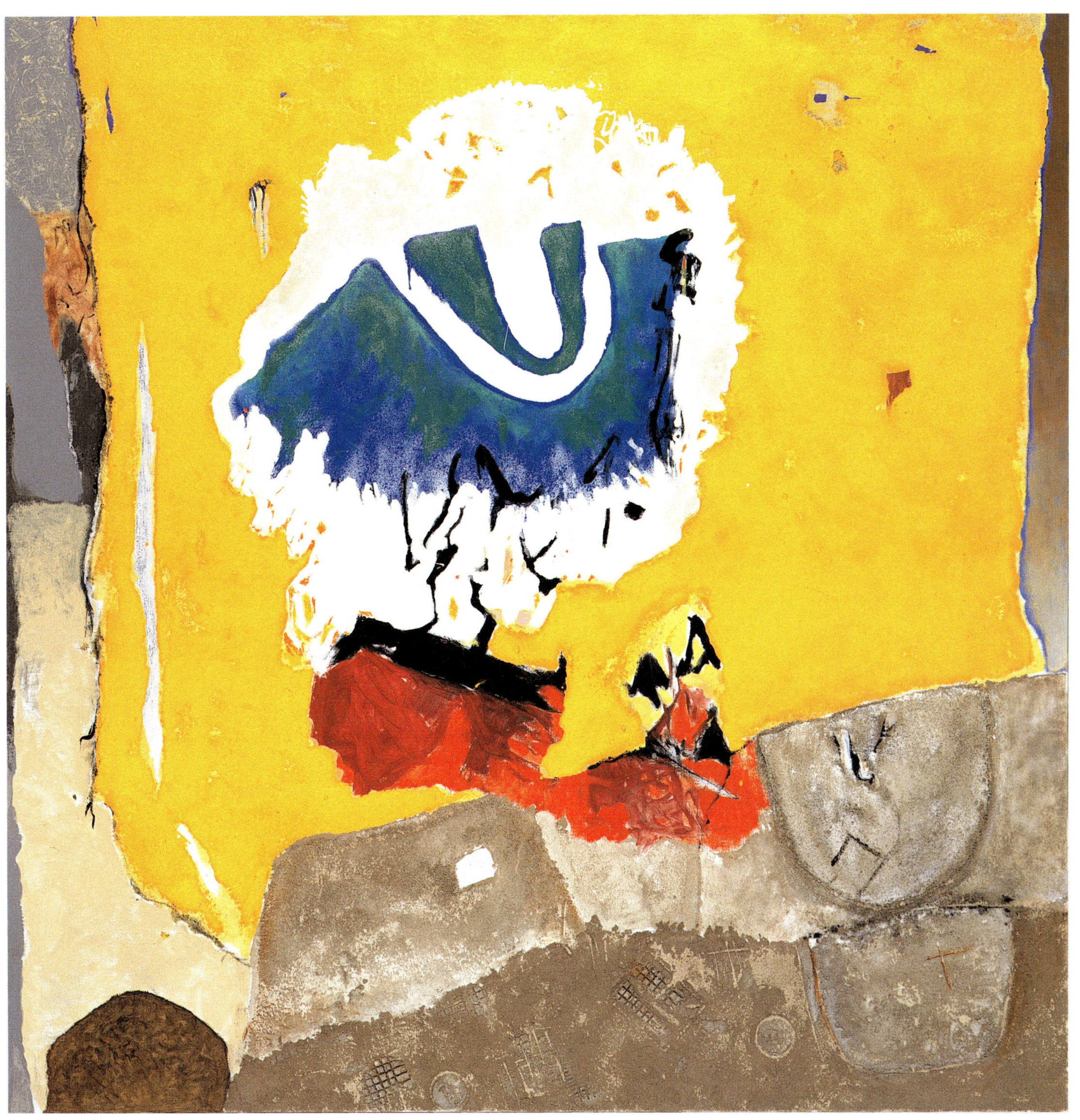

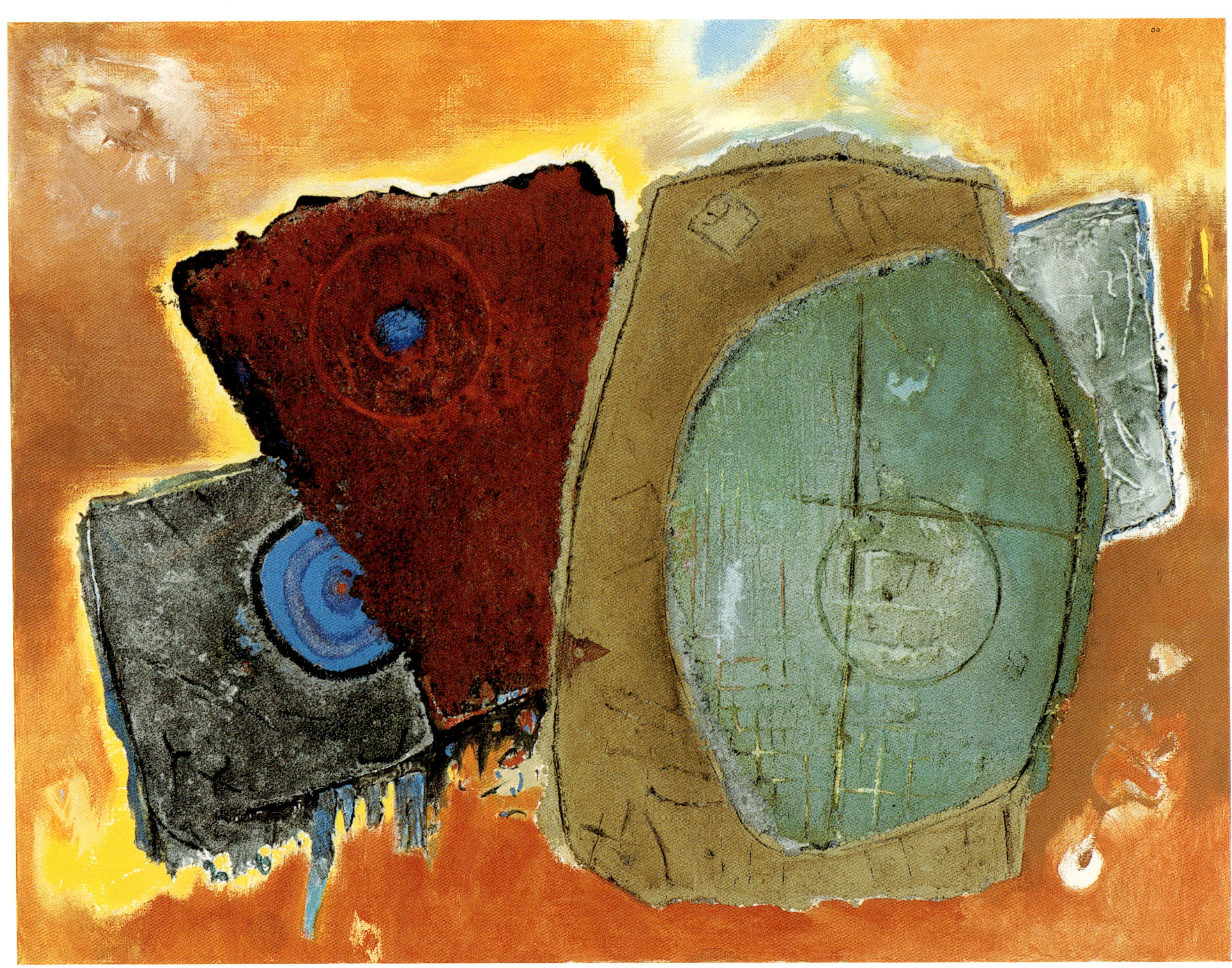

Composition (1990), 1990

Mixed media on canvas

30 × 40

Private collection

The resulting effect, combined with surface scratching and pitting, a few ancient, indecipherable inscriptions, and possibly a hint of a fossil or two, creates an extraordinary impression—especially when Donati also gives his love of color free rein.

The Walls of Thebes is an excellent example of how Donati puts this multiple effect to good use. In fact, few paintings in recent years have had surfaces as lovingly treated as this one. Even in reproduction, one responds warmly to its rich, granular textures, deep scratches and incisions—some of which the viewer is expected to believe were made by primitive man—occasional gleams of exposed under-layers of reds and oranges, and other evidences of the blue stone's hoary old age. Most remarkable of all, however, is the fact that Donati produced this geological and archaeological effect with the simplest of tools and, except for the title, without any literary or historical allusions.

Avant 'hier (1990), while not so heavily encrusted, nor, obviously, intended to appear as old, makes its point just as tellingly with a greater variety of forms and a more lighthearted choice of colors. *Composition '91,* on the other hand, takes a different tack entirely, and introduces, in conjunction with the usual textured forms and surfaces, an assortment of playful geometric shapes and structures that add an entirely new dimension to Donati's art.

For once, the addition of a new element to his work did not also indicate movement in a different direction. Henceforth, from roughly 1991 on, the changes that occurred would lead first to a gradual enlivening of his art and then to an updating of images from earlier periods.

The earliest of these changes took effect gradually. As already noted, *Composition '91* introduced a number of playful geometric structures and arrayed them against Donati's more traditional pictorial components. The result, while successful—indeed, *Composition '91* is one of the most charming of his

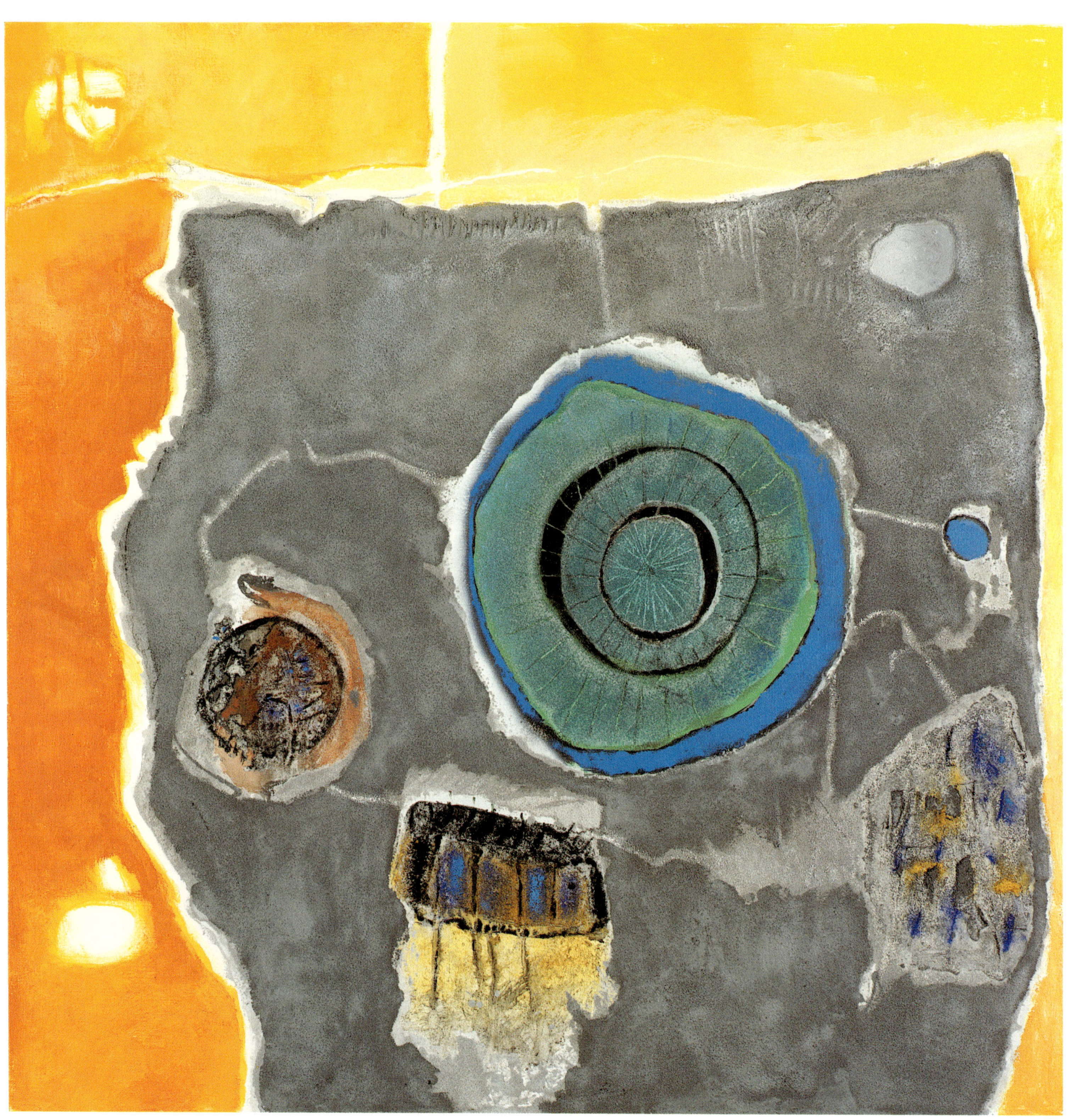

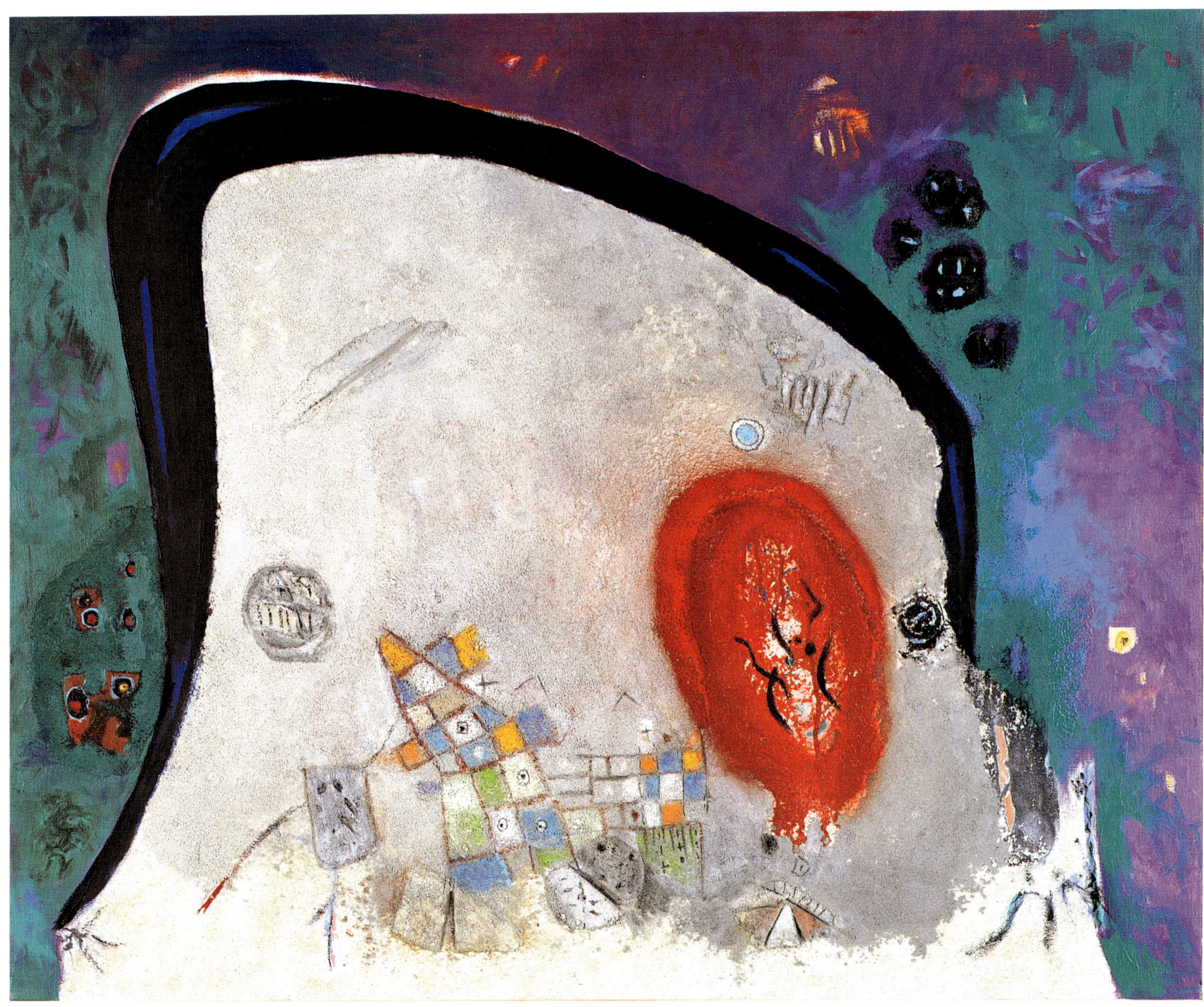

Composition '91, 1991
Mixed media on canvas
40 × 50
Collection Marilyn Ray and Robert Bassett

Facing page

Avant 'hier (Day before Yesterday), 1990
Mixed media on canvas
50 × 50
Collection Bruce Douglas

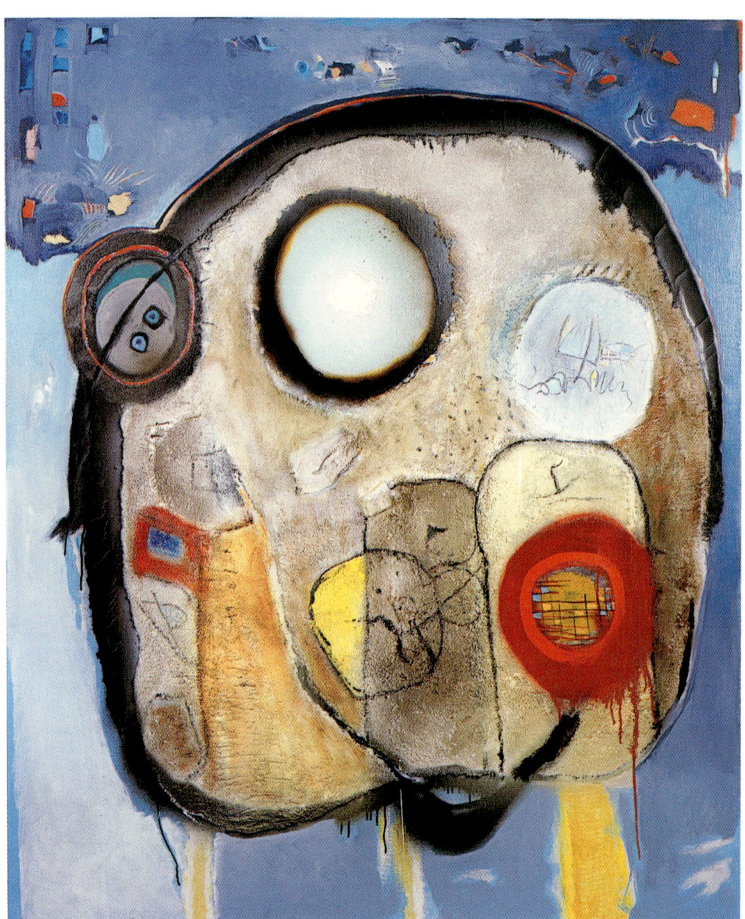

Happy Secret, 1993
Mixed media on canvas
50 × 60
Collection Susan and Jon Diamond

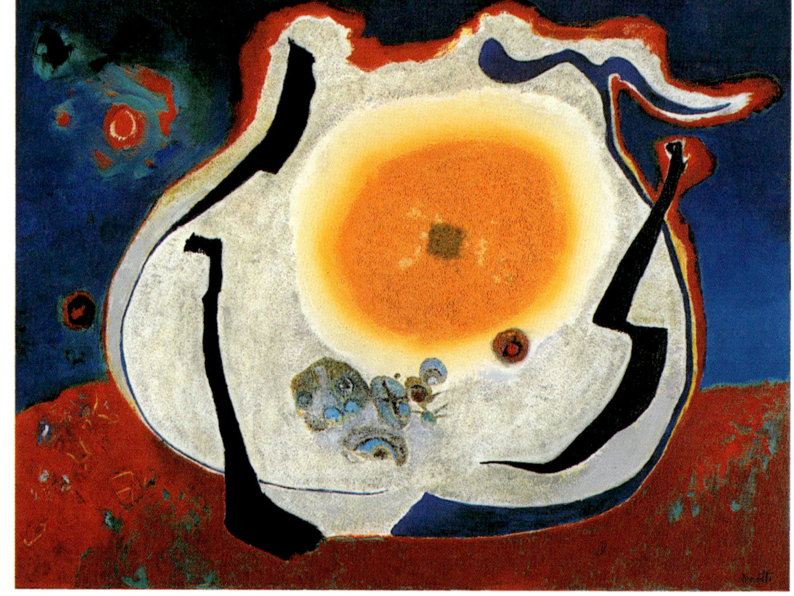

Blue Jays and Cardinals,
1993
Mixed media on canvas
30 × 40
Collection Stephen Nussdorf

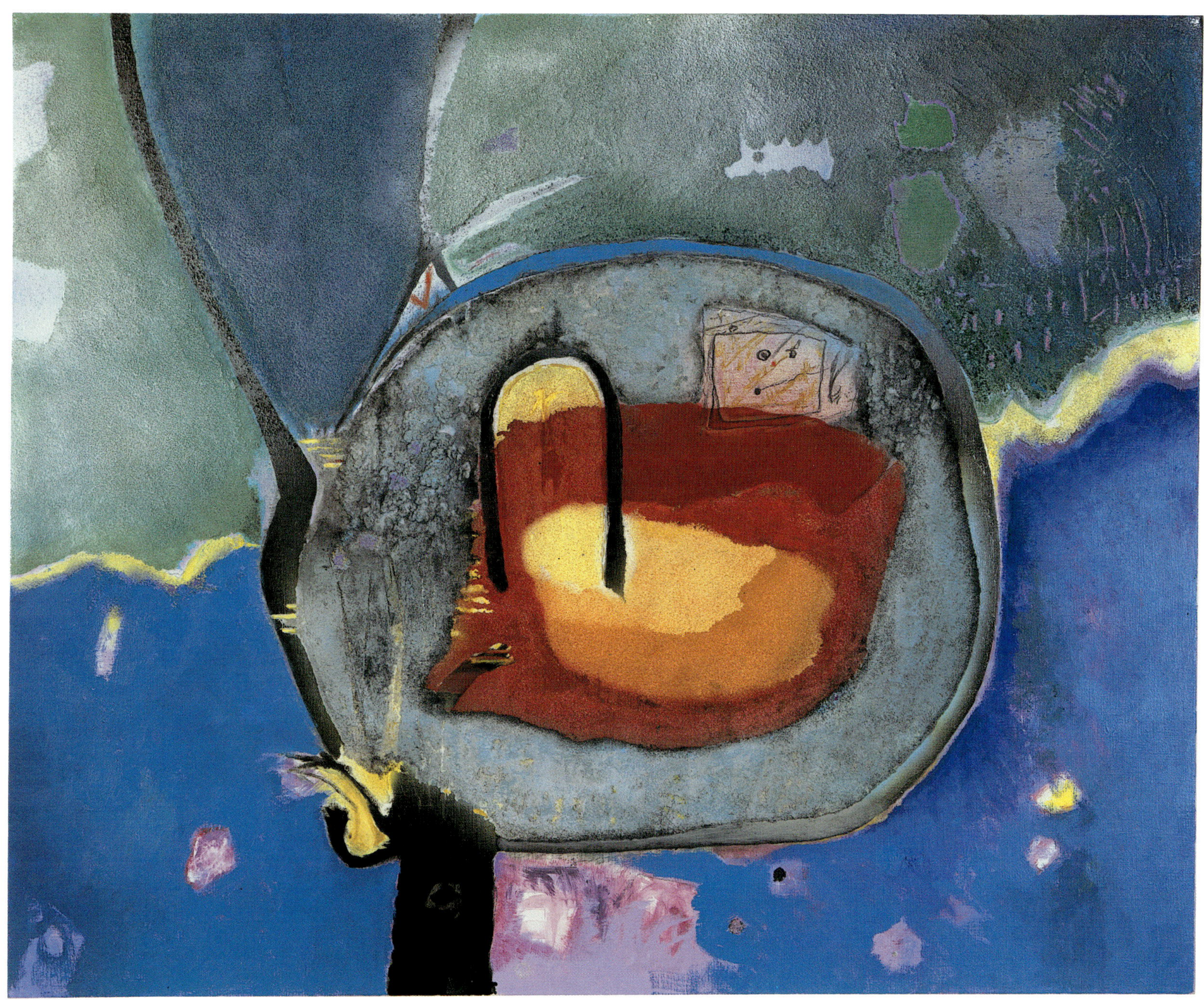

Flying Parrot, 1993
Mixed media on canvas
40 × 50
Collection Ted Townsend, Des Moines

recent canvases—depended to a large extent on a dark, elongated form for its formal resolution. Without it, these "playful" motifs would have remained isolated, and the composition itself would have lacked cohesion.

History Again (1994) utilizes an even more dominant dark form, this time to serve as backdrop for several small, frontally displayed objects as well as a larger, sunlike disk, but also to give the painting structure. It is a successful work, and yet, studying it carefully, one suspects that it represents Donati the Surrealist of the 1940s and early 1950s as much as it does the artist he has become in the 1990s. For one thing, the large dark form obviously originated as a huge puddle of black paint tilted vertically on the canvas and allowed to establish its final shape by dripping. Once the paint was dry, Donati simply added whatever other elements he needed to produce the result he desired. If that was not exactly the way he created some of his earliest Surrealist canvases, with their "accidental" effects and biomorphic forms, it certainly came close. In fact, the entire painting, black "puddle" and all, seems strangely anachronistic, as though it belongs as much to Donati's past as to his present.

That is hardly surprising, considering what was going on in his mind at the time. Already, in his 1991 *Anybody Can Figure It . . . ,* one senses a pronounced restlessness in the way he tackled its explosive imagery. And that impression is further strengthened by his 1992 *Lava à Pompeii,* a highly suggestive, quasi-Surrealist work with violent undertones that could represent (as the title hints), long-submerged creative forces about to erupt.

Be that as it may, it *is* clear that the early 1990s found Donati looking back with greater frequency to what he had painted in previous years. However, it was not to his Surrealist days that his mind returned most often at first but to those immediately following them that produced the large, purely geometric

Facing page
History Again, 1994
Mixed media on canvas
30 × 24
Courtesy Louis Newman Galleries,
Beverly Hills, California

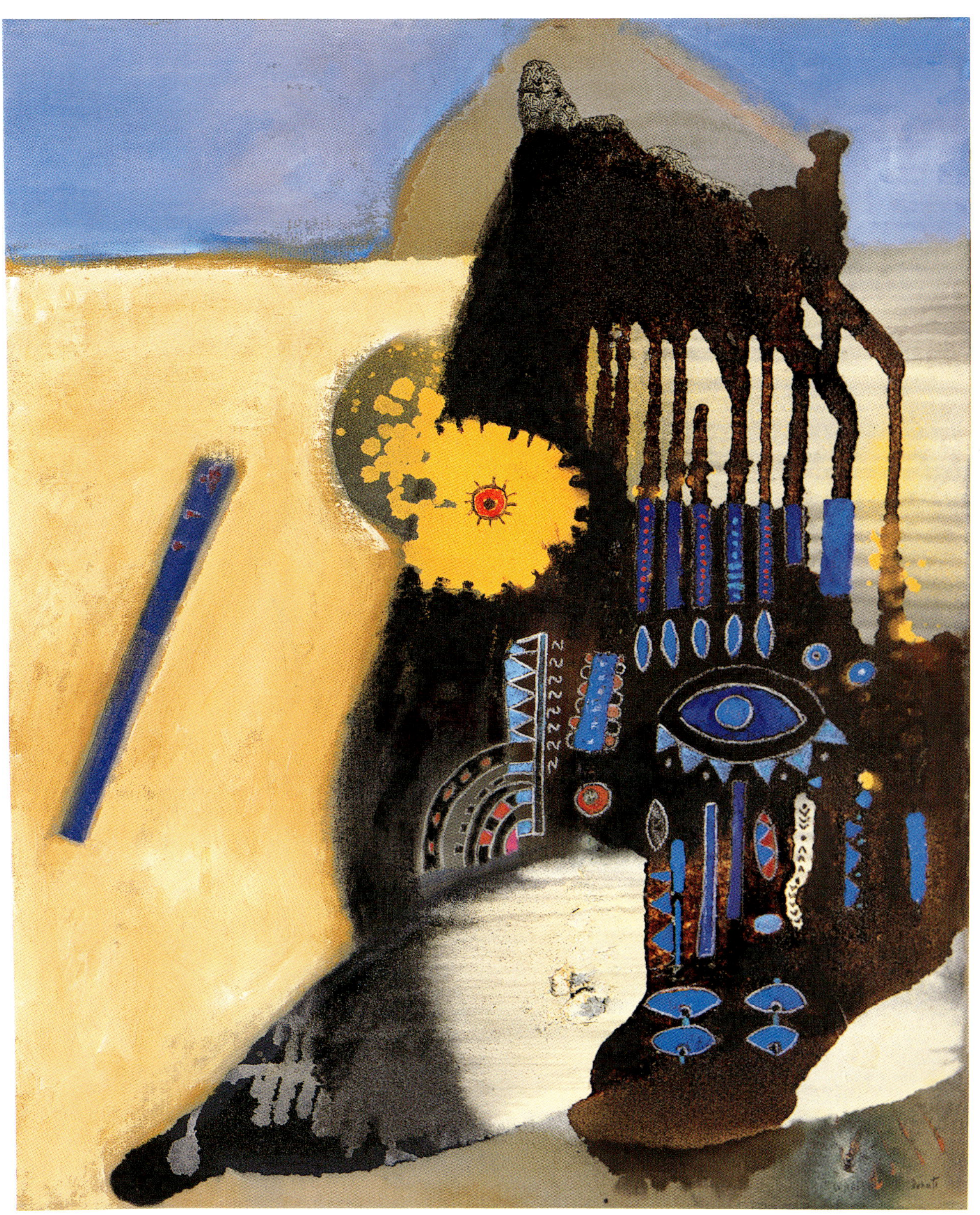

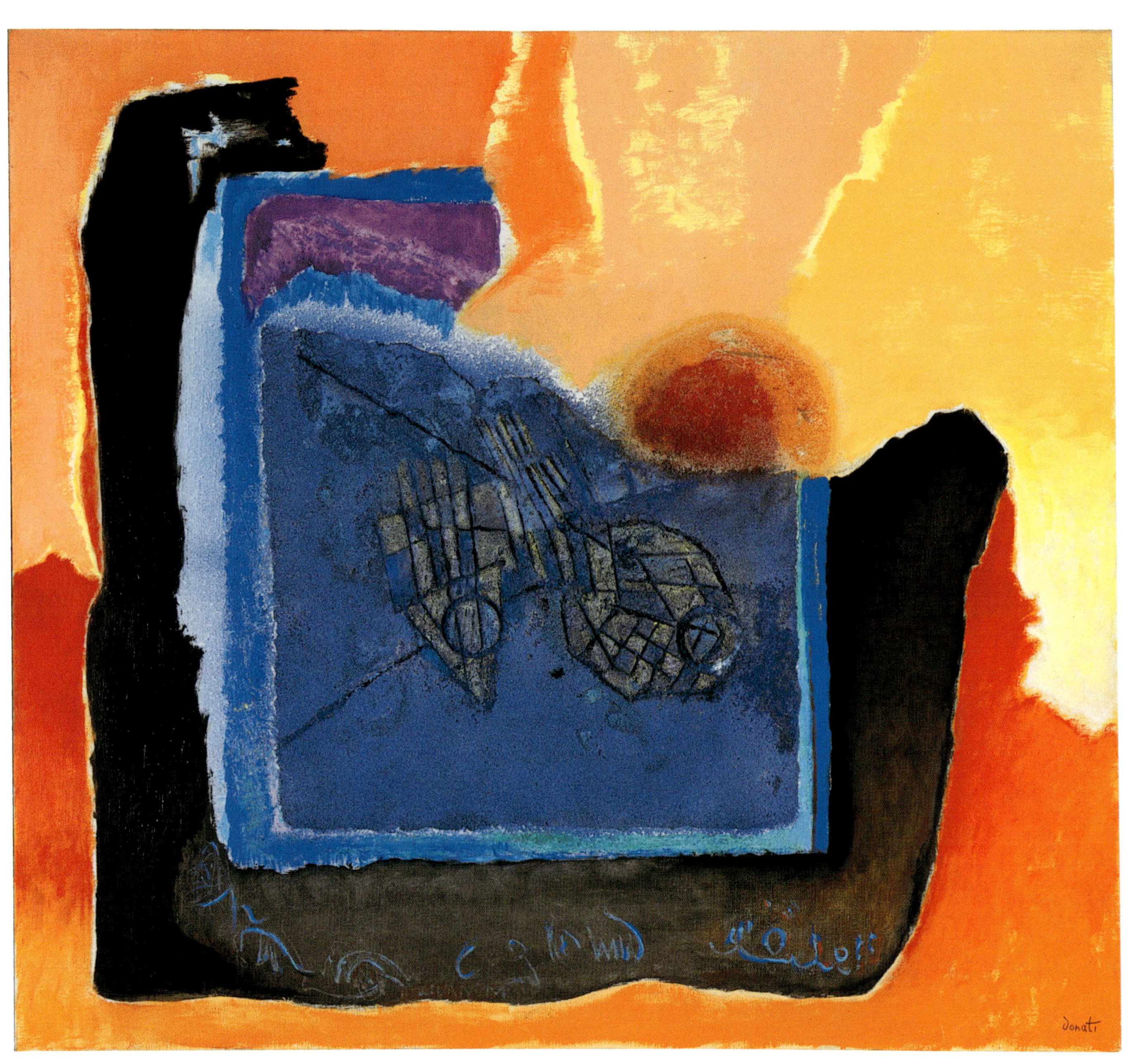

canvases he originally had shown only to close friends and that had not been exhibited until 1987.

For proof one can turn to *Launching Pad,* a totally geometric painting of 1994 that resembles nothing so much as his similarly geometric works of the late 1940s. In fact, Donati says the work was based on a drawing made in 1949 that seemed ideal for updating and translating into color.

Although *Launching Pad* was the only picture to be based so precisely on an earlier image, it pointed the way for others utilizing more selective borrowings from the past. Donati moved cautiously at first, permitting only small geometric configurations to appear in conjunction with his larger, more typical forms. But then, as he felt emboldened, he gradually allowed geometry to assume a greater role.

To see the results of this transformation, one need only compare *Grey Sun* and *Scrovegni Family* with *Carousel* and *Flying Trapeze,* all from 1994. In the first two, geometry still plays a supporting role and serves primarily as a technical device through which touches of wit, charm, and decorative color are introduced into the composition to enliven it. In the latter two paintings, all of that has changed. Miniature triangles, squares, diamonds, and straight lines—enclosed within extended geometric shapes—define the character of these works. Large, amorphous forms still exist, but they have been flattened and deprived of their subtly ominous power.

Donati's renewed interest in geometry did not preclude wit and charm, as had been the case with the hard-edged canvases of the late 1940s. Those paintings were severe and, more often than not, uncompromising in their insistence on structural grandeur and formal purity. The recent ones reflect a more relaxed and pleasantly idiosyncratic point of view, one that feels free to dip into the past for whatever might serve its current needs but that also would not hesitate

Facing page
Lava à Pompeii (Lava at Pompeii), 1992
Mixed media on canvas
36 × 40
Courtesy Horwitch Newman Gallery, Scottsdale, Arizona

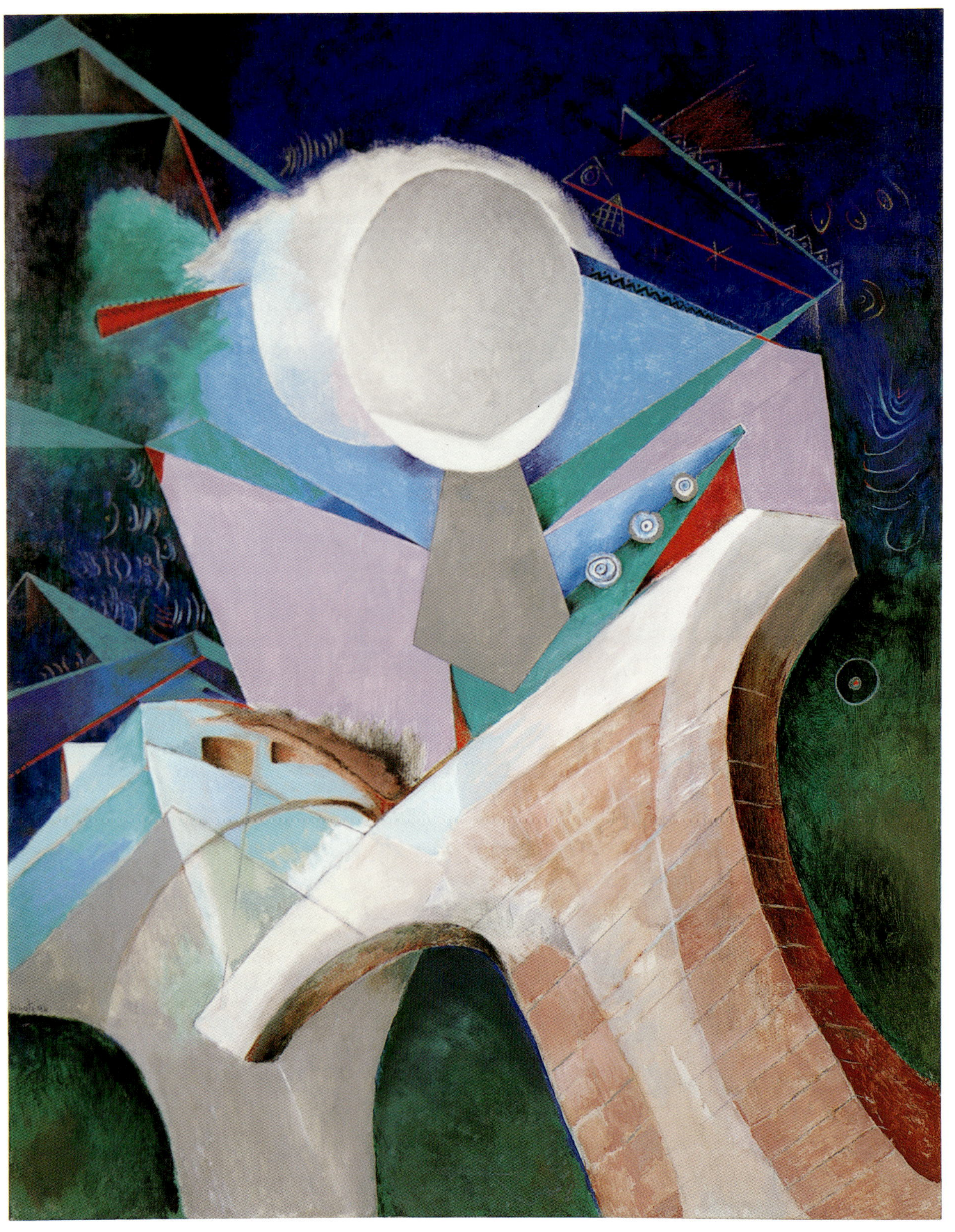

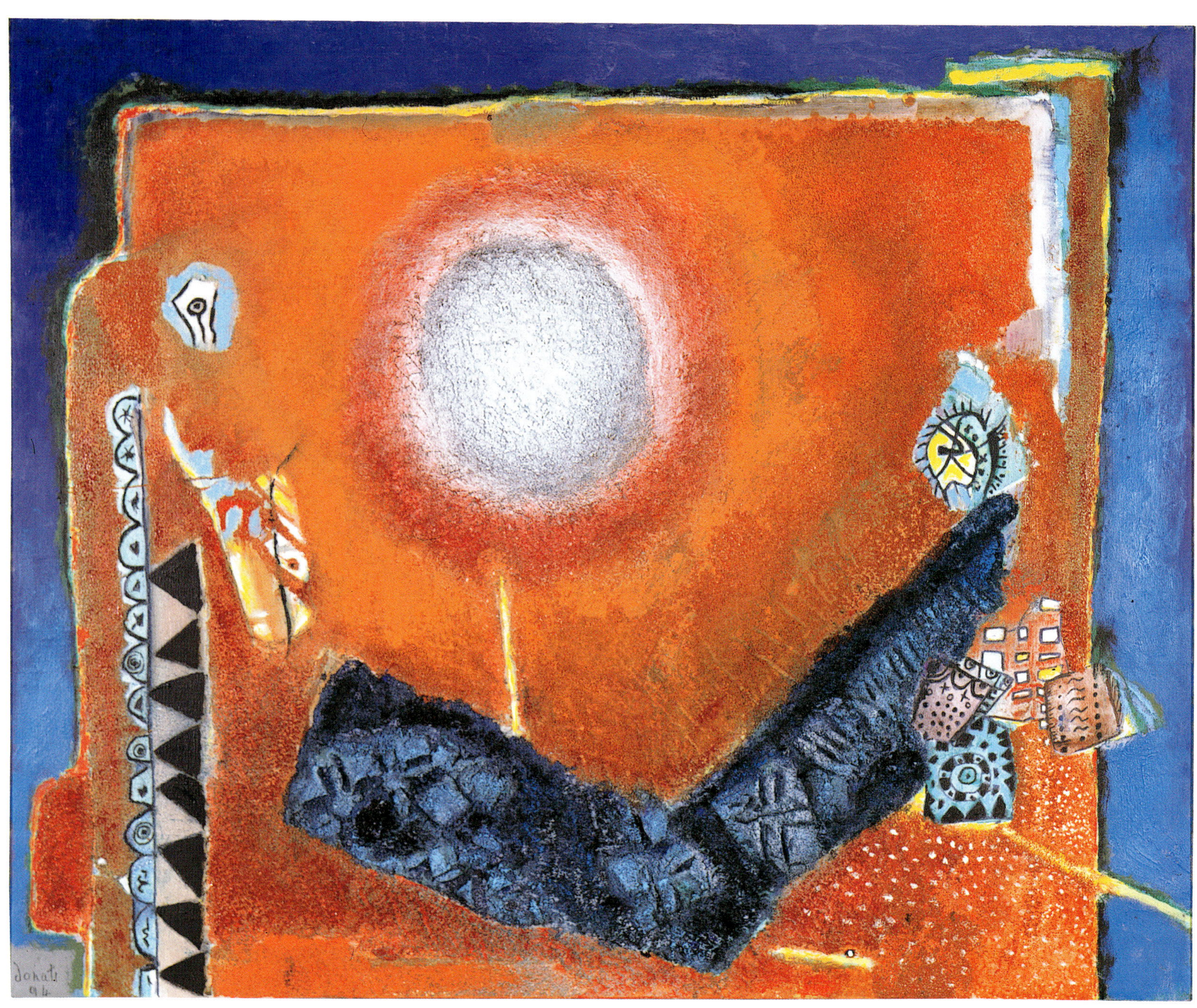

Grey Sun, 1994
Oil on canvas
24 × 30
Collection Philip D. Chapman

Facing page
Launching Pad, 1949–94
Acrylic on canvas
50 × 40
Courtesy Eric Davis

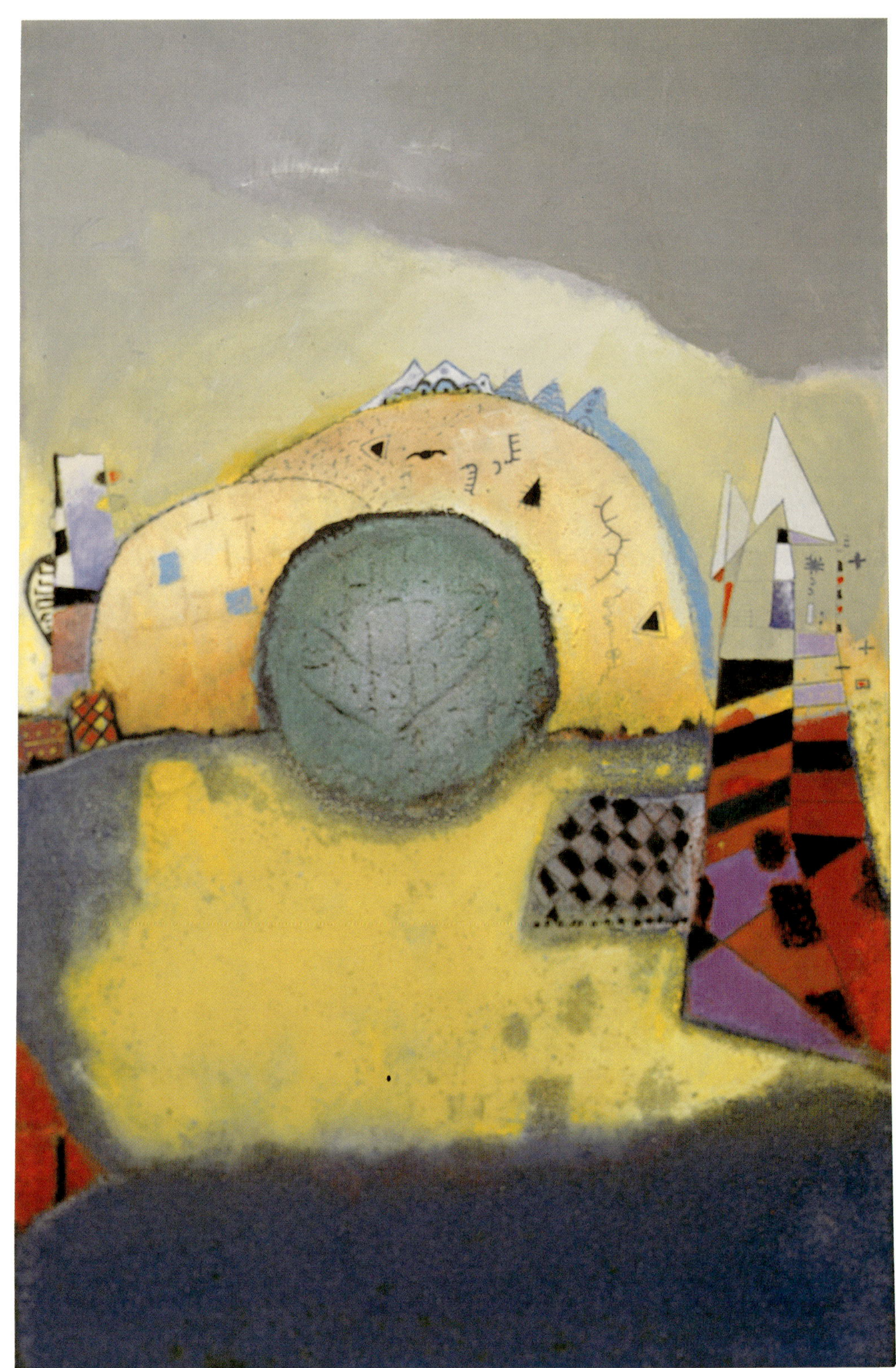

Scrovegni Family, 1994

Mixed media on canvas

36 × 24

Courtesy Horwitch Newman
Gallery, Scottsdale, Arizona

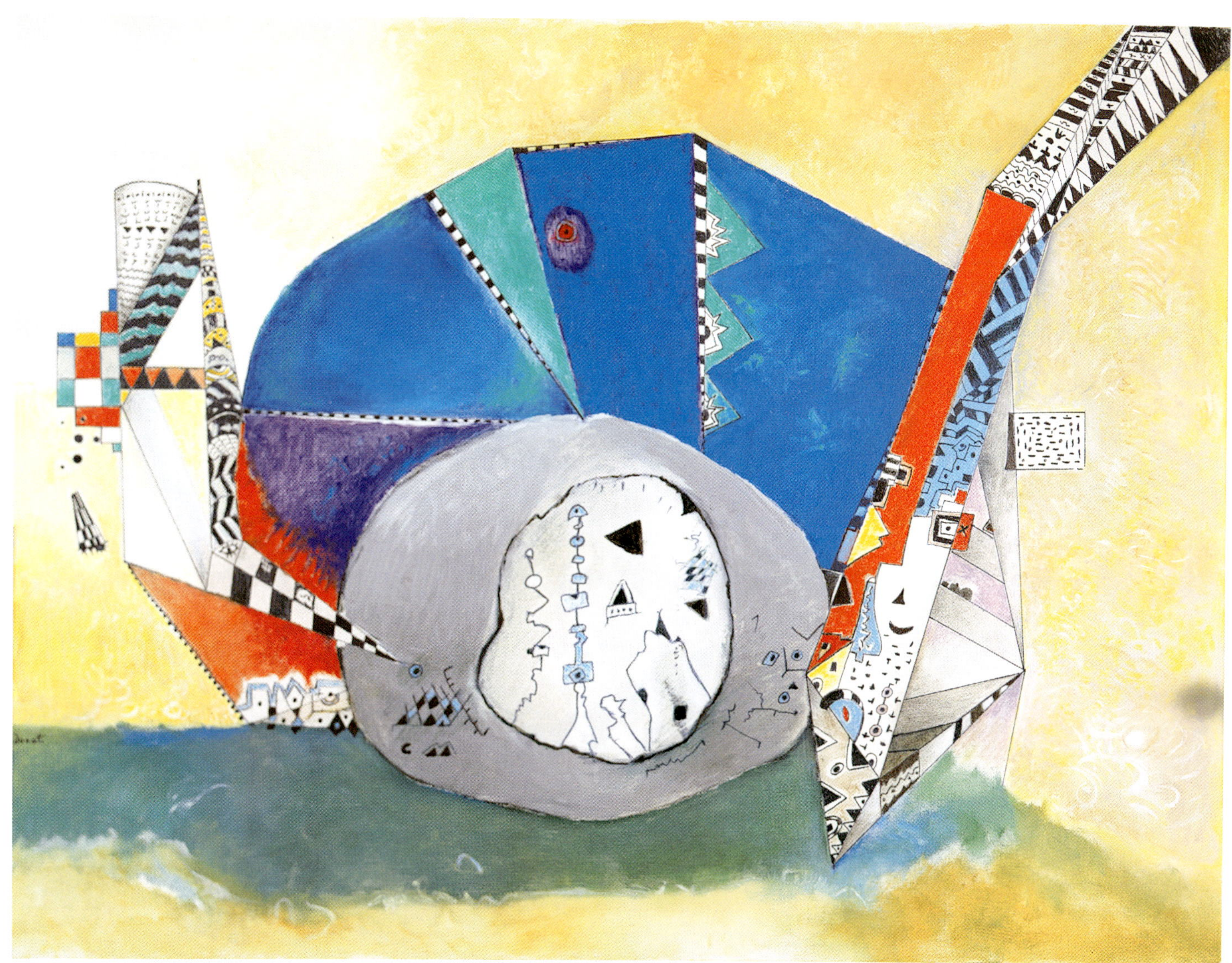

Carousel, 1994

Mixed media on canvas

30 × 40

Courtesy Maxwell Davidson Gallery,
New York

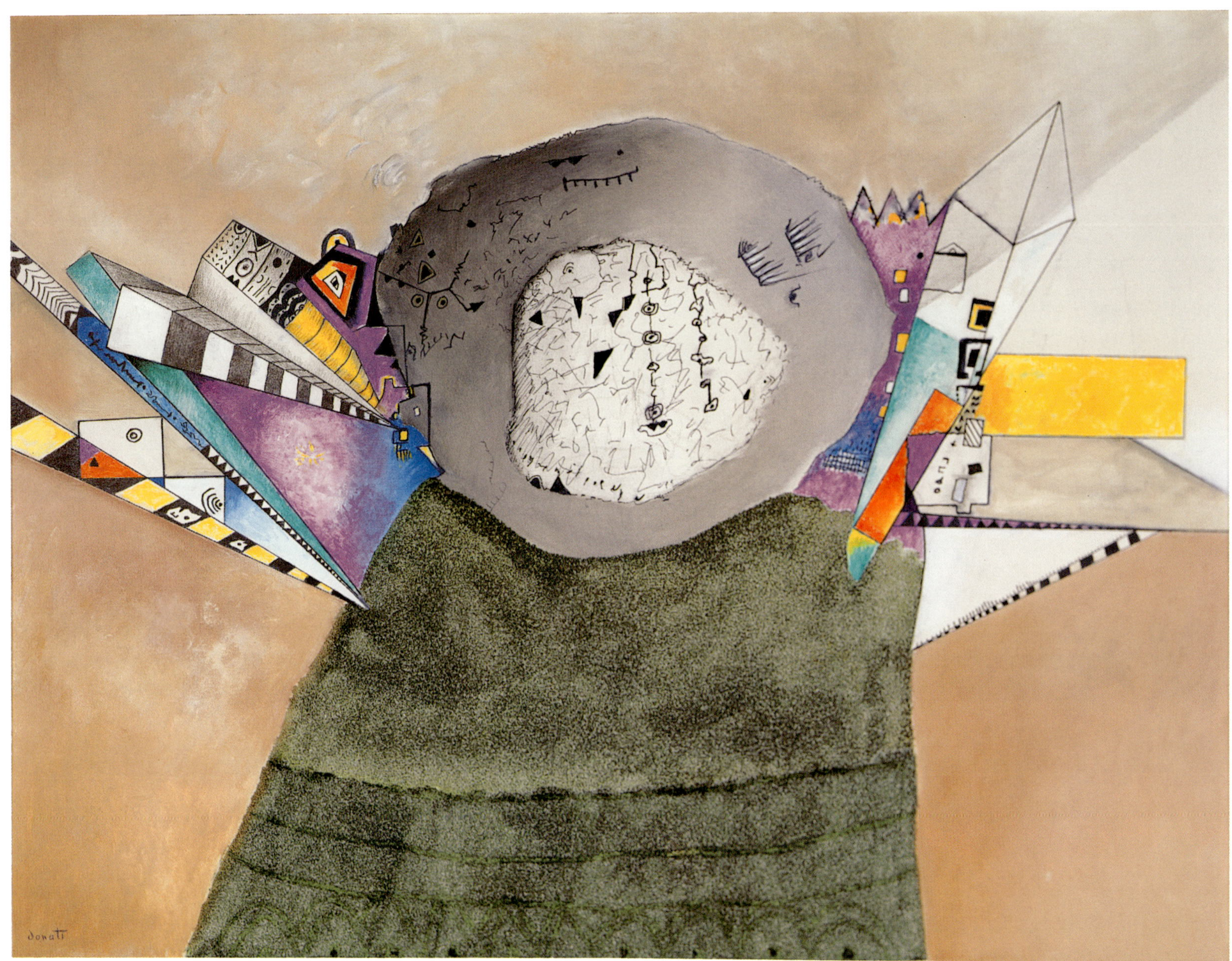

Flying Trapeze, 1994

Mixed media on canvas

30 × 40

Courtesy Maxwell Davidson Gallery,
New York

to turn whatever it found upside down if it served its purposes to do so. Thus, precisely defined geometric shapes that had achieved weighty, monumental importance in the 1940s became lighthearted, occasionally even delightfully frisky components of freely improvised compositions in the 1990s. And other aspects of Donati's earlier work, most particularly his use of transparent color and the results of lessons learned from Cubism, are translated into his recent idiom as well. But then, as he insists, "I wanted to combine the past and the present, and to use the best of both."

He also, one suspects, wanted to have some fun. In *Dinosaur's Eyes* (1994) he obviously succeeded. Only an artist who is a Surrealist at heart would have conceived—or dared to paint—a picture that so blatantly suggests that two large, anonymous-looking, circular whitish forms actually are eyes. And, as if that was not wickedly Surrealist enough, he then identifies them as such (and as dinosaur eyes at that) in the title.

Most of the time, however, his enjoyment of what he could do with paint led him in more purely pleasurable directions. For instance, in *Les tarots* (1995) he produces a colorful recapitulation of several of the thematic and formal devices that have served him so well over the years. At dead center stands the large bulky stone, complete with exposed interior surface and indecipherable inscriptions, that appears in so many of his canvases of the 1980s. Above and behind the stone, and extending away from it, are a number of pyramidal objects that come straight out of the late 1940s. And scattered about, on either side and below, are numerous simplified versions of linear configurations that have from time to time appeared in his work.

Two things set *Les tarots* apart from canvases of previous years from which Donati borrowed various devices: its lighthearted iconoclasm and its happy-go-lucky color. Nothing is sacred in this picture, least of all Donati's own creations.

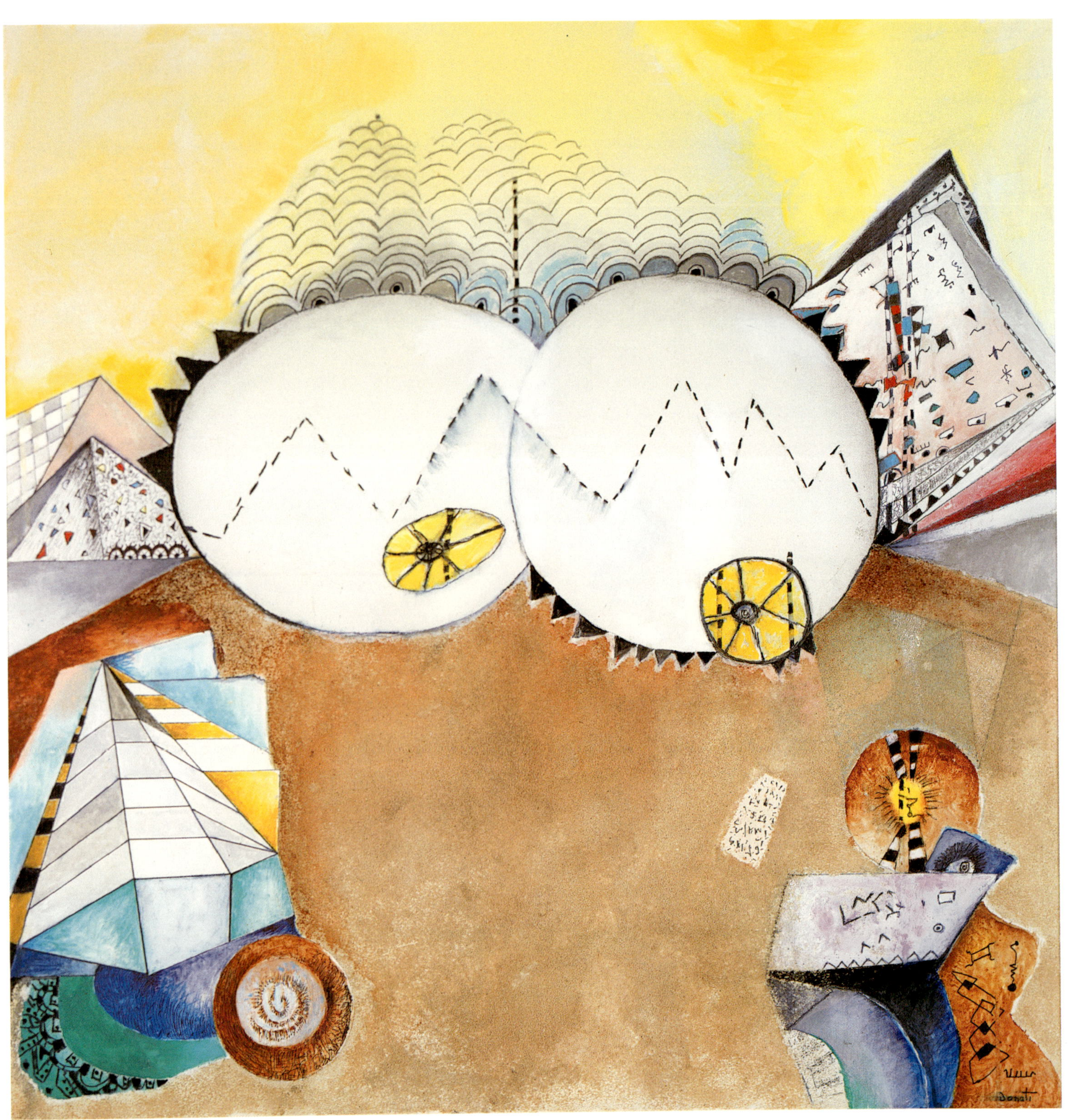

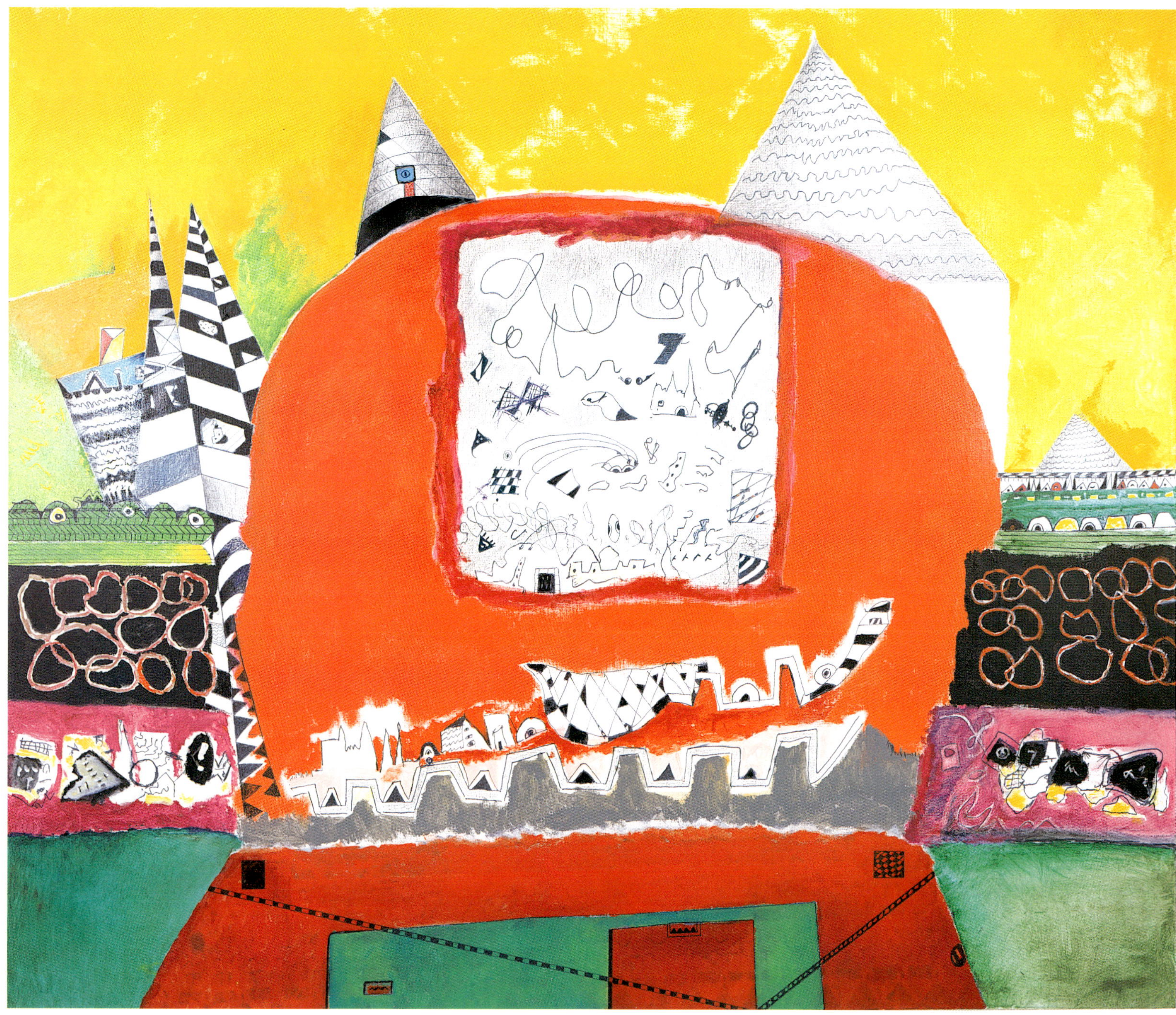

Facing page

Dinosaur's Eyes, 1994

Mixed media on canvas

36 × 36

Courtesy Maxwell Davidson Gallery, New York

Les tarots (Tarot Cards), 1995

Mixed media on canvas

50 × 60

Collection Nicholas C. Forstmann, New York

What was serious, even solemn in his earlier compositions becomes an object of fun and games in this one. Even the number 7, which played so persistent but mysterious a role in his younger days, here finds itself in the company of frisky calligraphic loops, whorls, and doodles on the stone's interior surface. And the triangular shapes that figured so importantly before now assume more playful identities as fairy-tale castles and objects that take on the appearance of upside-down ice-cream cones.

Topping it all is the painting's color—bright, varied, and wonderfully idiosyncratic. The stone is red, the sky is yellow, the adjacent areas are pink, green, and black; everything else is off-white. All in all, *Les tarots* is a delightful and charming work of art.

The year 1994 saw several other engaging variations on the stone-with-inscriptions theme. *Carousel,* in particular, succeeds brilliantly, with its two stones flanked by richly decorated, towerlike structures and its wide assortment of geometric details. And *Red and Purple Mesa,* undoubtedly the most radiantly life-affirming canvas of 1994, scores with its exquisite color, wonderfully inventive linear effects, and miniature organic forms.

Trip to the Future, on the other hand, veers off in another direction. More purely geometric than the other 1994 paintings, it also creates a slightly more serious impression. Most notable is its combination of both Surrealist and science-fiction devices to produce a spectral space-age image that slyly ridicules mankind's cosmic pretensions.

But it is to *Les souvenirs du passé,* also from 1994, that one must turn for the most successful realization of Donati's objective to combine the past and the present. Not only is it an attractive and provocative image in its own right, but it also exists as a remarkable synthesis of much of what is best and most fascinating about Donati's work of the distant and more recent past. Once

Facing page

Red and Purple Mesa, 1994

Mixed media on canvas

36 × 36

Courtesy Maxwell Davidson Gallery,
New York

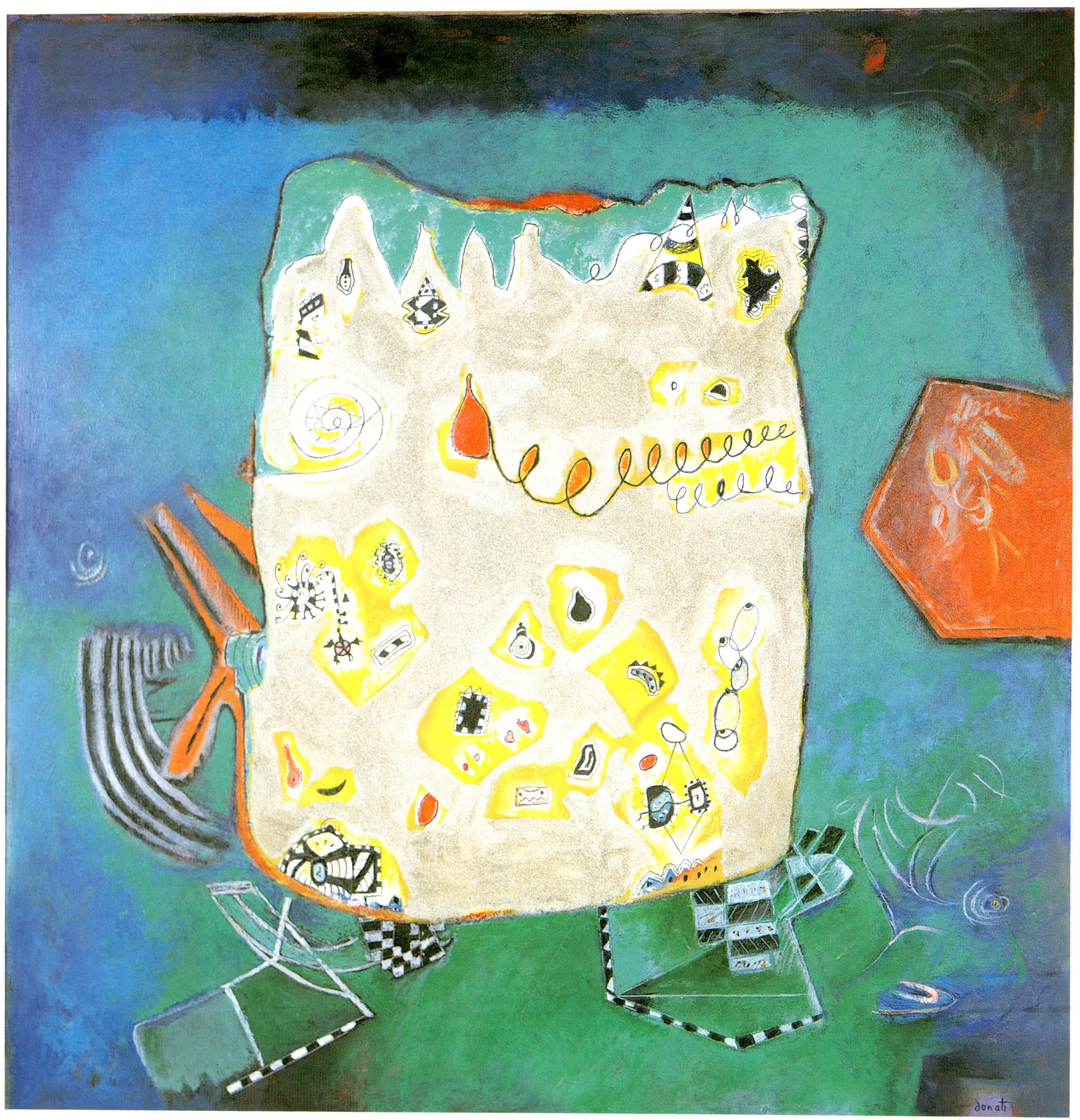

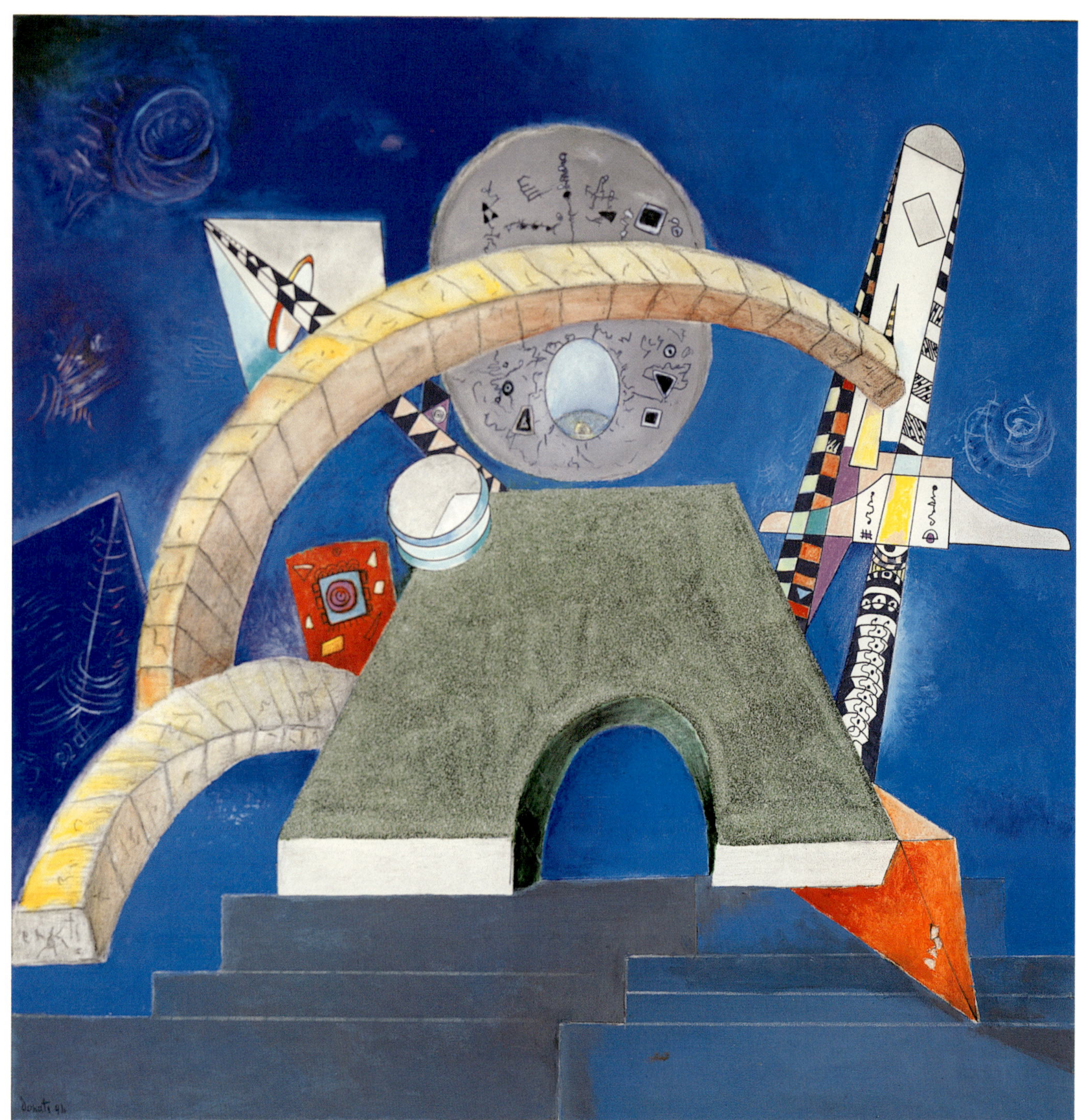

Trip to the Future, 1994

Mixed media on canvas

40 × 40

Courtesy Maxwell Davidson Gallery,
New York

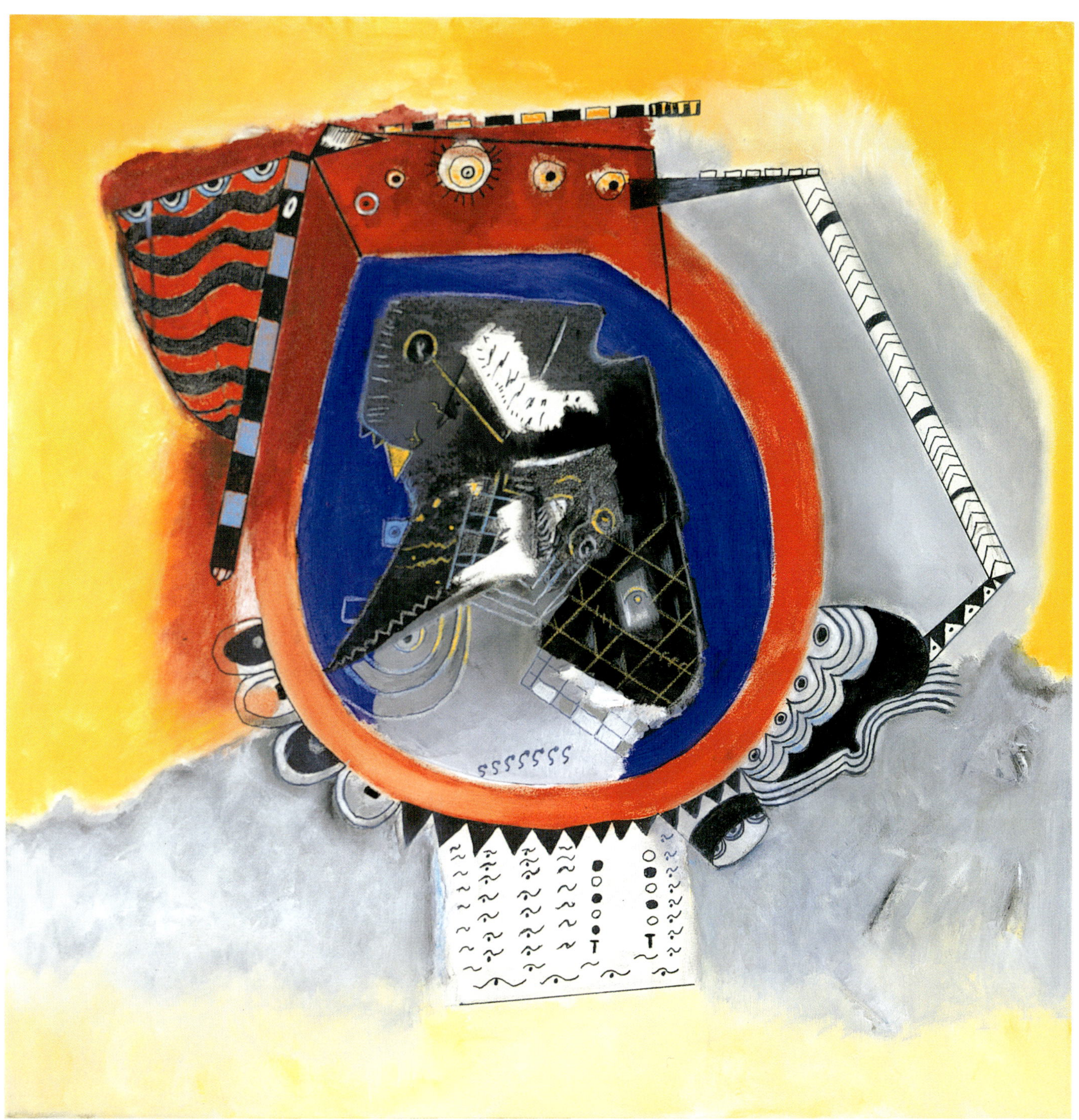

Les souvenirs du passé (Memories
of the Past), 1994
Mixed media on canvas
36 × 36
Courtesy Maxwell Davidson Gallery, New York

again, we are confronted by a large, dead-center stone. Here, though, it looms more as an abstract shape whose interior surface is dominated by a greyish black form with several of the attributes—but little of the character—of the grotesque biomorphic creatures inhabiting Donati's Surrealist canvases. Framing this updated and beguilingly humanized testament to the eternal power of the mythological mandragora root are two circular forms, one a deep blue, the other a bright red. Attached to these are various carefully selected formal elements drawn from other periods of Donati's creative life. Nothing could be simpler, more effective, or, indeed, more attractive. And yet this effect was achieved with a minimum of fuss and a lightness of touch that would be surprising were it not for the fact that Donati, especially at this stage of his career, was an artist who knew precisely the effect he wanted to get and the best way to get it.

Donati's skill and authority, as well as his willingness to take risks in his art, become even more apparent as one examines the canvases he produced in 1995. The majority of them utilize geometry almost as much, and certainly as effectively, as the ones he painted more than forty years before, partly as an act of technical discipline but mainly to gain greater control over the creative act. But 1995 was not 1947, and discipline and control were not high on his creative agenda. Facing new challenges and forging ahead into uncharted territory, however, were. So, after examining his various options, he decided to push ahead and explore a new avenue of expression, one that would focus primarily on geometric forms but in a more Surrealist fashion.

Plus beau encore was among the first of the 1995 works to enter uncharted territory. In this painting, space is more ambiguous and forms are less restrained by compositional logic than ever before in Donati's art. In none of his previous paintings, not even in the most uninhibited Surrealist or complex geometric canvases of his youth, had he exempted a picture's elements from the spatial

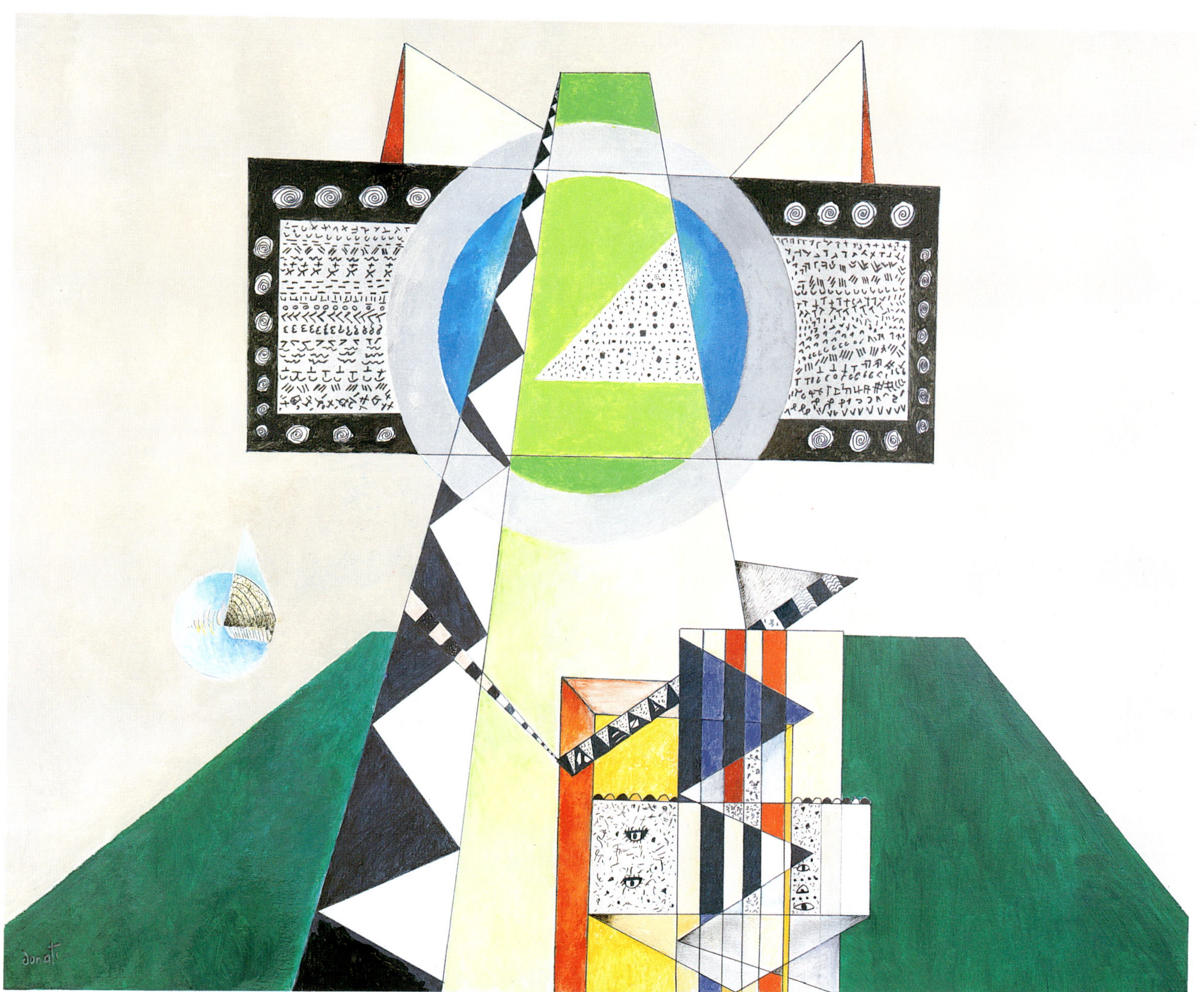

Temple déco (Deco Temple),
1994–95
Mixed media on canvas
40 × 50
Collection Mr. and Mrs. Stephen C.
Owen, Jr.

laws of linear or aerial perspective, nor permitted those elements to defy structural logic or common sense in their relationships with one another.

Thus in his 1944 *Trouble-fête,* one of the most wildly fanciful of his Surrealist creations, every object, no matter how extravagantly executed, is precisely situated in a space that is both "real" atmospherically and "correct" according to the rules of perspective. And in his 1947 *Tower of the Alchemist: Creation of the Sun,* one of the most complicated of his geometric constructions, a kind of architectural logic determines how each element relates to and affects every other element in the composition.

In *Plus beau encore,* however, and in almost every other painting of 1995, significant changes occur. In these works, Donati's traditional manner of defining and ordering space in his canvases is supplanted by a spatial and structural ambiguity that blurs the distinction between deep, illusionistic space and the flat, logically layered space he derived from Cubism.

Technically, this blurring results in an ever-shifting amalgam of devices Donati has used over the years to define pictorial space. Creatively, it sets the stage for, and helps make possible, a merger of considerable importance in the evolution of Donati's art—that of Surrealism and geometry.

To understand this need for a new method of defining space, one must go back to the end of 1994. Having successfully combined the past and present, and used the best of both in a number of charmingly idiosyncratic works, Donati was ready for an even more challenging undertaking: bringing together in one seamless whole as much as he could of both Surrealist and constructivist ideas and forms. His primary focus, as already noted, would be on the geometric, but it would be a world of circles, squares, and triangles that resonated with Surrealist mystery and magic.

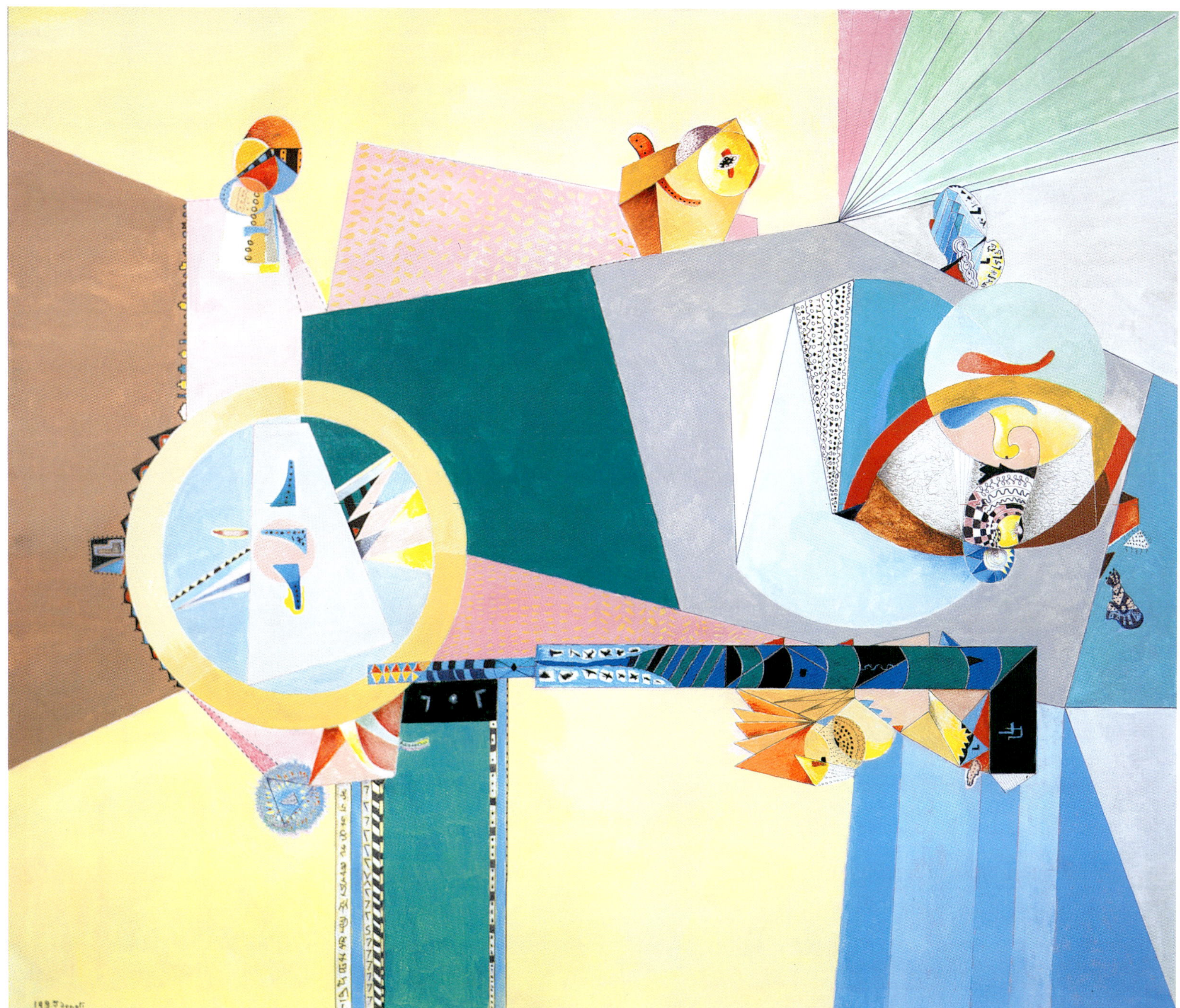

Plus beau encore

(More Beautiful Still), 1995

Mixed media on canvas

50 × 60

Courtesy Maxwell Davidson
Gallery, New York

138

E N R I C O

D O N A T I

To create such a world, however, he needed a more ambiguous spatial context, one that would itself reflect the kind of fusion he hoped to achieve between these two older modes of expression.

In *Plus beau encore* he not only succeeded in that objective, but he did so with wit and humor, managing, in the process, to cause objects to exist interchangeably in illusionistic and Cubistic space, and creating a wonderfully ambiguous transformation of reality very much in line with Surrealist intentions. (One wonders, for example, which of its sides really is up, whether it is an indoor or an outdoor scene, and just what the number 7, seen in the black rectangle left of center, signifies in this, its latest manifestation.)

In *Scarabeo* (1995) the indoors-outdoors conundrum is carried one step further—but with an even greater sense of paradox. And in *Symbiosis,* Donati combines a miniature version of his stone-with-inscriptions form with numerous loosely defined geometric elements to fashion a fanciful image reminiscent of some of his earliest and wildest Surrealist creations.

It is in *Le château des cartes* (1995), however, that Donati succeeded most dramatically, not only in establishing the spatial context he needed but also in bringing together, in one unified whole, vital aspects of both his Surrealist and constructivist periods. Placed between his Surrealist *Carnaval de Venise* (1946) and geometric *Chambre a décompression* (1948), *Le château des cartes* seems perfectly at home. True, this work obviously is closer in form to the latter painting, but careful examination should also make it clear that it is closer in spirit to the former.

For one thing, *Le château des cartes* is warmer and softer than its older hard-edged companion, and it is rather wicked and witty as well. Mostly it is a matter of ambiguities and transformations, of shifting perceptions of the nature and function of the forms involved: Is the large angular shape at bottom-center actu-

Facing page
Scarabeo, 1995
Mixed media on canvas
36 x 36
Collection Neil Fang

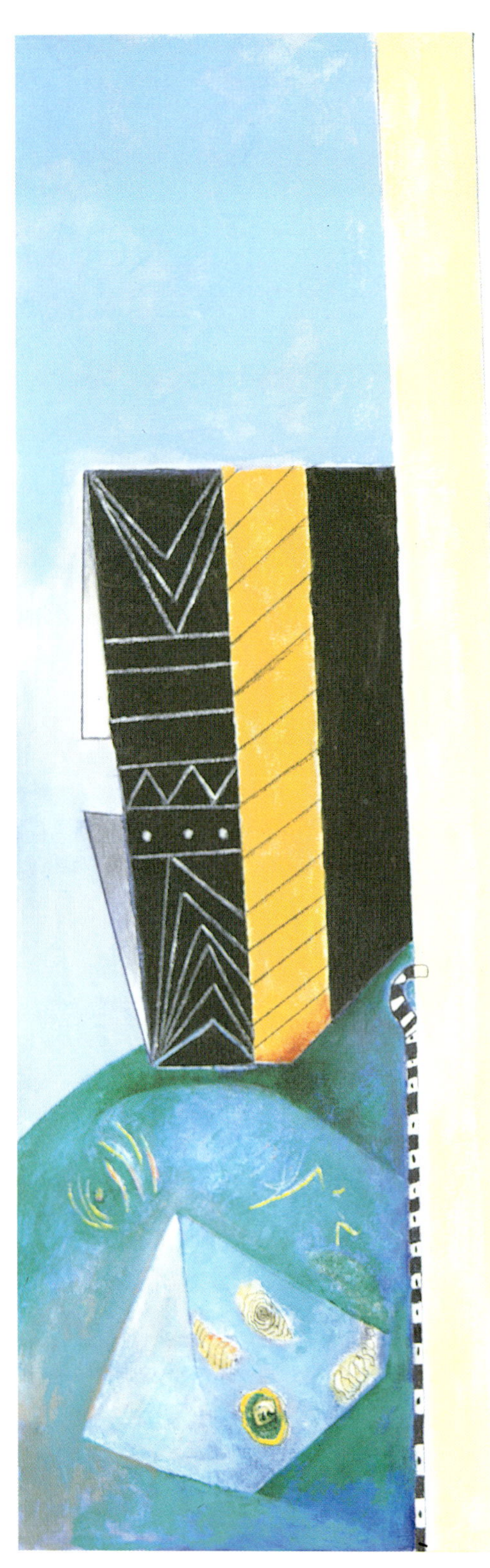
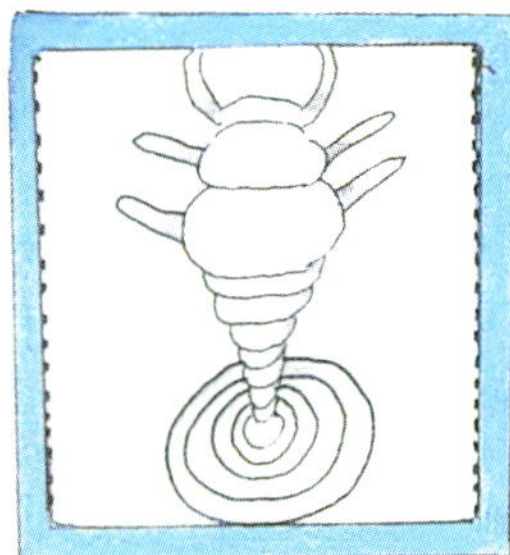
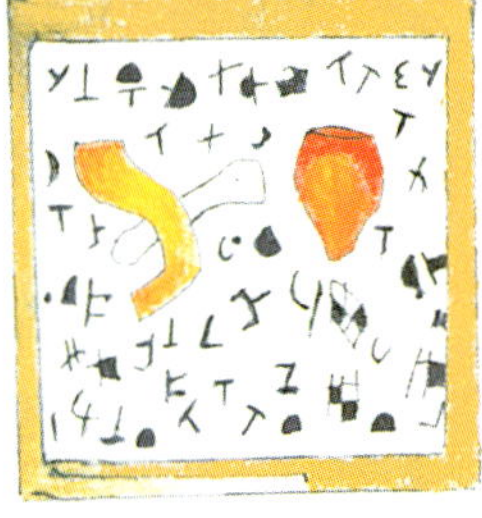
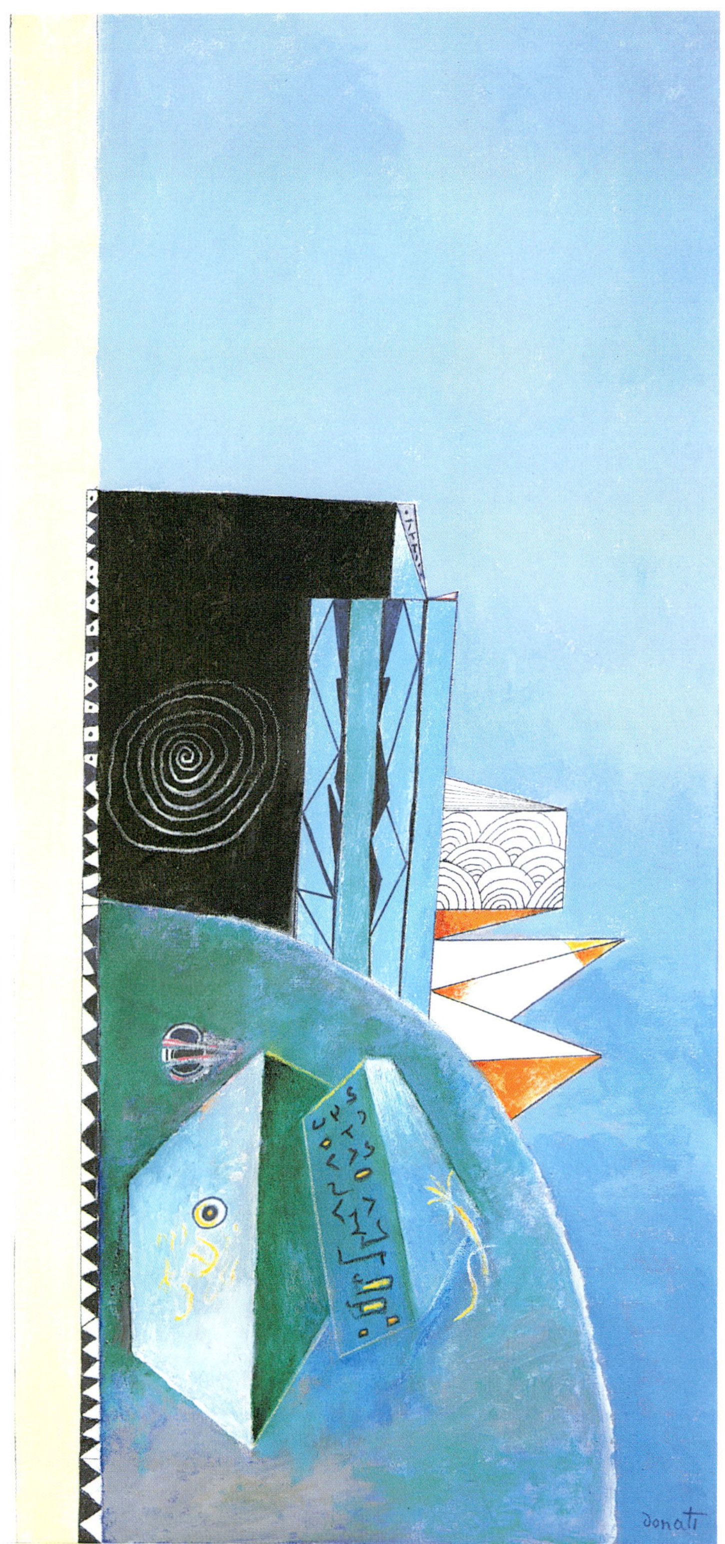
donati

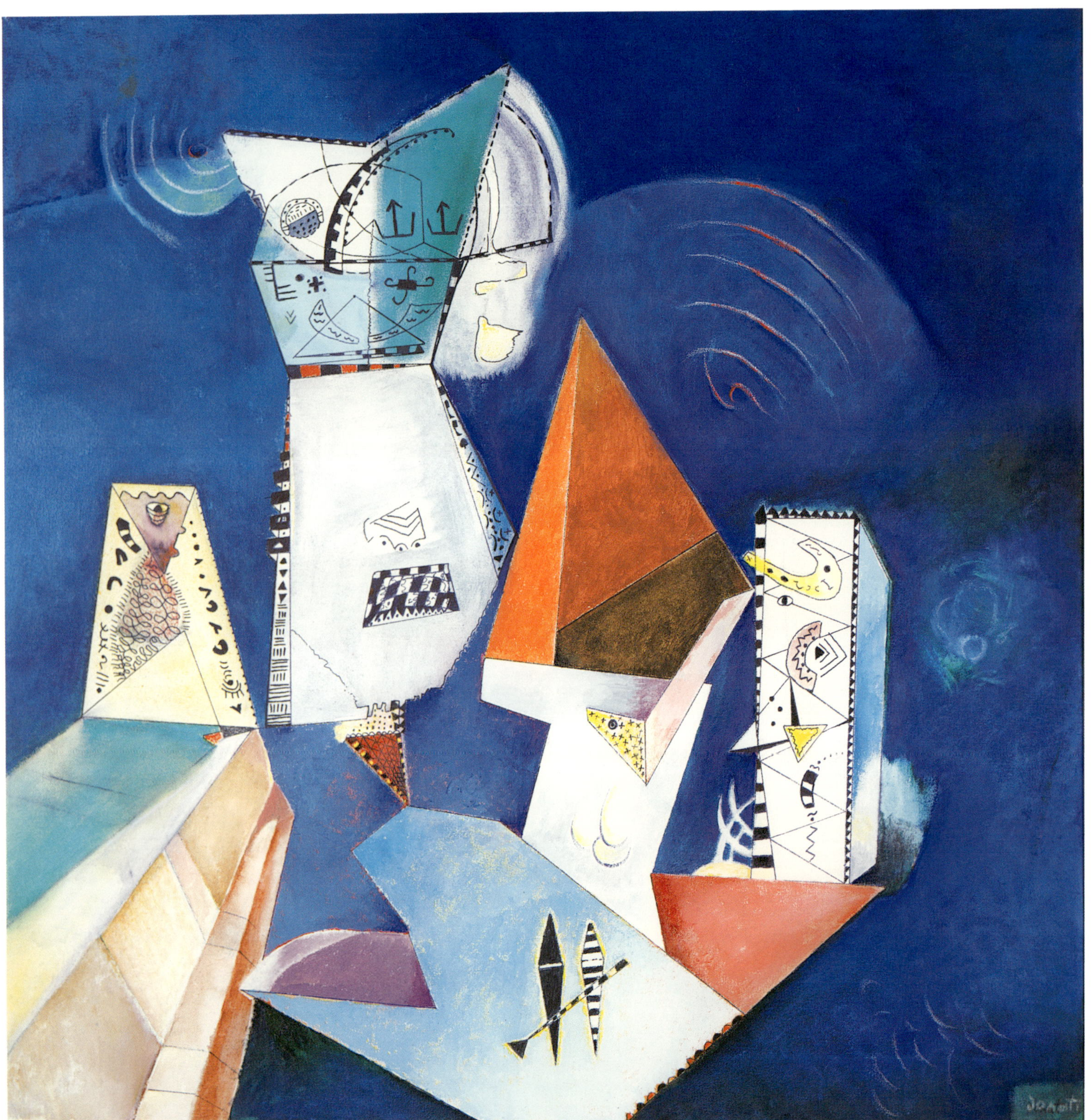

ally that of a light blue, open-mouthed fish? Should one see the narrow vertical object on the right as a funny head with a triangular nose or merely as a tall, decorated box—or possibly as a small cockeyed building? And is that dominant figure with downcast eyes facing left really a knight with a plume, or only a random combination of interesting shapes and scribblings?

When asked, Donati, not surprisingly, shrugs his shoulders and smiles. Good Surrealist that he is, he wants his art, above all, to retain its mystery and magic until the very end.

On the other hand, when asked if his art has come full circle in these recent works, he acknowledges that it has. He hastens to add, however, that he already is working on a number of new ideas. As yet, none has been given life on canvas, but that, he insists, is only a matter of time.

No one who knows Donati or his work can doubt the truth of that assertion. Throughout his career, it has been merely a matter of time before the need to attempt even better and more effective forms of painterly magic has reasserted itself. That was true at the height of his Surrealist period when he realized the necessity for greater technical discipline and control in his work, and it has been the case at every other critical point along the way. And whenever that need manifested itself, he invariably pulled up stakes and moved on. Not to have done so would have been inconceivable to an artist of his drive and imagination.

That imagination has served him well. It led him from the primal, darkly provocative Surrealist images of his early days to the witty and colorful iconoclastic paintings of the 1990s. And it did so by inducing him to concentrate his major efforts on producing works characterized by ever greater degrees of paradox and enchantment.

Translating these two attributes into art has always been his primary creative concern. Other artists have committed themselves to various aesthetic agen-

Facing page
Le château des cartes (The Castle of Cards), 1995
Mixed media on canvas
36 × 36
Private collection, courtesy Maxwell Davidson Gallery, New York

das, or have dedicated their art to social or spiritual ideals. But not Donati. For him, art has always been more a matter of paradox and enigma than of programs, dogmas, or beliefs. As a result, his paintings do not so much satisfy and explain as they stimulate and provoke.

But then, Donati's creative roots go deep into Surrealist soil. As he often says, "Once a Surrealist, always a Surrealist." André Breton was particularly impressed by the density and ambiguity of Donati's imagery, and by its wide range of possible meanings. The young artist's ability to provoke the viewer's imagination in several directions at once fascinated the elder Surrealist, and from all indications it was a crucial factor in Donati's acceptance into the movement.

Although his talent for suggesting a multiplicity of meanings has never deserted him, it did, as the illustrations in this book make clear, manifest itself differently in both manner and degree as his career progressed. This talent did not, however, modify the nature or significance of Surrealism's impact on his art. The dark, pulsating, subtly ominous mood that underlay so many of the paintings produced by that movement, and that played so vital a role in Donati's early work, still reverberates in many of his canvases today—although in a greater variety of forms and with considerably more color.

A significant side effect of Donati's open-ended approach has been his success at fusing a broad range of both European and American characteristics in his art. This internationalism is evident in the ease with which he combines European subtlety and elegance with an American predilection for large-scale images and open spaces. His profound involvement with the enigmas and mysteries of time and tradition, and his identity and posture as a painter-magician, also echo largely European interests and concerns—just as his preference for boldness and bluntness at various stages of his career echoes American ones.

Considering the complex and often enigmatic nature of his work, it is not surprising that Donati refused to sever his European connections. After all, the cultural soil within which his art first came to maturity is thousands of years old, and it still bears traces of the ancient myths and gods that nurtured it. And Surrealism itself, for all its acceptance by Americans, stems from an awareness of time and history that only a much older civilization or culture could fully comprehend.

On the other hand, Donati's optimism and expansiveness—he has never, for instance, permitted weariness or despair to enter his art—indicate how Americanized the artist in him has become. His creative origins may lie in the Mediterranean region of the world and in the deep, agonizing spaces of Surrealism. Yet the flower of his art, especially its most recent blossoming, has found its color and vitality in the United States.

But whatever its source, Donati's art is a rare and valuable creation whose various manifestations have enriched American art. From its Surrealist days to the present it has followed its own path, garnering honors along the way, but most important, providing meaningful aesthetic experiences for large numbers of art-loving individuals. That is not surprising, however, for his is an art that celebrates, mystifies, delights, enchants, and provokes all at the same time. Most of all, it is an art that moves its viewers to share Donati's wonder and awe at mysteries and realities as old as time and as challenging as any asked by the Sphinx.

To return for a moment to what Donati wrote many years ago about the significance of the fossil he discovered in 1949 on the beach at Dover: "There is a Latin word 'incubus' which I roughly describe in terms of a hammer which keeps tapping at your head. . . . You become aware of the knock but not of its significance. In order to find the source you must connect and relate various clues and fleeting insights."[13]

One must, in other words, seek that significance through whatever means are most truly at one's disposal. For Donati, of course, that would be through paint, color, shapes, textures, and lines—and through whatever imagery promises to yield the most clues and fleeting insights.

N O T E S

1 André Breton, Preface, *Paintings by Enrico Donati,* exh. cat. (New York: Passedoit Gallery, 1944), unpaginated.

2 All remarks by the artist not otherwise attributed are from conversations with the author.

3 Donati as quoted by Alan Jones, "Interview with Donati," *Arts* 65, no. 8 (April 1991): 17.

4 Ibid.

5 Maurice Nadeau in *Donati,* exh. cat. (New York: Durand-Ruel Galleries, 1949), 39, 54–55.

6 Nicolas Calas in ibid., 38.

7 Breton, Preface, *Enrico Donati.*

8 Jones, "Interview," 18.

9 Martica Sawin, "Spiritual and Electric Surrealism: The Art of Enrico Donati," *Arts* 61, no. 8 (May 1987): 28.

10 Ibid.

11 Peter Selz, *Enrico Donati* (Paris: Editions Georges Fall, 1965), 18.

12 Enrico Donati, unpublished manuscript in possession of the artist, unpaginated.

13 Ibid.

Selected Solo Exhibitions

1942 Passedoit Gallery, New York

1943 New School for Social Research, New York

1944 The Arts Club of Chicago

G Place Gallery, Washington, D.C.

Passedoit Gallery, New York

1945 Durand-Ruel Galleries, New York

1946 Durand-Ruel Galleries, New York

1947 Durand-Ruel Galleries, New York

Galerie Drouant-David, Paris

Gallery Studio, Chicago

Krouse College, Syracuse University, New York

1949 Durand-Ruel Galleries, New York

A. Weil, Paris

1950 Galleria Corso Vittorio Emanuele II, Milan

Galleria del Milione, Milan

Paul Rosenberg Gallery, New York

Galleria dell'Obelisco, Rome

1952 Alexandre Iolas Gallery, New York

Galleria d'arte del Cavallino, Venice

Galleria del Naviglio, Milan

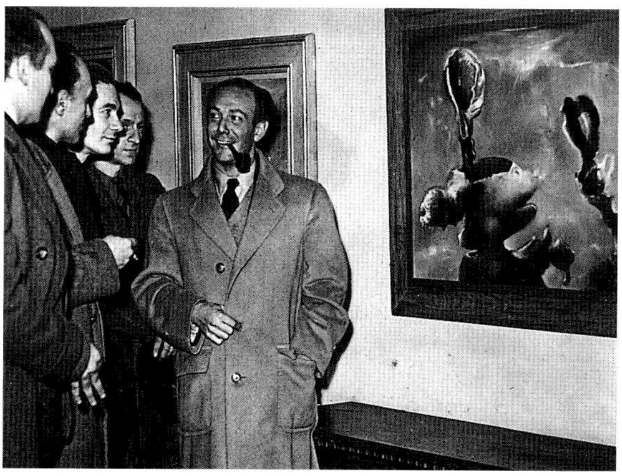

Left to right: Jacques Herold, Victor Brauner, Henri Goetz, Charles Etienne, and Donati at the opening of Donati's 1947 exhibition at Galerie Drouant-David, Paris.

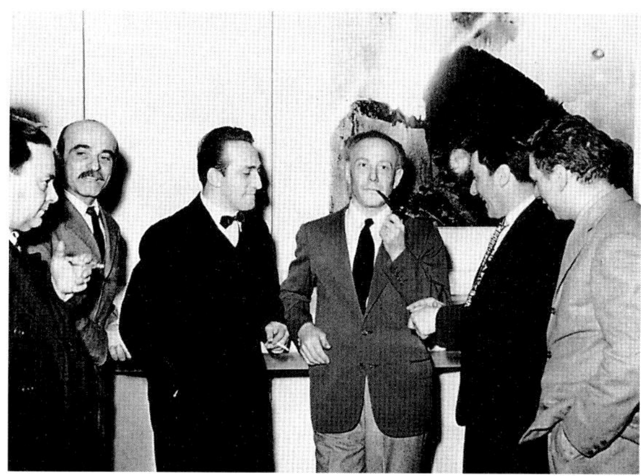

Left to right: B. Joppolo, Lucio Fontana, Robert Crippa, Donati, Matta, and Peverelli at the opening of Donati's 1950 exhibition at Galleria Corso Vittorio Emanuele II, Milan.

1953	Galleria d'arte del Cavallino, Venice
1954	Betty Parsons Gallery, New York
1955	Betty Parsons Gallery, New York
1956	Galleria del Naviglio, Milan
1957	Betty Parsons Gallery, New York
1958	Lowe Art Gallery, Syracuse University, New York
1959	Betty Parsons Gallery, New York
1960	Betty Parsons Gallery, New York
1961	Palais des Beaux-Arts, Brussels
1962	Neue Galerie im Kunstlerhaus, Munich
	Staempfli Gallery, New York
1963	Staempfli Gallery, New York
1964	J. L. Hudson Gallery, Detroit
	Hayden Gallery, Massachusetts Institute of Technology, Cambridge
1965	Obelisk Gallery, Washington, D.C.
1966	Staempfli Gallery, New York
	J. L. Hudson Gallery, Detroit
1968	Staempfli Gallery, New York
1970	Staempfli Gallery, New York
1972	Staempfli Gallery, New York
1974	Staempfli Gallery, New York
1976	Staempfli Gallery, New York
1977	Ankrum Gallery, Los Angeles
	Minnesota Museum of Art, St. Paul
	The Chrysler Museum, Norfolk, Virginia
	Fairweather Hardin Gallery, Chicago
	Tennessee Fine Arts Center, Nashville
1978	Davenport Municipal Art Gallery, Iowa
	Hunter Museum of Art, Chattanooga, Tennessee
	Wildenstein Art Center, Houston
1979	Ankrum Gallery, Los Angeles
	Norton Gallery of Art, West Palm Beach, Florida
	Osuna Gallery, Washington, D.C.
	The Phillips Collection, Washington, D.C.
1980	Palm Springs Desert Museum, California
	International Art Fair, Grand Palais FIAC (Foire internationale d'art contemporain), Paris
1982	Ankrum Gallery, Los Angeles
1984	Carone Gallery, Fort Lauderdale, Florida
	Gimpel & Weitzenhoffer Gallery, New York
1985	Georges Fall, Paris
1986	Gimpel & Weitzenhoffer Gallery, New York
	Louis Newman Gallery, Beverly Hills, California
1987	Gimpel & Weitzenhoffer Gallery, New York
	Zabriskie Gallery, New York
1989	Galerie Zabriskie, Paris
	Louis Newman Gallery, Beverly Hills, California
1990	Carone Gallery, Fort Lauderdale, Florida
1991	Louis Newman Gallery, Beverly Hills, California
1992	Carone Gallery, Fort Lauderdale, Florida
1994	Carone Gallery, Fort Lauderdale, Florida
	Louis Newman Gallery, Beverly Hills, California
1995	Horwitch Newman Gallery, Scottsdale, Arizona
	Maxwell Davidson Gallery, New York

Group Exhibitions

Bignou Gallery, New York, 1945, 1946, 1947

Carnegie International, Department of Fine Arts, Carnegie Institute, Pittsburgh, Pennsylvania, 1945, 1947, 1948, 1950, 1952, 1954, 1956

Corcoran Biennial, Corcoran Gallery of Art, Washington, D.C., 1945, 1947, 1957, 1959, 1961

Pennsylvania Academy of the Fine Arts, Philadelphia, 1945, 1947, 1957, 1964

The Art Institute of Chicago, 1945, 1954, 1957, 1960

Whitney Museum of American Art, New York, 1945, 1964

Albright-Knox Art Gallery, Buffalo, New York, 1946

John Herron Art Museum, Indianapolis, Indiana, 1946, 1963

University of Iowa Museum of Art, Iowa City, 1947

Galerie Maeght, Paris, 1947

Passedoit Gallery, New York, 1947

The Toledo Museum of Art, Ohio, 1947

Topicova Salon, Prague, Czechoslovakia, 1947

College of Fine and Applied Arts, Architecture Building, University of Illinois, Urbana, 1948, 1950, 1951, 1959

Biennale, Venice, 1950, 1986

Amici della Francia Gallery, Milan, 1951

Ninth Street Annual, New York, 1951

Third Tokyo Annual, Japan, 1951

Le Arti Figurative nell'Architettura, Milan, 1952

Galleria Casanova, Trieste, Italy, 1952

Galleria d'arte del Cavallino, Venice, 1952

Studio Paul Facchetti, Paris, 1952

Alexandre Iolas Gallery, New York, 1952

André Breton with Donati's sculpture *Fist*, which was included in the 1947 exhibition *Le Surréalisme en 1947* at Galerie Maeght, Paris.

Michel Tapié, Paris, 1952

Worcester Art Museum, Massachusetts, 1952

Bienal, São Paulo, 1953

Galleria del Calibano, Vicenza, Italy, 1953

Galleria del Naviglio, Milan, 1953

The Museum of Modern Art, New York, 1953, 1954, 1962

Stable Gallery, New York, 1953, 1954

University Galleries, University of Nebraska, Lincoln, 1953, 1964

Santa Barbara Museum of Art, California, 1954

Solomon R. Guggenheim Museum, New York, 1954, 1961

Whitney Annual, Whitney Museum of American Art, New York, 1954, 1956, 1958, 1961, 1963, 1965, 1966, 1970

Munson-Williams-Proctor Institute Museum of Art, Utica, New York, 1955

San Francisco Museum of Art, California, 1955

Indiana University Art Museum, Bloomington, 1957, 1959

Signa Gallery, East Hampton, New York, 1957

Gutai 9, Osaka, Japan, 1958

Inter-American Paintings and Prints Biennial, Mexico City, 1958

Pittsburgh International, Carnegie Institute, Pennsylvania, 1958, 1961

Tartaruga Gallery, Rome, 1958

Virginia Museum of Fine Arts, Richmond, 1958, 1962, 1970

American Federation of Arts, New York, 1959 (organized; traveled to nine United States venues)

The Arts Club of Chicago, 1959

De Cordova and Dana Museum, Lincoln, Massachusetts, 1959

Kresge Art Center, Michigan State University, East Lansing, 1959

Museum of Art, Rhode Island School of Design, Providence, 1959

Martha Jackson Gallery, New York, 1960

Minnesota Museum of Art, St. Paul, 1960

Pius XII Memorial Library, Saint Louis University, Saint Louis, Missouri, 1960

Walker Art Center, Minneapolis, 1960

Sibell Wolle Gallery, University of Colorado, Boulder, 1960

Decorative Arts Center, New York, 1961

Hayden Gallery, Massachusetts Institute of Technology, Cambridge, 1961

Krannert Art Museum, University of Illinois, Urbana, 1961, 1963

Mary Washington College Galleries, Fredericksburg, Virginia, 1961

Birmingham Museum of Art, Alabama, 1962

Galleria Civica d'arte Moderna, Torino, Italy, 1962

Allentown Art Museum, Pennsylvania, 1963

Columbia Museum of Art, South Carolina, 1963

Cincinnati Art Museum, Ohio, 1964

Pavilion of Fine Arts, New York World's Fair, 1964

Musées royaux des Beaux-Arts de Belgique, Brussels, 1965

Flint Institute of Arts, DeWaters Art Center, Flint, Michigan, 1966

Museum of Fine Arts, Boston, 1966

Aldrich Museum of Contemporary Art, Ridgefield, Connecticut, 1967

University Art Museum, University of California, Berkeley, 1968

Galleria d'arte Cortina, Milan, 1969, 1976

Château de Saint-Cirq-Lapopie, Lot, France, 1974

Ankrum Gallery, Los Angeles, 1976

Meredith Long Gallery, Houston, 1976

Staempfli Gallery, New York, 1976

University Art Museum, University of Texas at Austin, 1976

Rutgers University Art Gallery, New Brunswick, New Jersey, 1977

Orlando Museum of Art, Florida, 1978

American Academy and Institute of Arts and Letters Art Galleries, New York, 1981

Grace Borgenicht Gallery/Terry Dintenfass Gallery, New York, 1982

Artcurial, Paris, 1986

Bernice Steinbaum Gallery, New York, 1986

Centro Atlantico de Arte Moderno, Las Palmas, Spain, 1989

Palazzo Reale, Milan, 1989

Zabriskie Gallery, New York, 1989

Fundación Cultural Mapfre Vida, Madrid, 1990

ART/LA, International Contemporary Art Fair, Los Angeles, 1990, 1991

Musée National d'Art Moderne, Centre Georges Pompidou, Paris, 1991

Museo Nacional Centro de Arte Reina Sofía, Madrid, 1991

Miami International, Florida, 1991, 1992

Isidore Ducasse Fine Arts, New York, 1992

Hunter College Art Galleries, New York, 1994

Galleria d'arte Bergamo, Italy, 1995

Nassau County Museum of Art, Roslyn Harbor, New York, 1995

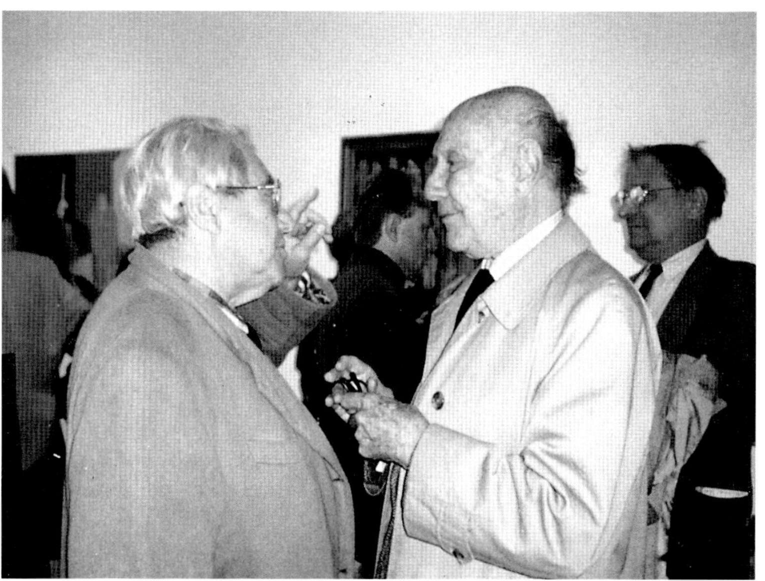

Left to right: Matta and Donati at the opening of the exhibition *André Breton: La beauté convulsive,* Centre Georges Pompidou, Paris, May 1991.

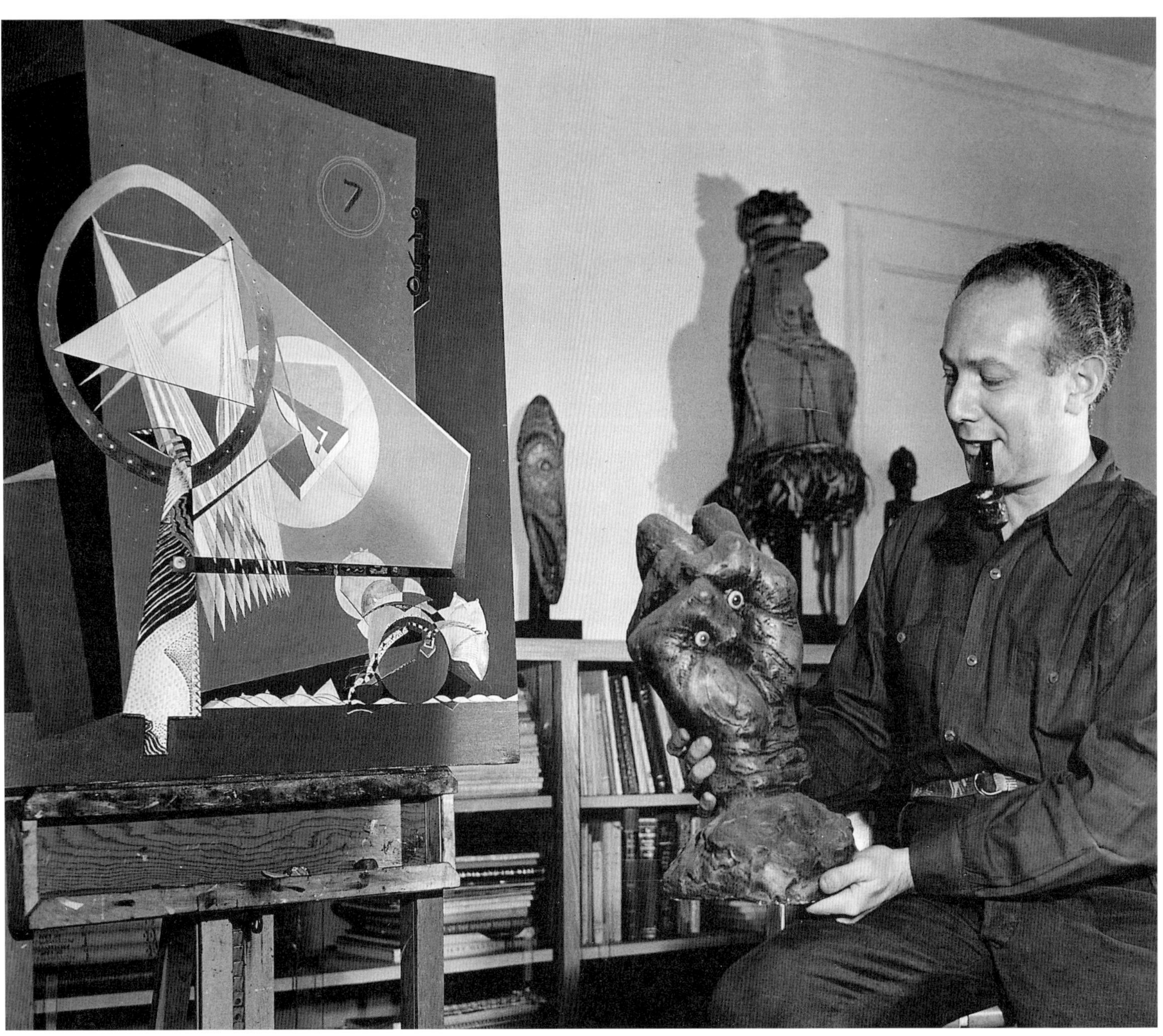

Donati with his sculpture *Fist,* 1946.

Selected Public Collections

Albright-Knox Art Gallery, Buffalo, New York

The Baltimore Museum of Art, Maryland

Musées royaux des Beaux-Arts de Belgique, Brussels

University Art Museum, University of California, Berkeley

The Detroit Institute of Arts, Michigan

Doane College, Crete, Nebraska

Museum of Art, Fort Lauderdale, Florida

Solomon R. Guggenheim Museum, New York

High Museum of Art, Atlanta, Georgia

Hirshhorn Museum and Sculpture Garden, Smithsonian Institution, Washington, D.C.

Housatonic Community College, Bridgeport, Connecticut

The Museum of Fine Arts, Houston, Texas

Archer M. Huntington Art Gallery, University of Texas at Austin

Museum of International Center of Aesthetic Research, Turin, Italy

The Israel Museum, Jerusalem

The Johns-Hopkins Hospital, Baltimore, Maryland

The Frances Lehman Loeb Art Center, Vassar College, Poughkeepsie, New York

The Lowe Museum, University of Miami, Florida

University of Michigan Art Gallery, Ann Arbor

Galleria Nazionale d'arte Moderna, Milan

MIT–List Visual Arts Center, Massachusetts Institute of Technology, Cambridge

The Museum of Modern Art, New York

Neuberger Museum of Art, State University of New York at Purchase

Newark Museum, New Jersey

Orlando Museum of Art, Florida

Palm Springs Desert Museum, California

Rockefeller University, New York

Galleria Nazionale d'arte Moderna, Rome

Museum of Fine Arts, St. Petersburg, Florida

Arturo Schwarz Surrealist Foundation, Milan

Seattle Art Museum, Washington

Swarthmore College Art Collection, Swarthmore, Pennsylvania

Tacoma Art Museum, Washington

Tougaloo College, Tougaloo, Mississippi

Oklahoma City Art Museum, Oklahoma

Washington University Gallery of Art, St. Louis, Missouri

Whitney Museum of American Art, New York

Yale University Art Gallery, New Haven, Connecticut

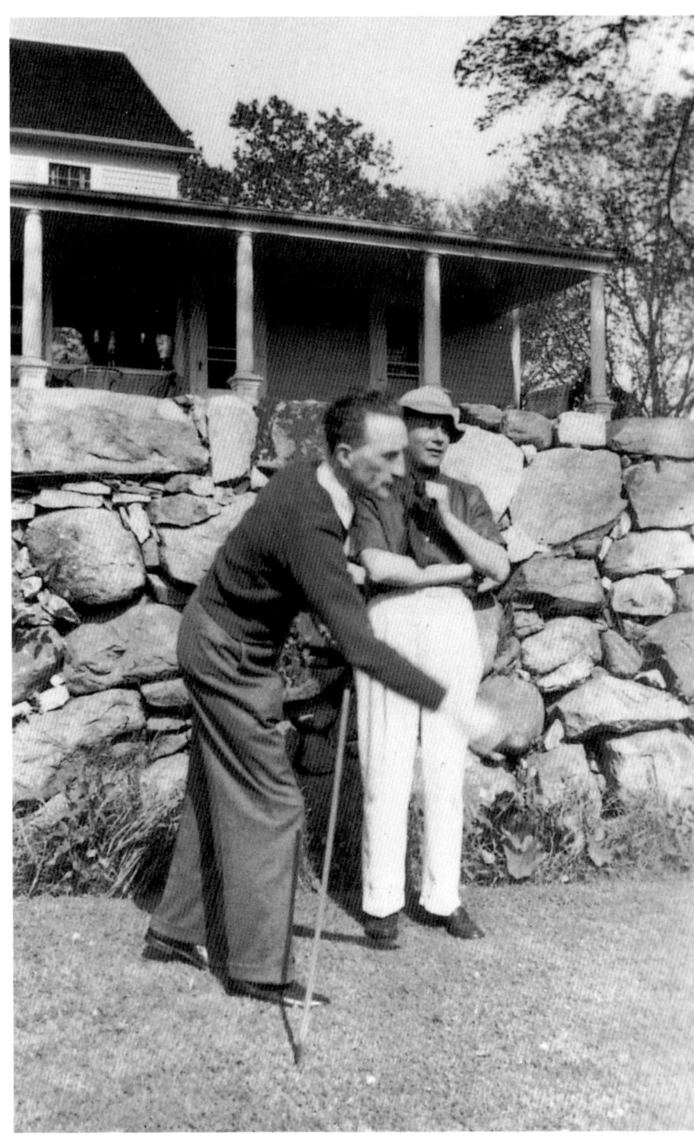

Left to right: Marcel Duchamp and Donati at Yves Tanguy's house in Woodbury, Connecticut, 1945.

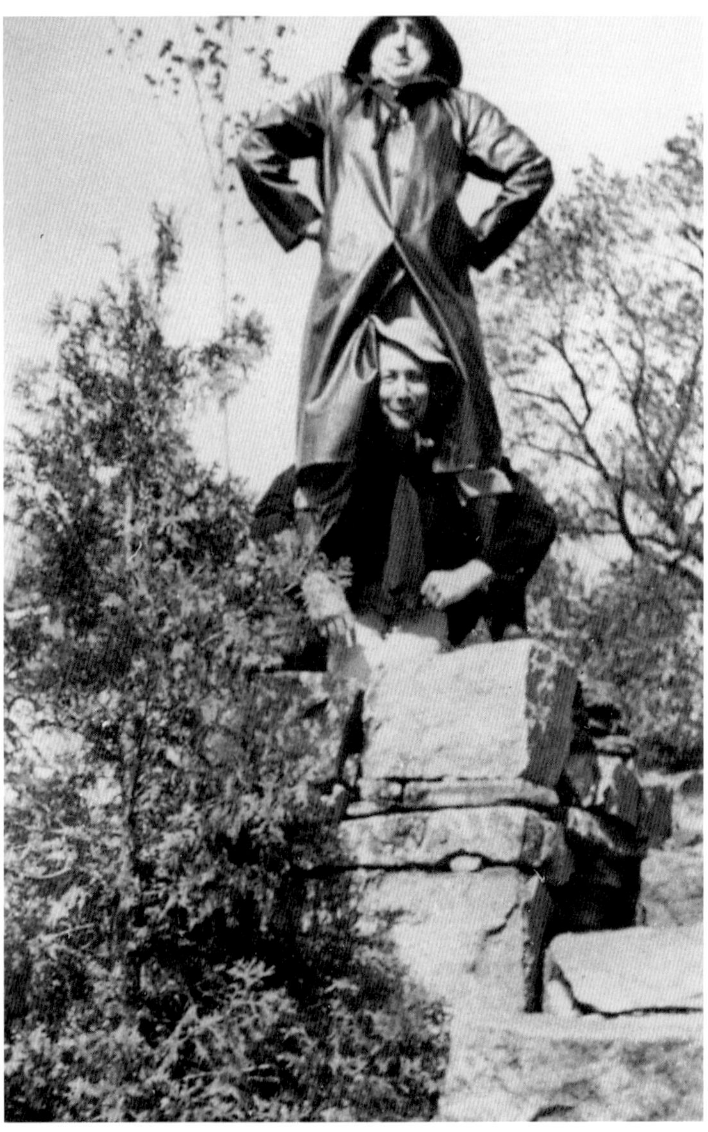

Yves Tanguy (top) and Donati at Tanguy's house in Woodbury, Connecticut, 1945.

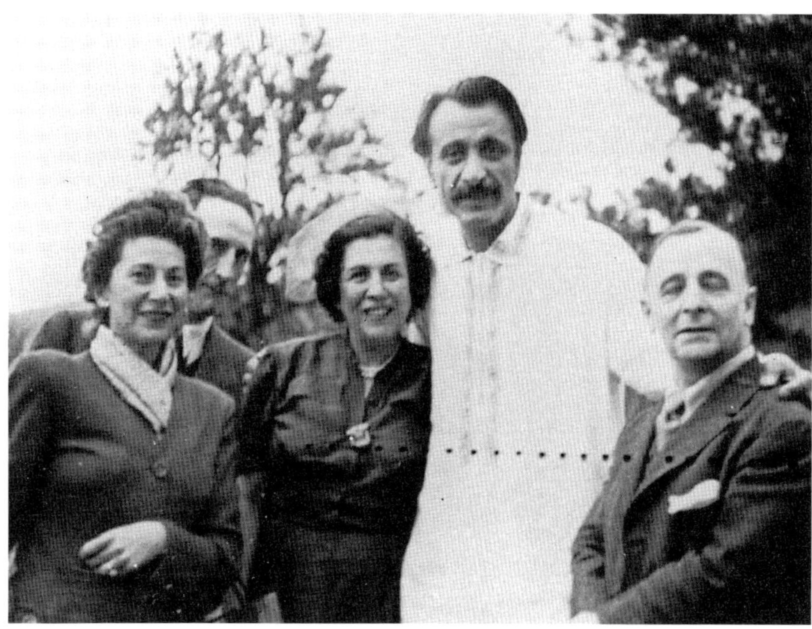

Left to right: Claire Donati, Marcel Duchamp,
Maria Martins, Arshile Gorky, and Frederick
Kiesler at Gorky's house in Connecticut,
1946. Photo by Enrico Donati.

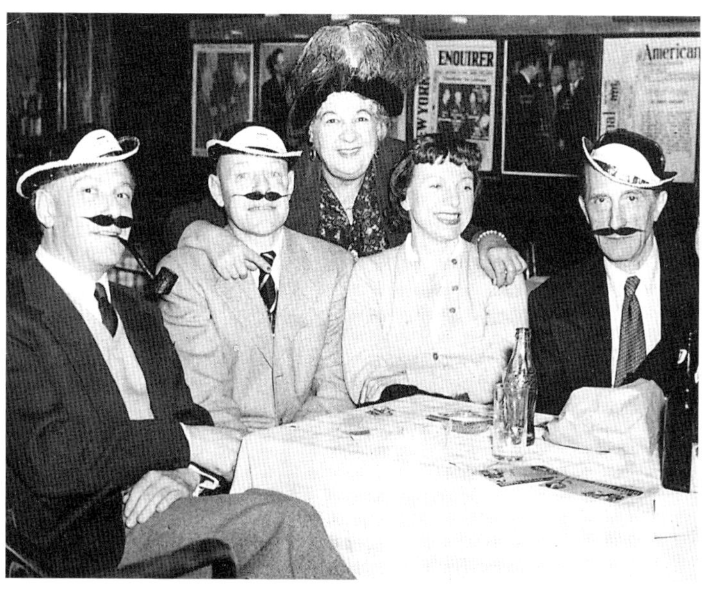

Left to right: Donati, M. and Mme Jean
Dubuffet, and Marcel Duchamp at the
Bowery Follies, New York, about
1951. Unidentified woman wearing
hat is a member of the Follies troupe.

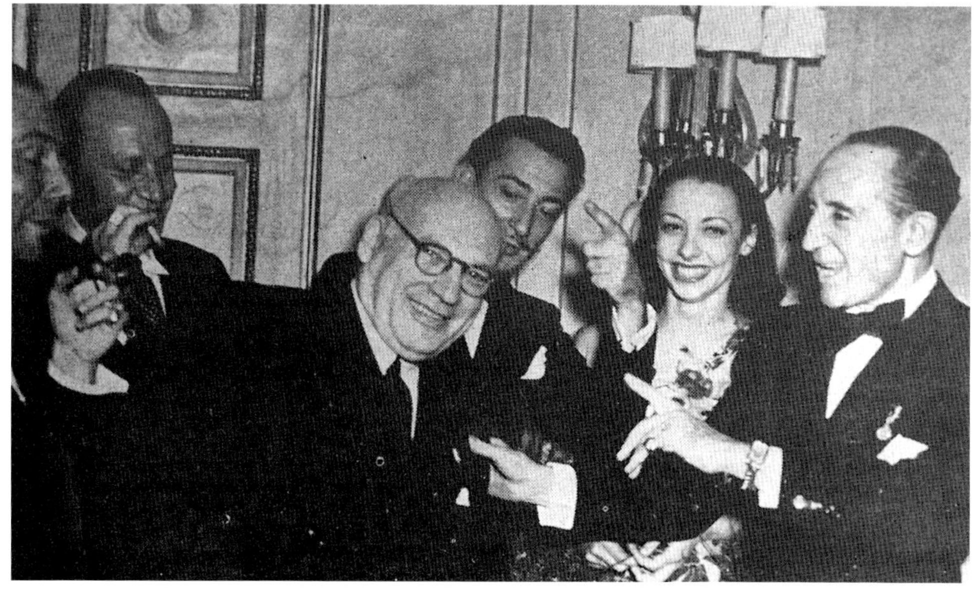

Left to right: Donati, Marcel Vertes,
Sol Hurok, Salvador Dalí, unidentified
ballerina, and the Marquis of Cuevas
after the first performance of a 1945
New York staging of the ballet version
of Maurice Ravel's *Bolero,* for which
Donati created the settings.

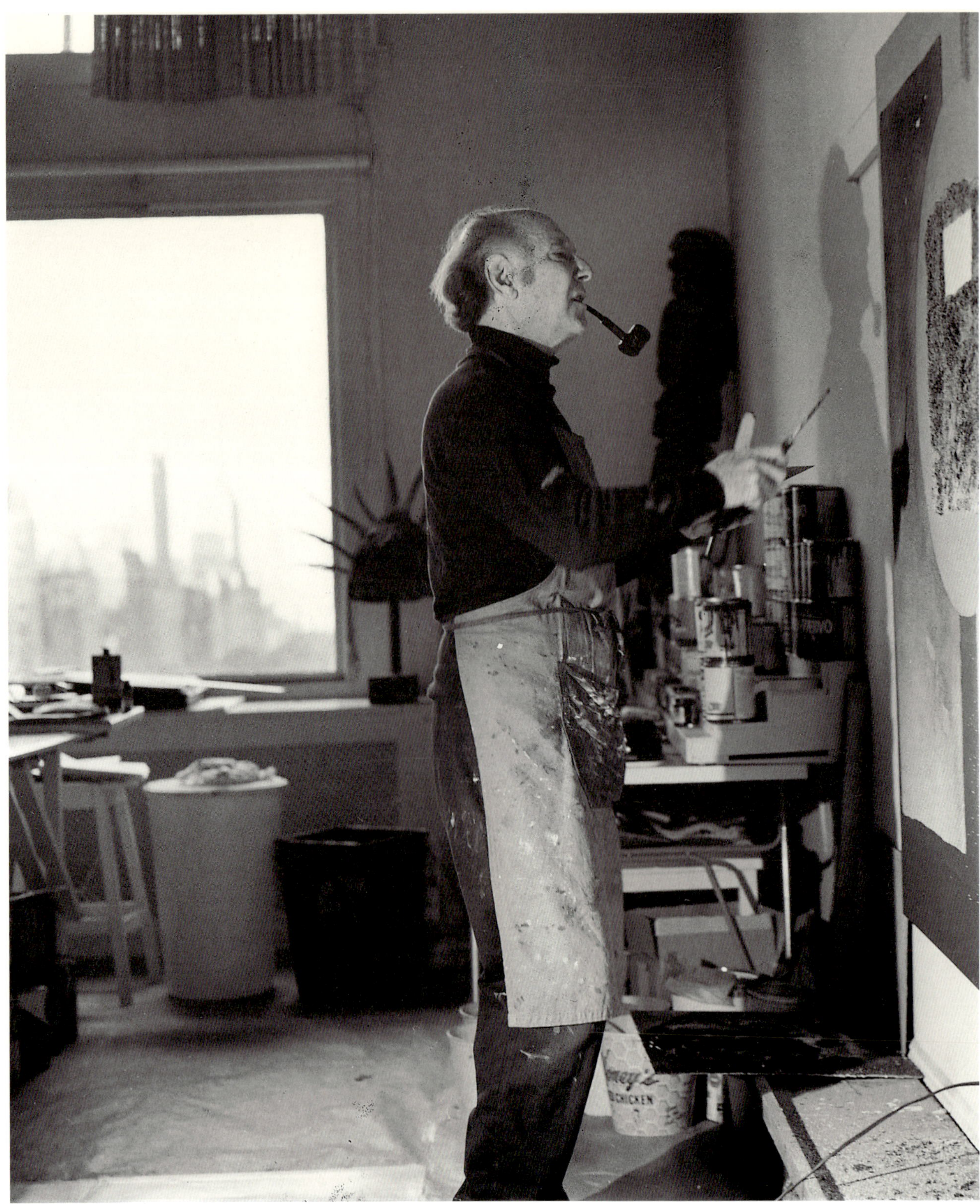
Donati, 1965.

Selected Bibliography

BOOKS AND EXHIBITION CATALOGUES FEATURING OR CONTAINING REFERENCES TO WORK BY ENRICO DONATI

Alexandrian, Sarane. *Surrealist Art.* New York: Praeger, 1970.

André Breton y el surrealismo. Exh. cat. Madrid: Museo Nacional Centro de Arte Reina Sofía, 1991.

Annual Exhibition 1954: Contemporary American Painting. Exh. cat. New York: Whitney Museum of American Art, 1954.

Annual Exhibition 1956: Contemporary American Painting. Exh. cat. New York: Whitney Museum of American Art, 1956.

Annual Exhibition 1958: Sculpture, Painting, Watercolor, Drawing. Exh. cat. New York: Whitney Museum of American Art, 1958.

Annual Exhibition 1961: Contemporary American Painting. Exh. cat. New York: Whitney Museum of American Art, 1961.

Annual Exhibition 1963: Contemporary American Painting. Exh. cat. New York: Whitney Museum of American Art, 1963.

Annual Exhibition 1965: Contemporary American Painting. Exh. cat. New York: Whitney Museum of American Art, 1965.

Annual Exhibition 1966: Sculpture and Prints. Exh. cat. New York: Whitney Museum of American Art, 1966.

Annual Exhibition 1970: Contemporary American Painting. Exh. cat. New York: Whitney Museum of American Art, 1970.

Apollonio, Umbro. *Enrico Donati.* Exh. cat. Milan: Edizioni del Milione, 1950.

Arnason, H. H. *Sixty American Painters: Abstract Expressionist Painting of the Fifties.* Exh. cat. Minneapolis: Walker Art Center, 1960.

______. Introduction. In *American Abstract Expressionists and Imagists.* Exh. cat. New York: Solomon R. Guggenheim Museum, 1961.

Atlantic Richfield Collection. New York: Atlantic Richfield Corporation, 1969.

Baron, Jacques. *Anthologie plastique du surréalisme.* Paris: Editions Filipacchi, 1980.

Barr, Alfred H., Jr., ed. *Painting and Sculpture in the Museum of Modern Art.* New York: Museum of Modern Art, 1948.

Baur, John I. H. *Catalogue of the Collection of the Whitney Museum of American Art.* New York: Whitney Museum of American Art, 1973.

Biro, Adam, and René Passeron. *Dictionnaire général du surréalisme et de ses environs.* Paris: Presses Universitaires de France, 1982.

Breton, André. Preface. In *Paintings by Enrico Donati.* Exh. cat. (New York: Passedoit Gallery, 1944), unpaginated.

______. *Le Surréalisme et la peinture.* New York: Brentano's, 1945.

______. *Le Surréalisme en 1947.* Exh. cat. Paris: Galerie Maeght, 1947.

Breton, André, Nicolas Calas, and Maurice Nadeau. *Donati.* Exh. cat. New York: Durand-Ruel Galleries, 1949.

Calas, Nicolas. Preface. In *Enrico Donati.* Exh. cat. New York: Staempfli Gallery, 1962.

Chadwick, Whitney. *Women Artists and the Surrealist Movement.* Boston: Little, Brown, 1985.

Clarac-Serou, Max. *Donati.* Venice: Edizioni del Cavallino, 1953.

Collection of the American Republic Insurance Company. 1967.

Colt, Eleanore Phillips. *Going Strong.* New York: Arcade Publishing, 1991.

De Rosa, Stefano. *Roberto Crippa.* Exh. cat. Bergamo: Galleria d'arte Bergamo, 1994.

Duchamp, Marcel. Preface. In *Enrico Donati.* Exh. cat. Brussels: Palais des Beaux-Arts, 1961.

______. Preface. In exh. cat. New York: Alexandre Iolas Gallery, 1952.

Giani, Giampiero. *Spazialismo.* Milan: Conchiglia, 1956.

Godwin, Blake-More. Introduction. In *Thirty-fourth Annual Exhibition of Contemporary American Paintings.* Exh. cat. Toledo Museum of Art, 1947.

Gomez Correa, Enrique. *El Pleno Dia.* Illustrations by Enrico Donati. Santiago: Edition Mandragora, 1948.

Goodrich, Lloyd, and John I. H. Baur. *American Art of Our Century.* New York: Praeger, 1961.

Greenberg, Clement, and Nicolas Calas. *Donati.* Milan: Edizione del Milione, 1954.

Gruen, John. Preface. In *Enrico Donati: A Retrospective Exhibition.* Exh. cat. New York: Staempfli Gallery, 1976.

Hall, Lee. *Betty Parsons: Artist, Dealer, Collector.* New York: Harry N. Abrams, 1991.

Inventions Surréalistes. New York: Isidore Ducasse Fine Arts, 1992.

Jean, Marcel. *Histoire de la peinture surréal-iste.* Paris: Editions du Seuil, 1959.

Jouffroy, Alain. "Donati between Two Worlds." In *Enrico Donati.* Exh. cat. Detroit: J. L. Hudson Gallery, 1964, unpaginated.

LeKatsas, Barbara. *Surrealism.* Exh. cat. Roslyn Harbor, N.Y.: Nassau County Museum of Art, 1995.

Marangon, Dino, and Toni Toniato. *Spazialismo.* Desenzano del Garda: Edizioni Nuovi Strumenti, 1989.

Martin, Richard. *Fashion and Surrealism.* New York: Rizzoli, 1987.

Maulpoix, Jean-Michel. *XXe Siècle après 1950.* Paris: Hatier, 1991.

McCabe, Cynthia Jaffee. *Artistic Collaboration in the Twentieth Century.* Exh. cat. Washington, D.C.: Hirshhorn Museum and Sculpture Garden, Smithsonian Institution, 1984.

McNamee, M. B. *Paintings from the Collection of Mr. and Mrs. Morton May.* Exh. cat. Saint Louis: Pius XII Memorial Library, Saint Louis University, 1960.

Moretti, Luigi. *Strutture e Stile.* Exh. cat. Torino: Galleria Civica d'arte Moderna, 1962.

Musée National d'Art Moderne. *Yves Tanguy.* Exh. cat. Paris: Editions du Centre Pompidou, 1982.

______. *André Breton: La beauté convulsive.* Exh. cat. Paris: Editions du Centre Pompidou, 1991.

Neff, Terry Ann R., ed. *In the Mind's Eye: Dada and Surrealism.* Exh. cat. Chicago: Museum of Contemporary Art, 1985.

Noel, Bernard. "L'oeil surréaliste." In *La Planète affolée: Surréalisme, dispersion et influences, 1938–1947.* Marseilles: Editions Flammarion, 1986, 15–24.

Passeron, René. *Encyclopédie du surréalisme.* Paris: Editions Somogy, 1975.

Pierre, José. *L'Aventure surréaliste autour d'André Breton.* Paris: Artcurial, 1986.

______. "Le Surréalisme en 1947." In *La Planète affolée: Surréalisme, dispersion et influences, 1938–1947.* Marseilles: Editions Flammarion, 1986, 283–307.

Poma, Fernando. *Modern Art Looks Ahead.* New York: Beachhurst Press, 1947.

Powell III, Earl A. *Abstract Expressionists and Imagists: A Retrospective View.* Exh. cat. Austin: University of Texas at Austin, 1976.

Rathbone, Perry T. *Selections from the Collection of Susan Morse Hilles.* Exh. cat. Boston: Museum of Fine Arts, 1966.

Read, Herbert. *A Concise History of Modern Painting,* New York: Praetor, 1959.

Robert-Jones, Philippe. *Arts of the Twentieth Century.* Brussels: Palais des Beaux-Arts, 1977.

Rubin, William. *Dada, Surrealism, and Their Heritage.* Exh. cat. New York: Museum of Modern Art, 1968.

Sawin, Martica. "Aux Etats-Unis." In *La Planète affolée: Surréalisme, dispersion et influences, 1938–1947.* Marseilles: Editions Flammarion, 1986, 105–44.

______. *Surrealism in Exile.* Cambridge: MIT Press, 1995.

Schwarz, Arturo. "Art and Alchemy." In *La Biennale di Venezia.* Exh. cat. Venice: Edizioni la Biennale, 1986, 77–109.

______. *I Surrealisti.* Exh. cat. Milan: Gabriele Mazzotta and Palazzo Reale, 1989.

Selection 1968: Recent Accessions to the University Art Collections. Berkeley: University Art Museum, University of California, Berkeley, 1968.

Selz, Peter H. *Enrico Donati.* Paris: Editions Georges Fall, 1965.

______. *American Painting.* Exh. cat. Richmond: Virginia Museum of Fine Arts, 1970.

Staempfli, Georges. Preface. In *Enrico Donati.* Exh. cat. New York: Staempfli Gallery, 1979.

Steinbaum, Bernice. *Elders of the Tribe.* Exh. cat. New York: Bernice Steinbaum Gallery, 1986.

El Surrealismo entre Viejo y Nuevo Mundo. Exh. cat. Madrid: Sala de Exposiciones de la Fundación Cultural Mapfre Vida, 1990.

Sweeney, James Johnson. Preface. In *Younger American Painters.* Exh. cat. New York: Solomon R. Guggenheim Museum, 1954.

Tapié, Michel. Preface. In *Enrico Donati.* Exh. cat. Munich: Neue Galerie im Kunstlerhaus, 1962.

______. *Espaces Abstraits.* Exh. cat. Cortina: Edizioni della Galleria d'arte Cortina, 1969.

Venturi, Lionello. *Pittura Contemporanea.* Milan: Editore Ulrico Hoepli, 1946.

Washburn, Gordon Bailey. *Pittsburgh International.* Exh. cat. Pittsburgh: Department of Fine Arts, Carnegie Institute. 1958.

______. *Pittsburgh International.* Exh. cat. Pittsburgh: Department of Fine Arts, Carnegie Institute. 1961.

Wechler, Jeffrey. *Surrealism and American Art, 1931–1947.* Exh. cat. New Brunswick, N.J.: Rutgers University Art Gallery, 1977.

______. *Abstract Expressionism: Other Dimensions.* Urbana: University of Illinois Press, 1989.

Weller, Allen S. *Contemporary American Painting.* Exh. cat. Urbana: University of Illinois Press, 1951.

______. *Contemporary American Painting.* Exh. cat. Urbana: University of Illinois Press, 1959.

______. *Contemporary American Painting.* Exh. cat. Urbana: University of Illinois Press, 1961.

______. *Contemporary American Painting.* Exh. cat. Urbana: University of Illinois Press, 1963.

Weller, Allen S., and Frank Roos. *Contemporary American Painting.* Urbana: University of Illinois Press, 1948.

Williams, Hermann Warner, Jr. Introduction. In *Twentieth Biennial Exhibition of Contemporary American Painting.* Exh. cat. Washington, D.C.: Corcoran Gallery of Art, 1947.

______. Introduction. In *Twenty-seventh Biennial Exhibition of Contemporary American Painting.* Exh. cat. Washington, D.C.: Corcoran Gallery of Art, 1961.

Wolff, Theodore F. *Enrico Donati: The Most Recent Work.* Paris: Editions Georges Fall, 1984.

______. *The Many Masks of Modern Art.* New York: Christian Science Monitor Publishing Society, 1989.

______. Preface. In *Enrico Donati.* Exh. cat. New York: Maxwell Davidson Gallery, 1995, unpaginated. (Originally published in Wolff, 1984.)

Zabriskie, Virginia. *Conspiratorial Laughter. A Friendship: Man Ray and Duchamp.* Exh. cat. New York: Zabriskie Gallery, 1989.

ARTICLES AND REVIEWS IN MAGAZINES AND NEWSPAPERS

Alcancz, F. "Arte senza frontiere alla Biennale di Pittsburgh." *Giornale del Popolo* (Bergamo), December 7, 1952.

"Animal Party." *Look,* June 6, 1949, 30.

Apollonio, Umbro. "Il surrealismo e Donati." *Il Giornale di Napoli,* December 19, 1950.

______. "Enrico Donati ha 'epurato' il surrealismo dalle scorie." *Giornale del Lunedi* (Trieste), December 26, 1950.

"Artist to Be Entertained." *Times Herald* (Washington, D.C.), May 25, 1944.

"Art News in Paris." *New York Herald Tribune,* November 29, 1946.

"Art: On the Couch." *Time,* April 24, 1950, 82.

"Les Arts." Review, *Echoes de France* (Paris), December 4, 1946.

"Arts Club Show Today," Review, *Chicago Sun,* November 3, 1944.

Ashton, Dore. "Un romantique du XXe Siècle: Le peintre Enrico Donati." *Les Beaux-Arts* (Brussels), October 20, 1961, 8.

Beckelmann, J. "Enrico Donati." *Deutsche Woche* (Munich), March 12, 1962.

______. "Sinfonie in drei Farben." *Rhein-Zeitung* (Koblenz), March 22, 1962.

Berryman, Florence S. "Review of 'A Night in May' at the G Place Gallery." *Sunday Star* (Washington, D.C.), May 28, 1944.

Bolis, Maria Sirtori. "Convegni d'arte." *Corriere degli artisti* (Rome), October 31, 1951.

Boswell, Helen. "Enrico Donati's Colorful Paintings." *Art Digest,* June 1, 1943.

Braff, Phyllis. "Nassau Museum Explores Surrealism's Achievements." *The New York Times.* January 29, 1995, 14.

Brizio, A. M. "La pittura moderna." *La Nouva Stampa,* February 8, 1948.

Budigna, Luciano. "Il pupillo del Surrealismo." *Settimana* (Milan), November 18, 1950.

Burrows, Carlyle. "The Week in Art." *The New York Times,* March 18, 1945.

"By One and by Groups." *The New York Times,* May 16, 1943.

Calas, Nicolas. "Enrico Donati." *Art International,* March 1962, 42.

Canaday, John. "Art: A Wild, but Curious, End-of-Season Treat." *The New York Times,* June 6, 1960.

______. "The Blind Artist." *The New York Times,* October 2, 1960.

______. "Art: The Whitney Annual." *The New York Times,* December 13, 1961.

Chancy, Michael, and Dolores Tropiano. "Valley and State." *Arizona Republic,* March 10, 1995, B8.

Chevalier, Denis. "Enrico Donati." *Arts,* December 20, 1946.

Coates, Robert. *The New Yorker,* December 27, 1958.

______. "The Art Galleries." *The New Yorker,* April 21, 1962.

______. *The New Yorker,* January 4, 1964.

Cooper, Robert. "Part of Atlanta's High Museum Collection on View at UTC Gallery." *Detroit Free Press,* May 8, 1969.

"Cordon Bleu." *The New York Times,* April 20, 1952.

Costigliore, M. "Esprit des formes." *Plaisir de France,* December 1947.

Cyr, Don. "A Conversation with Enrico Donati." *Art News,* May 1972.

Delanglade, F. "Enrico Donati." *La France au Combat* (Paris), November 28, 1946.

Devree, Howard. "Kindred Modernists." *The New York Times,* February 27, 1944.

Diehl, Gaston. "Les Arts." *Liberation-Soir* (Paris), November 29, 1946.

Donati, Enrico. "Statement." *It Is* (winter–spring 1959), 27.

"Donati." Review of solo exhibition at Galerie Drouant-David, Paris. *Arts,* November 22, 1946.

"Donati." *Look,* September 23, 1953, 116.

"Donati." Review of solo exhibition at Galerie Drouant-David, Paris. *L'Ordre* (Paris), November 20, 1946.

"Donati." Review of group exhibition at Amici della Francia Gallery, Milan. *L'Unità* (Milan), November 3, 1951.

"Donati." Review of solo exhibition at Neue Galerie im Kunstlerhaus, Munich. *Die Zeit* (Hamburg), March 12, 1962.

"Donati—Airy Improviser." *Art News,* March 15–31, 1945, 18–19.

"Donati at Passedoit." *New York World-Telegram,* February 26, 1944.

"Donati Crits Students; Sites *(sic)* 'Lack of Invention.'" *Blockprint* (Rhode Island School of Design, Providence), May 16, 1962.

"Donati Has His Night." *Art Digest,* May 15, 1944, 11.

"Donati Impresses." Review of solo exhibition at Betty Parsons Gallery, New York. *New York Herald Tribune,* December 4, 1960.

"Donati Show Scheduled." *Washington Post,* May 14, 1944.

"Donati, Surrealist or Not, Intrigues the Eye." *Art Digest,* March 1946, 53.

Driver, Morley. "Abstraction Can Lead to Distraction." *Detroit Free Press,* February 9, 1964.

Duché, Jean. "Enrico Donati." *L'Ordre* (Paris), November 20, 1946.

Duflo, Pierre. "Magie de l'absurde." *Reforme* (Paris), July 19, 1947.

"D'une galerie à l'autre." *L'Ordre* (Paris), December 7, 1946.

"Early Arrivals." Review of solo exhibition at Passedoit Gallery, New York. *The New York Times,* March 19, 1944.

"English Speaking Union, Arts Club Both Holding Teas Week from Today." *Chicago Daily News,* November 27, 1944.

"Enrico Donati." Review of solo exhibition at Passedoit Gallery, New York. *Art Digest,* February 15, 1944.

"Enrico Donati." Review of solo exhibition at Betty Parsons Gallery, New York. *Art Digest,* May 15, 1954.

"Enrico Donati." Review of solo exhibition at New School for Social Research, New York. *Art News,* June–July 1943, 51.

"Enrico Donati." Review of solo exhibition at Passedoit Gallery, New York. *Art News,* February 15–29, 1944, 21.

"Enrico Donati." Review of solo exhibition at Durand-Ruel Galleries, New York. *Art News,* March 1946, 53.

"Enrico Donati." Review of solo exhibition at Durand-Ruel Galleries, New York. *Art News,* March 1947, 42.

"Enrico Donati." Review of solo exhibition at Betty Parsons Gallery, New York. *Art News,* March 1959, 13.

"Enrico Donati." Review of solo exhibition at Staempfli Gallery, New York. *Art News,* May 1962.

"Enrico Donati." Review of solo exhibition at Staempfli Gallery, New York. *Art News,* December 1963.

"Enrico Donati." Review of solo exhibition at Staempfli Gallery, New York. *Art News,* March 1968.

"Enrico Donati." Review of solo exhibition at A. Weil, Paris. *Arts* (Paris), May 6, 1949.

"Enrico Donati." Review of solo exhibition at Betty Parsons Gallery, New York. *Arts Magazine,* December 1960.

"Enrico Donati." Review of solo exhibition at Staempfli Gallery, New York. *Arts Magazine,* April 1966.

"Enrico Donati." Review of solo exhibition at Staempfli Gallery, New York. *Art/World* (New York), March 19–April 18, 1979.

"Enrico Donati." Review of solo exhibition at Galerie Drouant-David, Paris. *Côte d'Azur* (Cannes), December 8, 1946.

"Enrico Donati." *L'Express* (Paris), April 21–27, 1989.

"Enrico Donati." *Il Giornale del Mezzogiorno* (Rome), November 5, 1950.

"Enrico Donati." Review of solo exhibition at Norton Gallery of Art, West Palm Beach. *Miami Herald,* April 13, 1979.

"Enrico Donati." *New York Herald Tribune,* April 3, 1949.

"Enrico Donati." *New York Herald Tribune,* November 30, 1963.

"Enrico Donati." Review of solo exhibition at Staempfli Gallery, New York. *New York Post,* March 2, 1968.

"Enrico Donati." *The New York Times,* December 1, 1963.

"Enrico Donati." Review of solo exhibition at Staempfli Gallery, New York. *The New York Times,* April 1, 1972.

"Enrico Donati." Review of solo exhibition at Staempfli Gallery, New York. *The New York Times,* May 7, 1976.

"Enrico Donati." Review of solo exhibition at Staempfli Gallery, New York. *The New York Times,* March 28, 1980.

"Enrico Donati." *Nouvelle Gazette* (Brussels), October 24, 1961.

"Enrico Donati." *Time,* February 4, 1966.

"Enrico Donati." Review of solo exhibition at Staempfli Gallery, New York. *Time,* March 8, 1968.

"Enrico Donati." Review of solo exhibition at Galleria dell'Obelisco, Rome. *L'Unità* (Milan), November 5, 1950.

"Enrico Donati." Review of solo exhibition at Durand-Ruel Galleries, New York. *View,* May 1945.

"Enrico Donati at Milione." *Domus,* May 1950, illus.

"Enrico Donati Opens at Norton Gallery." *Palm Beach Daily News,* April 8, 1979, 6.

"Enrico Donati's Double Life." *Fortune,* July 17, 1978, 84.

Etienne, Charles. "Enrico Donati." *Combat* (Paris), November 20, 1946.

"Europe at the Whitney." *The New York Times,* March 18, 1945.

"Faces behind the Figures." *Forbes,* October 1, 1972, 68.

"Famous Visitor." *Fort Lauderdale* (Florida) *News,* March 21, 1963.

Figel, Nancy. "Donati Norton Exhibition Showcase of Surrealism." *Palm Beach* (Florida) *Times,* April 20, 1979.

Fitzgerald, Adeline. "These Charming People." *Chicago Herald,* November 3, 1944.

Fitzsimmons, James. "Stable Group Sets a Smart Pace." *Art Digest,* June 1, 1954, 11.

"D'une rive à l'autre." *Nouvelles Littéraires,* November 21, 1946.

"Further along the Trail." *The New York Times,* March 10, 1946.

Geist, Sidney. "Enrico Donati." *Art International,* October 25, 1960, 39.

Genauer, Emily. "Artists Stress New Ideas in Art Shows." *New York Herald Tribune,* January 4, 1959.

Glueck, Grace. "To Lend or Not to Lend." *The New York Times,* January 24, 1965, 22.

Goebel, M. M. "Enrico Donati." *Town and Country,* January 1967.

Goll, Yvan. "Enrico Donati." *France-Amérique* (Paris), March 17, 1946.

Gray, Christopher. "The Gainsborough Studios." *Architectural Digest,* November 1991, 98.

Gruen, John. "Enrico Donati." *Art International,* March–April 1976.

Hager, Moses. "Donati Still Clings to Surrealism." *Jersey Journal,* February 4, 1970.

Hakanson, Joy. "New York Artist's Exhibition Opened at Hudson." *Detroit News,* February 3, 1964.

______. "Enrico Donati: Images in Sounds." *Detroit News,* February 9, 1964.

Horn, Helen. "Art Collections." *Reno* (Nevada) *Evening Gazette,* November 9, 1965.

Hunter, Sam. "Guggenheim Sampler." *Art Digest,* May 15, 1954.

Hurlburt, Roger. "Mandrake Root Grows Deep in Donati's Heart." *Sun-Sentinel* (Fort Lauderdale), December 9, 1984.

______. "Surrealism Meant to Free Artists from Restraints of Past Beliefs." *Sun-Sentinel* (Fort Lauderdale), February 15, 1987, 1G.

______. "Goodbye, Dali." *Sun-Sentinel* (Fort Lauderdale), January 24, 1989.

______. "Last of Original Surrealists Joyfully Depicts Earth's Past." *Sun-Sentinel* (Fort Lauderdale), April 4, 1990.

______. "Surrealist Emeritus." *Sun-Sentinel* (Fort Lauderdale), March 23, 1993.

______. "Donati Gave Surrealism Another Voice in the '40's." *Sun-Sentinel* (Fort Lauderdale), April 13, 1994, 3E.

______. "Painting for All Palettes." *Sun-Sentinel* (Fort Lauderdale), October 15, 1995, 18.

______. "Carone Presents Local Artists, Season Review." *Sun-Sentinel* (Fort Lauderdale), December 14, 1995, 3E.

Hynes, Betty. "Painting Exhibition to Be Presented." *Times Herald* (Washington, D.C.), May 11, 1944.

Imbourg, Pierre. "Les Expositions." *Toujours Paris,* December 4, 1946.

______. "Donati." *Une Semaine de Paris,* June 1, 1949.

Jaquer, Edouard. "Le surréalisme par-dessus l'ancien et le nouveau monde." *Opus International,* April–May 1991, 82–88.

Jewett, Eleanor. "Arts Club Puts Two Moderns' Works on View." *Chicago Daily Tribune,* November 4, 1944.

Jones, Alan. "Enrico Donati: A Painter and His Surrealist Entitlements." *Arts Magazine,* April 1991, 17.

Joron-Derem, Christophe. "La Belle Renommée de la province." *Les Beaux-Arts* (Brussels), September 1987.

"Joseph L. Hudson, Jr.: Detroit's Merchant Prince." *Detroit News,* September 12, 1965.

Kochnitzky, Leon. "Surréalisme et peinture." *La Victoire* (Paris), November 24, 1945.

Kohen, Helen L. "Donati Space: A Retrospective." *Miami Herald,* April 27, 1979.

Kramer, Hilton. Review of solo exhibition at Staempfli Gallery, New York. *The New York Times,* November 16, 1974, 24.

______. Review of solo exhibition at Staempfli Gallery, New York. *The New York Times,* May 7, 1976, 12.

______. Review of solo exhibition at Staempfli Gallery, New York. *The New York Times,* March 28, 1980, 27.

Lansford, Alonzo. "Escapist Surrealism." *Art News,* March 15, 1947.

Lebel, Robert. "Surréalisme, années américaines." *Opus International,* April–May 1991, 76–81.

"Les Arts." Review in *Echoes de France* (Paris), December 4, 1946.

Lewis, Jo Ann. "The Cellar Surrealist." *Washington Post,* December 4, 1979.

Lipson, Karin. "The Surrealist Stars and Others, on Parade." *Newsday* (New York), January 20, 1995.

MacCormac, John. "Viennese Find No Differences in Art Works by Surrealists and Schizophrenic Patients." *The New York Times,* April 11, 1950.

Malone, Eileen. "Toledo Corporation Supports Contemporary Art." *Impresario,* April–May 1970, 22.

Mannoni, Angelo. "L'americana incontrò in piazza di Spagna Nando Galleri." *Gazzetta Sarda-Sassari* (Rome), December 11, 1950.

Mathew, Roy. "Donati World." *Art/World* (New York), April 22–May 20, 1982.

Mezio, Alfredo. "Technicolor." *Il Mondo* (Rome), November 25, 1950.

Michel, Georges. "Surréalistes attardés." *L'Ordre* (Paris), December 3, 1946.

Modugno, Bruno. "D'all'Obelisco." *Lo Studente d'Italia via Delle Botteghe* (Rome), November 30, 1950.

Monahan, Julie A. "Houbigant Takes a Classic Approach." *Women's Wear Daily,* September 11, 1987, S42.

Moser, Charlotte. "Reality of Surrealism." *Houston Chronicle,* May 21, 1978, 15.

"Mostre d'arte." *Gazzettino Sera* (Venice), October 23, 1952.

"Mostre d'arte." *Giornale di Trieste,* November 15, 1952.

"Mostre d'arte." Review of group exhibition at Amici della Francia Gallery, Milan. *L'Italia* (Milan), November 7, 1951.

"Mostre d'arte." Review of group exhibition at Amici della Francia Gallery, Milan. *Il Popolo* (Milan), November 9, 1951.

"Mostre d'arte a Firenze." *La Nazione* (Florence), May 18, 1952.

Nadeau, Maurice. "Enrico Donati." *Cahier d'art* (Paris), 1945–46.

"A New Look for RCA." *Newsweek,* January 29, 1968.

"New Means for Moderns." *Life,* November 22, 1954, 160–62.

"New York World Art Center." *Look,* June 8, 1948, 54–55.

"Norton Gallery Exhibition: Paintings by Enrico Donati." *Palm Beach* (Florida) *Chronicle,* April 18–24, 1979, 10.

"Norton Gallery to Exhibit Enrico Donati Paintings." *Lake Worth* (Florida) *Herald,* April 5, 1979.

"Nostalgie du surréalisme." *Le Monde,* April 12, 1989, 30.

"Oggi gli artisti spaziali alla Galleria Casanuova." *Il Corriere di Trieste,* November 15, 1952.

Parks, Steve. "Portrait of a Young Museum; The Nassau County Museum of Art Is Thriving, Five Years after Its Separation from Local Politics." *Newsday* (New York), February 6, 1995, B04.

Petset, Wolfgang. "Alchemist Donati." *Moderne,* July 1962, 16, illus.

Pfeiffer-Belli, Erich. "Kosmische Kunde." *Die Abendzeitung* (Munich), March 15, 1962.

Piquet, Philippe. "Le surréalisme en Amérique." *L'Oeil* (Paris), May 1986, 61–64.

Preston, Stuart. "Two Painters." *The New York Times,* December 4, 1960.

Ratcliff, Carter. "Artist's Dialogue: Enrico Donati." *Architectural Digest,* November 1988, 94–104, illus.

______. "Manhattan Transfer." *Art in America,* May 1989, 174–81.

Rausch, Gary. "Visit to Scottsdale Gallery Will Be Surreal—Literally." *Scottsdale Tribune,* March 12, 1995.

Reilly, Maude. "Donati Extravaganza." *Art News,* March 1, 1945.

Review of solo exhibition at Betty Parsons Gallery, New York. *Apollo,* April 1959, 124.

Review of solo exhibition at Durand-Ruel Galleries, New York. *Art Digest,* March 1, 1945, 11.

Review of solo exhibition at Durand-Ruel Galleries, New York. *Art Digest,* March 1, 1946, 16.

Review of solo exhibition at Durand-Ruel Galleries, New York. *Art Digest,* April 1, 1949, 12.

Review of solo exhibition at Paul Rosenberg Gallery, New York. *Art Digest,* November 1, 1950, 18.

Review of solo exhibition at Alexandre Iolas Gallery, New York. *Art Digest,* May 1, 1952, 19.

Review of group exhibition at Bignou Gallery, New York. *Art News,* January 1945.

Review of solo exhibition at Paul Rosenberg Gallery, New York. *Art News,* November 1950, 68.

Review of solo exhibition at Alexandre Iolas Gallery, New York. *Art News,* May 1952, 44.

Review of solo exhibition at Palais des Beaux-Arts, Brussels. *Les Beaux-Arts* (Brussels), October 1961, 8.

Review of group exhibition at Bignou Gallery, New York. *Brooklyn Eagle,* January 14, 1945.

Review of solo exhibition at Neue Galerie im Kunstlerhaus, Munich. *Handelblatt* (Dusseldorf), March 23, 1962.

Review of solo exhibition at Neue Galerie im Kunstlerhaus, Munich. *Munchener Merkur* (Munich), March 18, 1962.

Review of solo exhibition at Durand-Ruel Galleries, New York. *New York Herald Tribune,* March 17, 1946.

Review of solo exhibition at Durand-Ruel Galleries, New York. *New York Sun,* March 9, 1946.

Review of solo exhibition at Durand-Ruel Galleries, New York. *New York Telegram,* March 9, 1946.

Review of Red Cross benefit, *The New York Times,* April 30, 1944.

Review of group exhibition at Bignou Gallery, New York. *The New York Times,* January 14, 1945.

Review of solo exhibition at Durand-Ruel Galleries, New York. *View,* February 1946.

"La Ruota ha posato." *Milano Sera,* March 8, 1952.

Sawin, Martica. "Spiritual and Electric Surrealism: The Art of Enrico Donati." *Arts,* February 1987, 28.

Scattola, Virgilio. "Carena—Canal—Donati." *Minosse* (Venice), October 11, 1952.

Schwarz, Arturo. "Biennale '86" *Epoca,* July 1986.

Shirey, David L. Review, *The New York Times,* June 8, 1975, 86.

Smith, Tim. "Palm Beach Opera's 'Lucia' Shines." *Sun-Sentinel* (Fort Lauderdale), March 13, 1995, 3D.

______. "*Lucia* Closes Season for Palm Beach Opera." *Sun-Sentinel* (Fort Lauderdale), March 5, 1995, 4D.

"Society." *Chicago Sunday Tribune,* November 12, 1944.

"Solidly Surrealistic." *Arizona Republic,* March 10, 1995.

Soupault, Philippe. "Enrico Donati." *Lettre Française,* November 27, 1946.

"Surrealist Show to Open with Donati as Guest." *St. Paul* (Minnesota) *Dispatch,* January 20, 1977.

"Today's Calendar." *Chicago Daily Tribune,* November 3, 1944.

"Tour d'expositions." *Spectateur* (Paris), November 5, 1946.

"À travers les galeries." *Lettres Françaises,* December 6, 1946.

"True, Quite Different." *The New York Times,* March 11, 1945.

Upton, Melville. "New Art and Old." *New York World-Telegram,* May 15, 1943.

______. Review, *The New York Times,* February 11, 1944.

Urbania, E. "The Exhibition of Enrico Donati at Gallery Passedoit," *Progresso Italo-Americano,* March 2, 1944.

Van Rosen, R. "Exhibition of Donati's Work." *Russian Daily* (New York), May 23, 1943.

Wehy, Siegfried. "Modern Art Puts Khrush on Canvas." *Newark* (New Jersey) *Star Ledger,* February 28, 1963.

Wilson, Wendy. "Southwest Painting: It's Hung up on the Past," *Santa Fe* (New Mexico) *Reporter,* January 10, 1980, 19.

Wolff, Millie. "Surrealist Donati Has Norton Show." *Palm Beach* (Florida) *Daily News,* April 9, 1979.

Wolff, Theodore F. "How Do You Rank a Fine Artist Who Is Not Quite at the Top?" *Christian Science Monitor,* May 22, 1982, 15.

______. "Where Have All the Painterly Painters Gone?" *Christian Science Monitor,* December 21, 1982, 18.

______. "The Many Masks of Modern Art: Putting It on the Line." *Christian Science Monitor,* September 1, 1983, 20.

______. "Gouged, Scratched, Scumbled, Beautiful." *Christian Science Monitor,* April 5, 1984, 38.

______. "'Realism' Found a Staunch Adherent." *Christian Science Monitor,* April 7, 1986, 29.

______. "Kokoschka's Art and Life Celebrated in Major Retrospective." *Christian Science Monitor,* December 26, 1986, 21.

______. "Donati: The Surrealist Years." *Christian Science Monitor,* January 21, 1987, 27.

______. "The Pleasure of His Painting." *Christian Science Monitor,* March 12, 1987, 30.

UNPUBLISHED ARTICLES ABOUT ENRICO DONATI

Clarac-Serou, Max. "In Praise of Barrenness," 1953.

Crehan, Hubert. "From Dust to Dust," 1960.

Serpan, I. "Where It Is a Question of a Geography without Shores," 1952–53.

Tyler, Parker. "A Harmony in Paint," 1945.

Index

Page numbers in *italics* refer to illustrations.

E N R I C O

D O N A T I

Photograph Credits

Ronnie Abrams, pages 23, 35, 58, 108 left, 111, 114, 116, 119, 120, 122–26, 128, 129, 131–33, 135, 137, 139, 140

Albright-Knox Art Gallery, 87

Geoffrey Clements, 82

A. C. Cooper Ltd., 92

Detroit Institute of Arts, 86

Peter A. Juley & Son, 62, 63 bottom, 71 top, 74 left, 75, 84

Marcel Lannay, 43

Earl Leaf, 153 bottom

Robert Mates, 27

Charles Mayer, 85

Gjon Mili, 10

Sally Ritts, 80

Marina Schinz, 154

Speltdoorn et Fils, 73

Lee Stalsworth, 88

Tetsu Sueyoshi, 21, 22, 25, 26, 31, 32, 34 left, 36, 37, 38 right, 41, 42, 44, 46–53, 55–57, 59, 62–63 top, 65–67, 69, 71 bottom, 72, 76–79, 90, 97, 99–101, 103, 105, 115

Tony Vaccaro, frontispiece